About the author

Jane Teresa Anderson has a BSc Honours degree in Zoology, specialising in developmental neurophysiology, from the University of Glasgow, Scotland. She has worked as a dream analyst and dream therapist since 1992, basing her work on her independent research into dreams and dreaming. She has written five other books on dreams: *Sleep On It and Change Your Life; Dream It: Do It; The Shape of Things to Come; 101 Dream Interpretation Tips* and the previous edition of this book, entitled *Dream Alchemy.*

Jane Teresa is the host of The Dream Show, a long-running podcast series, and regularly appears on radio and national television talking about dreams and dream interpretation. She created The Dream Academy at dream-academy-online.com to house her online courses, and blogs and consults through her website.

She lives in Brisbane, Australia.

www.janeteresa.com

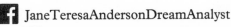 JaneTeresaAndersonDreamAnalyst

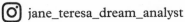 jane_teresa_dream_analyst

JANE TERESA ANDERSON

the
dream
handbook

HIGH LIFE HIGHLAND	
3800 17 0037620 9	
Askews & Holts	07-Mar-2018
154.63	£12.99

piatkus

PIATKUS

Previous edition *Dream Alchemy* first published in Australia
and New Zealand in 2003 by Thomas C. Lothian Pty Ltd
This edition first published in Australia and New Zealand in 2018
by Hachette Australia, an imprint of Hachette Australia Pty Limited
First published in Great Britain in 2018 by Piatkus

1 3 5 7 9 10 8 6 4 2

A CIP catalogue record for this book
is available from the British Library.

ISBN 978-0-349-42031-8

Printed and bound in Great Britain by
Clays Ltd, St Ives plc

Papers used by Piatkus are from well-managed forests
and other responsible sources.

MIX
Paper from
responsible sources
FSC® C104740

Piatkus
An imprint of
Little, Brown Book Group
Carmelite House
50 Victoria Embankment
London EC4Y 0DZ

An Hachette UK Company
www.hachette.co.uk

www.improvementzone.co.uk

Dedication

To Michael.
I followed the rainbow and there you were. Pure gold.

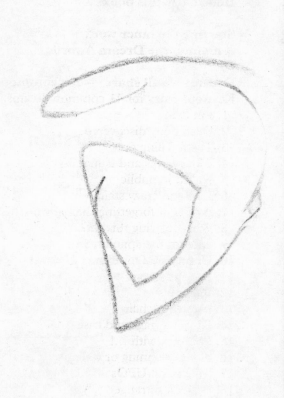

Contents

How to use this book

For maximum impact, start at the first chapter and keep reading. Or, if you want to get to the bottom of what your dream means and to make it work for you:

1 Use the contents page to look up the 'Dreams we all share — our common dreams' section and find the dream that resembles yours most closely. If you have a recurring dream that is listed, start with that.

2 Read all about that common dream. Your dream is unique, but the questions included will lead you to discover what your personal dream means.
   ◆ Each common dream starts with an inspirational quote. Think of each quote as being the silver lining in each possibly dark or puzzling dream. As you explore the meaning of your dream, contemplate the quote and let it guide you towards making positive changes in your life. Let it be your quest, your alchemy riddle or task, your unfolding insight, your path to alchemical gold. Think of each quote as a way of initiating a meditation leading to personal and spiritual insight, or the Philosophers' Stone guiding you towards the life-changing revelations each dream offers you.
   ◆ You may or may not see your variation of a common dream in the 'In your dream perhaps …' list. Don't worry if your dream isn't there! The examples included are memory prompts.
   ◆ In the 'How do you feel in your dream?' list, pick out the feelings unique to your dream. Some people find it difficult to find words to describe feelings. This list helps you to express how you felt, because how you feel in a dream is a vital part of its interpretation.
   ◆ Next comes the 'How does your dream end?' section. Select the ending closest to your dream to see how near you are to seeing positive changes coming into your life, or to see if you need to look at a new approach to the situation your dream is puzzling over. You'll also find this

section helpful in comparing your dream ending to other common dream endings. Reading the positive endings helps to program your unconscious mind for positive change — the dream symbols communicate, by way of positive example, directly with your unconscious mind.

◆ Most common dreams are about solving waking-life situations or issues, so they show what is holding you back as well as how to free things up for yourself. Check out the 'What your dream means' sections to explore which may apply to your life and which can guide you towards unblocking your way forward.

◆ Each common dream section features a detailed dream interpretation ('What your dream means') to help you understand the symbols and issues prevalent in each dream.

◆ Following this section are examples of the kinds of situations that people experiencing this dream may be in. Use 'In your life this could be about ...' as a checklist or general orientation to help you identify your particular circumstances.

◆ Even though each of these 41 dreams is common to most people, your own dream holds the hallmarks of your personal situation. The section 'Your unique dream contains personal clues only you may recognise' helps you to identify and understand the symbols in your dream that are clues to your personal case. Use these to help you pinpoint the exact area of your life your dream is addressing.

◆ By answering the questions in 'Why has this dream come up for you now?' you will become clearer about why your dreaming mind is keen to address this situation *now!* This section also helps you to identify the spiritual questions (usually issues of fear and love) that you are facing at this time.

◆ Finally, each common dream presents you with three dream alchemy practices. What these are and how they work is covered on pages 9–12 and also in the 'Dream alchemy practice guide' on pages 329–38.

3 Do the dream alchemy practices that go with your dream. Affirmation and visualisation dream alchemy

practices require repetition over a set period of time to be effective. But while too few repetitions will simply not work for you, it is not necessary to do any more than the recommended number.

For affirmations, repeat thirty times a day for the first week and then only twice a day (once in the morning and once before you go to sleep) for three more weeks. You may wish to do your thirty repetitions in one session or to space them throughout your day.

For visualisations (which should take you less than thirty seconds to do), repeat twenty times a day for the first week, then ten times a day for the second week and twice a day for the next month. Space your visualisations throughout your day.

4   If your dream does not fit any of the 41 common dreams, start by reading the first three common dreams in any case. Even though these are not your dreams, these sections communicate the art of dream interpretation. The more you read, the more you awaken and nourish your natural ability to interpret your uncommon dreams.

5   Move on to the section 'Our uncommon dreams' on page 289. These chapters show you how to interpret all your uncommon dreams and how to design dream alchemy practices to help you achieve your unique goals.

   Each chapter starts with a quote to introduce the dream interpretation methods that will help you to 'precipitate' your unique alchemical solutions from your puzzling uncommon dreams.

6   Do your dream alchemy practice! Avoid the temptation to interpret a dream and then move on to your next dream and your next without doing this.

7   Feel free to jump ahead and read the 'Dream alchemy practice guide' on pages 329–38 for a deeper understanding of how and why dream alchemy works.

8   Use the keyword index on pages 23–24 for common dreams and the general index to help you track down whatever else you need to know.

Starting the inner work

Let the magic begin

I have been waiting many moons for you to open your eyes to dreamlight. Welcome. Step this way. We have work to do. Let the magic begin.

Everybody dreams, and dreams — like fresh air — are free. Your days begin and end with the gift of dreams, even if you have forgotten how to remember them or how to unwrap them. The weirdness of a dream is only its wrapping, its language. Once you have cracked the code, the meaning of your dream is revealed.

Your dreams are messages about you and your life, in code. Your dreams reveal how you picture the world and how you envisage your place in it. They show how your early experiences shaped your beliefs about the way the world works and about who you are. Every night your dreams update the data, consolidating, refining, questioning or changing your understanding of the world according to the events of the day.

Imagine standing at the bottom of a mountain, looking up at its peak. You see an overhanging rock and a snowy precipice. Your belief is that this mountain is hard to climb. Next to you stands a man, and next to him stands a woman and so on as you are one of thousands of people forming a circle around the base of the mountain. You are all looking up at its peak.

The man next to you sees a slightly different view. He too sees the overhanging rock and the snowy precipice but he has climbed many mountains tougher than this one. His view of the mountain and his belief is that it is relatively easy to climb. The woman standing next to him looks up at the peak in fear. In her younger days she lost a lover to a mountaineering

1

accident. Her view of the mountain is one of fear and grief and it is her belief that the mountain is best left alone. Around the other side of the mountain, a child looks up at the peak. He sees a gentle slope leading all the way to the top, all green grass glistening in the sunshine. He holds his mother's hand as they step forward to take the cable car all the way to the top. His view is that the mountain is an easy, fun adventure and his belief is about to be confirmed and strengthened.

The mountain is life — or perhaps it is all the secrets of the universe. We each look at the mountain every day. What we each see depends on where we stand, on our past experiences and on our beliefs. Every night your dreaming mind adds your experiences of the day into your mountain picture. Your dream updates the information on your mountain — your view and beliefs about life — but it does this in code. Every rock and every stone that forms the mountain is captured in dream code. Every pebble, every grain of sand of your belief about life is there in your dreams. Just as a mountain of desert sand can be blown away, so too mountains can be moved and life — as you think you know it — can shift and change slowly or suddenly.

When you understand your dreams you understand why your life is the way it is. You understand the grains of sand that are your beliefs, the pebbles that are your experiences, the stones that are your insights, the rocks that are your foundations, the peaks that are your goals, and the climbs that represent your feelings about how easy or difficult life is. When you understand your dreams you understand how your fears and beliefs shape the mountainous path ahead of you, and in understanding all of this you have the beginnings of magic. You have the ability to change what you see. The mountain, your life, your path, your self is yours to change. Are you ready to let the magic begin?

This book shows you how to unwrap your dreams, to crack the code, so that you can see with greater clarity the way your life is and why it might be so. With the gift unwrapped and your life revealed, the next choice is yours. If you wish to make changes, this book can help.

The dream alchemy practices are unique, inspirational and simple exercises to help you move mountains or, at least, to rearrange the pebbles to make your climb easier. They are very powerful life-changing practices.

The formula for using this book to decode *your* dreams and for choosing or designing *your* dream alchemy practices to improve *your* life is covered later in this chapter, but before applying the formula it's best to acquaint yourself with the basic elements of dreaming and dream alchemy.

What is a dream?

A dream is a snapshot of how you see your life and your place in it on any given night, based on your conscious and unconscious experiences of the last 1–2 days. Usually it focuses on a question or problem in your life, but why is it presented in such a bizarre code?

You have a deeper and more complex mind than the one you use every day. This is the key to understanding the function of dreams, why they are in code and how you can use the material of your dreams to make deep and lasting positive changes to your life. Dream alchemy practice will help you.

You are aware of about 10–15 per cent of your mind's thoughts, experiences, feelings, memories and beliefs. This is your conscious mind. The other 85–90 per cent of your mind is like the underwater part of an iceberg, out of sight and, as the saying goes, 'out of your conscious mind'. This other 85–90 per cent of yourself is your unconscious mind. The word unconscious simply means 'what you are not conscious of'. This book does not use the word subconscious. It assumes that at any given moment you are either consciously aware of something or not. Your unconscious mind is just the greatest part of your mind and you're not aware of it.

There you are, going about your life, only aware of the tip of the iceberg of your mind! Maybe this would be okay if your unconscious mind was inactive. But it's not. Your unconscious mind is incredibly powerful.

Whenever you have an experience or feeling you don't enjoy and don't wish to confront, it goes straight into your unconscious mind. Straight to the 'don't want to know' department in the basement of your mind. There it sits and grows and festers with all the other 'don't want to know' memories and feelings.

Even the flip side of your so-called good thoughts and beliefs head down to the basement too. For example, if you have been taught to be polite then there are probably some extremely impolite thoughts and feelings lurking about down there. If you have been taught that it's bad to express feelings of anger then there will be some very angry memories and feelings there too.

Other inhabitants of your unconscious mind include negative self-talk (I'm not clever, I'm not beautiful, I'm useless) and a kaleidoscope of life beliefs absorbed during your early years (Money doesn't grow on trees, It's all work and no play).

In the basement they may be, but asleep they are not. Your unconscious mind is very much in control of your life. Here's an example. Imagine you want to lose weight. Your conscious mind holds a picture of a slim new you. You want that body! You are prepared to do what it takes. But somehow you stay the same weight or you even get fatter, no matter what you do. The culprit is your unconscious mind hanging onto a belief it has stored since last time you were slim and things didn't work out too well for you. Perhaps it believes, based on your last experience, that if you are slim you will attract attention and end up being hurt again, so the best way to protect your feelings is to stay under cover of fat — to keep the padding on. Whenever your unconscious mind has an opposite belief to your conscious mind, it will sway the result of your efforts.

There are also many wonderful things about your unconscious mind that are revealed in your dreams. It is brilliantly creative and a fantastic problem-solver, so when you interpret a dream you can discover some great ideas to put into action. It is also where many of your potential gifts and talents sleep, awaiting discovery, along with a multitude of other wonderful facets of your greater being.

Your unconscious mind can also occasionally reach out and connect with the minds of others, resulting in telepathic dreams; and it can reach into the past and into the future, unearthing information you didn't think you knew, sometimes leading to precognitive dreams.

So, returning to the question, What is a dream?

To add to the earlier definition, a dream is a snapshot of how your conscious and your *unconscious* minds see your life and your place in it on any given night. Usually a dream focuses on a question or problem in your life. When you decode your dream you see *both* your conscious and *unconscious* views of your life — and of the question or problem.

Your dreams are incredibly powerful because if you can decode them you will catch your unconscious mind at its own game. Suddenly you will get the full picture. Suddenly you see the unconscious beliefs that are undermining your life goals. Suddenly you see the unconscious beliefs that have been shaping your life and what has helped or hindered you. Suddenly you see the amazing unawakened parts of your greater being.

Knowledge is power! You can apply dream alchemy practices to change those unconscious beliefs revealed by your dream, or to awaken and release your sleeping magnificence. Let the magic begin! But first you must crack that bizarre code.

Why are dreams in bizarre code?

Why can't a dream just say what it really means?

Dreams are recorded mostly by your unconscious mind. It uses a different language simply because it is an ancient part of your mind, one not wired for logic, reasoning or everyday communication as your conscious mind is.

Look at it this way. You are asleep and dreaming. Your unconscious mind is busy processing the events of the day, comparing them to past experiences, memories and beliefs and generally updating the information on your view of the world and your place in it. It has to find an easy way to store all this information, a shorthand way of compressing feelings and words so that they can be easily retrieved when needed.

Imagine looking at a detailed painting or picture. Every picture tells a whole story using emotion. Imagine listening to music. Every melody spins a tale with feeling. Imagine smelling a long-lost scent from childhood. Every smell delivers a deluge of memories. This is the way dreams code, in shorthand parcels of pictures, shapes, sounds, smells, emotions and so much more.

Your task is to wake up and look at the big picture of your dream until it speaks its thousands of words and feelings back to you. (They are your feelings so you will eventually recognise them. You forgot about them the moment you dropped them into your unconscious mind.) This book shows you how to do that looking. Your most important tool will be the dream alchemy practices included in this book. Resist the urge to refer to a dream dictionary, as these can be misleading.

What's wrong with using a dream dictionary?

It would be great if dream dictionaries worked for individual dreams, but they generally don't. The blue teacup in your dream is not the same as the blue teacup in anyone else's dream because *your* experiences and memories of blue teacups are special to you. Your unconscious mind has stored away 'blue teacup' as shorthand for something about you.

Some symbols have similar meanings for many people. For example, water in dreams often represents your emotions. Why? Because when you look at water you often describe it in emotional terms: the turbulent river, the calm pool, the raging sea or the refreshing waterfall, for example. So you can look at the water in your dream and see what kind of feeling the water showed you — and there you have it, an emotion of yours pictured as water.

Many people might have similar feelings about cats (independent, intuitive) but others might disagree, seeing cats as perhaps irritating (causing allergies), hurtful (scratching) or comforting (acting as a warm cushion on your lap). If all these people dreamed of a cat, the meaning of the cat would depend on these feelings, and this kind of explanation is rarely within the scope of a dream dictionary.

While some dream dictionaries can be useful to give you ideas, they mostly lead you away from becoming an expert on your own dreams because they encourage the habit of looking up a dream instead of *exploring* your unique dream. They can also lead you very far along the wrong track by giving the impression that the dictionary meanings are absolute. It's more accurate to learn the methods of cracking *your* dream code.

What is a recurring dream?

Your dreams recur when you keep coming up against the same old blocks or issues without resolving them. Recurring means you are stuck, repeating, can't get past go. That's why most recurring dreams have unsatisfying endings. Your dreams show you as stuck, stuck, stuck ... so something needs to change, change, change.

What's your recurring dream? Do you find yourself back at school again thinking, 'I thought I left here years ago?' Or are you continuously running for that plane and missing it? How about that one where you can't get the elevator to stop at the floor you want? And how about that magic moment when you suddenly dream the way out? You finally leave school, catch the plane or step out of the elevator onto your chosen floor? Those dreams are your solutions, your keys, your way out.

Here's part of the secret. You know your dream is about your experiences of the last two days, so think back and take a few notes. What were the difficult moments? Where did you feel stuck? Who or what irritated you? Where did you feel uncomfortable and with whom? Now — next time you have the recurring dream, do the same. Over several repeats you'll be able to see what the days leading up to the dream shared in common. You may even be able to name the issue.

To blast the recurring dream into the past and leave it there you need to be able to interpret it so you can apply dream alchemy practices. In this way you will be able to make the changes that move you on to new adventures both in your dreams and in your life.

What is a nightmare?

Nightmares are dreams, like any other dream, but they can be blood-freezing, teeth-chattering, heart-thumping and paralysingly scary. But why do dreams sometimes choose such terrifying material as death, falling, wild animals and the stuff of sheer horror?

Nightmares are about fear. Your dreams address the problems, questions and conflicts you meet in waking life, looking to make sense of it all. What holds you back most in life is fear. What moves you forward most in life is love. Your conflicts and worries mostly revolve around your fears. Your dreams show you what you fear (in dream code) and may come up with new ways of overcoming your fears. Sometimes your dreams show you that when you face your fears they disappear.

If you run away from something frightening in a dream, you'll keep running. Nothing is solved. If you run away from something in waking life, you'll keep running. Nothing is solved. If you turn away from something fearful in a dream, it will continue to haunt you. If you turn away from something fearful in waking life, it will continue to haunt you.

What you fear in waking life will haunt you in your dreams, begging you to face up to it. If you fear your personal power, it may frighten you in a dream, dressed as a shadowy power or as a huge scuttling spider. If you fear asserting yourself in waking life, you may find yourself expressing violent anger in your dream or being confronted by a dark, angry force.

When you wake up from a disturbing dream, pulse racing, soaked in sweat, gulping air like you've been holding your breath and feeling a heavy weight on your chest, try not to panic. All that's happening is that when you experience fear in a dream your body responds with an adrenaline rush just as it does when you have a fright when you're awake. Your body doesn't know the difference between dreaming and being awake when it comes to fear. That adrenaline response is as old as dreaming, designed to equip your body to fight the wild animal or flee it.

Should you fight your nightmare fears or run from them?

Neither really. It's better to quietly *name* your fears. Like Rumpelstiltskin, once named they vanish. To name your fears and banish your nightmares you'll need to start by interpreting your dreams and then apply dream alchemy practices.

Dream alchemy

Dream alchemy is the process of working with your dreams to transform your spiritual, emotional, mental and physical life into alchemical gold. The dream alchemy practices in this book work directly on your unconscious mind to 're-program' unconscious beliefs, thoughts and patterns that are not working well for you and your life. These practices are successful because they employ the language of your unconscious mind: and your unconscious mind responds.

The dream alchemy practices include visualisations, affirmations, dialogues, artwork, gut-reaction poetry, bodywork, giving back beliefs, story telling, writing and other adventures. There are many variations of dream alchemy practice because each practice is uniquely tailored to *your* dream and your needs. (For detailed descriptions of these practices see the 'Dream alchemy practice guide' on pages 329–38, and for examples see the practices given for each of the 41 common dreams in this book.)

Alchemy and dream interpretation

In mediaeval times, alchemy was the quest to understand and master the elements of nature and to demonstrate this mastery by turning base metal into gold. In its study of elements and substances, real and conjectured, it is often seen as being the forerunner of chemistry and perhaps of quantum physics. But it was far more than a pre-scientific or material quest. The mental and physical discipline required to dedicate years towards the seemingly impossible task of transforming base metal into gold tested the spirit, making of alchemy a spiritual discipline. The trials each apprentice encountered advanced his spiritual understanding of himself and the world. The base metal was his self and his experience of life. The task was to transform his self as well as his waking life into gold. The gold, symbolising the sun (consciousness and enlightenment), was his personal and spiritual transformation.

The main outcome of transmuting physical matter into gold and to transforming the base soul was the Philosophers' Stone. The Philosophers' Stone (also known, among many other names, as the *lapis elixir*) was the holy grail of alchemy. The possessor of the stone was promised eternal youth, freedom from death or sickness, and total inner knowledge, including that of how to transform base metal into gold. The Philosophers' Stone could never be dissolved or lost — once it was found. But first, it had to be found.

Alchemists believed matter was made up of four elements — earth, air, fire and water — held together, or unified, by a fifth element, invisible to the uninitiated. This fifth element was known as the quintessence. It was the secret of secrets with which one could control nature. The quintessence and the Philosophers' Stone were symbols for the same grail.

An important part of alchemy, then, was to find the Philosophers' Stone, the grail or the quintessence — then all was possible, physically, mentally, emotionally and spiritually.

Initiates, both men and women, practised alchemy through study and the practical work of mixing elements, compounds and substances, encapsulating their findings in symbols, drawings and mystical formulae. Much of the work was carried out in laboratories — places equally fitted out for practical and mystical activities. The symbols and mystical formulae constituted a secret language, a way of hiding the metaphysical and spiritual work of alchemy from the attention of the church and the uninitiated.

As an example, an important compound in alchemy is vitriol, a sulphate or sulphuric acid that burns away matter. Part of its function was to burn away matter to reveal the quintessence. The word *vitriol* is composed of the first letters of the words in this Latin phrase: '*visita interiora terrae rectificandque invenies occultum lapidem*'. This translates as 'Visit the interior of the earth and, by rectifying, you will discover the hidden stone.' The metaphysical meaning of vitriol in medieval alchemy was the process of visiting the inner self to purify the soul by burning away the dross, thereby discovering the secret of life itself.

Dreams, once interpreted, reveal the inner self in all its tarnished and bruised beauty. By interpreting our dreams we can then act on the insights we gain about ourselves to burn away the tarnish, heal the bruises and hurts, and polish the soul so it shines. In this way we can become masters of our spiritual, emotional, mental and physical worlds.

Our dreams can be seen as being like base metal, and the process of interpreting them as a process of spiritual discipline. The insights we gain about ourselves as a result are all part of the grail, the Philosophers' Stone, the magic with which we can choose to transform our lives.

How exactly do the dream alchemy practices work?

The dream alchemy practices included in this book work on your unconscious mind, which is far more powerful than your conscious mind in shaping your life. Your dreams show you the differences between your conscious and unconscious beliefs and give you clues about how you can resolve these differences. This can be tricky, as your unconscious mind is powerful and very adept at countering your attempts to change things. In the battle of wits between your conscious and unconscious minds, the unconscious wins hands-down.

The dream alchemy practices work to undo the unconscious patterns and themes that are standing in the way of you achieving your goals. People from all walks of life use affirmations but these are usually based on what the conscious mind wants and they are created using everyday (conscious-mind) language. Dream alchemy practices involving affirmations communicate with your unconscious *in its own language*. In all the dream alchemy practices (not only the affirmations) you are working with the symbols from your dreams, subtly conversing with your unconscious beliefs using the language they understand.

To understand exactly how each kind of dream alchemy practice works, see the 'Dream alchemy practice guide' on pages 329–38.

How easy is it to do the dream alchemy practices?

Most of the dream alchemy practices are easy to do, but others are more challenging. It's best to start by finding one of the 41 common dreams (see 'Dreams we all share — our common dreams', pages 21–288) that you have experienced. Read all about the dream and then choose one of the prescribed dream alchemy practices. Each common dream has three for you to choose from — or you may wish to do all three. Then move on to the next of the 41 common dreams that you have experienced, and do the same. You will see how easy the practices are and you will reap the benefits of doing them.

Designing dream alchemy practices to suit your uncommon dreams

The best way to become an excellent dream alchemist is to read through all the 41 common dreams in this book, even if you have not experienced all of these yourself. As you read the combination of dreams and practices you will easily recognise the patterns and absorb the skills you need to design your own practices. The 'Dream alchemy practice guide' includes design guidelines to help you choose the most suitable dream alchemy practice for your dream situation, and to create it and use it.

How to remember your dreams

Everybody dreams. If you let someone sleep but prevent them from dreaming, they suffer extreme physical and mental symptoms. Dreams, whether you remember them or not, keep you sane. But when you *do* remember them, interpret them and act on them, they also provide you with life-changing insight and capabilities. So how can you remember your dreams?

The most common reasons for bad dream-recall include:

* Your parents soothed your nightmares by telling you they were 'only dreams' so you learned not to bother remembering them.
* You have blocked dream-recall because you had a series of scary dreams.
* You jump out of bed in the morning when the alarm goes off, jumping straight into your conscious world — not giving yourself time to bask in the twilight zone and remember your dreams.
* Deep down you don't want to look at, let alone change, anything about your life.

To remember your dreams:

* Tell yourself your dreams are important. Buy an exercise book or another special book to use as your dream journal and expect to remember your dreams.
* Keep paper and pen by your bed and jot down a couple of words of the dream you have had as a memory jogger to read in the morning. Or keep a tape recorder by your bed to record your dream in the middle of the night.
* When you wake up in the morning, lie in the position you usually dream in. Your body muscles hold memories of your dream so lying in the same position often triggers your memory.
* Set two alarms. Set the second one for the time you must get out of bed. Set the first one for about twenty minutes before. When your first alarm goes off, lay in your dreaming position and float along in the twilight zone. Banish any thoughts about the day. Think of the first alarm as waking you up to your dreams and the second alarm as waking you up to your day.
* Write something in your dream journal every day, even if you can't remember a dream. Write about your waking feelings. These are often a hangover from the feelings in your dream, so writing about these gradually triggers your dream recall over several weeks.
* Continue reading this book. It is likely to bring back

your dream memory because it emphasises the importance of your dreams.

How to record your dreams

To get the most benefit from interpreting your dreams you
will need to write them down. Buy yourself a book with
blank pages. Make it a special book, something to treasure.
This is your dream journal.

Use the righthand pages to record your dreams. Start
with the date and then choose a title for each dream. Write
your dream exactly as you remember it. Use the first words
that come into your head. You will discover that these first
words are a major key to interpretation. Don't be tempted
to edit or choose better words. Your unconscious came up
with the dream — stick with the language it chose! If you
misspell a word, don't correct it. This mistake will also be a
key to your dream interpretation. Add in as many feelings as
you can remember from your dream, as they too are keys to
your interpretation.

Divide the lefthand pages into two columns. Use one
column to write your dream interpretations. Use the other
column to record notes about what happened during the
day: your feelings, questions, problems and insights as these
can help you to identify the situations your dreams may be
processing and addressing.

At the back of your dream journal keep a few pages to
use as an index. Each day write the date and then the titles
of all your dreams for that night under the date. When you
need to look back for a particular dream you will be able to
scan the titles and access the dream quickly. The date will
give you an idea of where it is in your book.

As your dreams are in date order they will be easy to
find, but if you really want to be efficient you can number
the pages of your dream journal and write the page numbers by your dream titles.

Your dream titles also act as memory joggers. Every six
weeks look through your index, reading the titles of your
dreams for the last six weeks. This review can help you to

identify cycles of recurring dreams or to see your patterns of breakthrough and progress.

As well as recording your dreams, you might like to buy a smaller exercise book to use for your dream alchemy practices.

Expect changes and synchronicities

Expect positive changes to occur in your life just through reading this book. Many of the dreams you will read here deal with life's major processes and rites of passage. The life lessons and insights we gather along the way enrich and transform us personally and spiritually. Reading and contemplating the types of dreams that accompany these processes may trigger profound positive change for you, even if you haven't yet experienced the event or dream yourself.

You may experience synchronicities before you finish reading this book. A synchronicity is a coincidence or series of coincidences that are not really coincidences at all. (A coincidence is a chance thing, but a synchronicity feels far too meaningful to be due to chance alone.) When you experience a synchronicity you may feel as though you've got goosebumps. Typically you are also completely puzzled by what the synchronicity *means* even though it feels amazingly meaningful. So what is synchronicity and why might you experience it while reading *The Dream Handbook*?

Think of synchronicity as being like a dream you have while you're awake. Of course, it's a real event, but think of it as something that needs interpreting (like a dream) before you can understand it. Synchronicities are events rich in symbolism. If you think of them as everyday events, they are bizarre. If you interpret them as dreams they make sense.

Synchronicity happens to you when something in your unconscious mind shifts and changes — as it will do while you read this book, interpret your dreams and do your dream alchemy practices. It happens when you are on the verge of an exciting insight, a new understanding about your life.

A night
at the Dream Awards

Thank you. I've got a piece of paper here somewhere. Oh, the tears! It's been quite a journey from base metal to Dream Award! Now, where was I?

Thank you. I'd like to thank my dreams for the spiritually inspiring alchemist's stones they delivered that helped me in precipitating the solution that became my awakening. I see it all so clearly now.

In a good night's sleep you have about five big dreams, usually all concerning the same question. Each one contains a Philosophers' Stone — an insight previously unknown to you that you can use to transform your waking life from base metal into gold. What treasure! What potential!

Each night as you fall asleep you teeter on the verge of bringing home the gold. After ninety minutes of deep sleep, the first big dream is — well, let's say the first dream is 'screened'. The first big dream of the night is usually the most vivid and surreal.

Imagine the excitement down in the basement of your deep unconscious — maybe tonight's the night! Picture this. Your dream director paces in the dark:

'Maybe tonight's the night!'

'Maybe tonight's the night to bring home the gold. Maybe tonight we'll screen the dream of a lifetime. Maybe tonight she'll finally get the message. Maybe tonight we can pull out all our best stops. Maybe tonight it's Dream Awards all round! What's the theme for the night?'

'The theme?' echoes a rumbling voice from the Script Development Department in the depths of the dark unconscious. 'We thought we might have another look at the self-esteem question tonight. We laid some good foundations with the power issue last night, so we're ready to take a fresh look at self-esteem.'

'Ah, big one,' replies the dream director, one eye on the clock. 'We're ten minutes down and the clock's ticking. Eighty minutes and we need the first big dream up and ready to go. Order up the early life memories please — run a combined search on "power" and "self-esteem".'

The staccato splutter of modems firing up to download the memory neurons of the brain mingles with the smell of start-of-shift coffee.

The dream director taps her microphone. 'Metaphors Department, you in yet?'

'In and rolling. We've got a good round-table blitz group in today. Should come up with some crackers tonight. I hear the Puns and Wordplay Department has a top-class crossword puzzle expert on the job tonight. We might be up for the Dream Awards with tonight's screenings.'

The dream director drums her fingers on her desk. 'Seventy-five minutes and counting. Casting Department, you on board? We need a big cast for tonight: the best you can, we're going for the Dream Awards. Theme is self-esteem and power. I want people from waking life, people from the past and a couple of characters from fiction. Stick to theme, but think extremes; even go as far as caricatures. Oh, and we'll need two extras. Make-up are standing by to archetypecast the extras.'

At ninety minutes exactly the first big dream is screened and recorded for posterity in the Unconscious Memory Archives Department. At the same time a copy is sent, as always, to the Conscious Recall Database but with no expectation of success as the IT technicians are still chasing the dream deletion virus that entered the system at the same moment in history as the Industrial Revolution.

After the screening, brief congratulations are exchanged and then all heads are down to create the second dream. This time conditions are tighter. The deep sleep interval between dreams decreases as the night goes on *and* the dreaming periods get longer. With less time for creativity and production and longer stories to shoot, it's no surprise that dreams closer to morning tend to be a little more mundane.

By morning the film crew are partying and retiring to doze at the Back Burner Inn for the day. You stir, fleetingly in contact with Conscious Recall Database, battling the dream deletion virus to archive the data over to the permanent conscious memory store. Somewhere between dreaming and getting out of bed a partial victory is declared, a dream or two are remembered and the still vigilant dream director wonders, before hitting the sack, if her movies have worked their magic.

Stop right there! So your dream director pulled off an award-worthy dream of a lifetime? So you've remembered most of it? So you're going to entertain a few people with it today? So you're going to interpret it too? That's excellent, but remember: you can interpret your dream and learn heaps about yourself and your life, but unless you take action based on what you learn you're missing gold by a million miles.

And that's not all! You can take action, but to counteract those unconscious beliefs that can still powerfully trip you up, you need to do your dream alchemy practice.

It's *doing* the dream alchemy practice that *undoes* any unconscious beliefs that are in your way.

Reading the dream alchemy practices is not going to do it for you. Half-doing the dream alchemy practices is not going to do it. Thinking the dream alchemy practices are too simple, silly or time-consuming is not going to do it either.

Rushing to remember and interpret your next dream is certainly not going to do it for you if you haven't done your dream alchemy practice on the gift you have already been given.

Each dream remembered is a gift. Each one contains a 'Philosophers' Stone' or profound insight to enable you to transform your waking life and, above all, your self from base metal into gold. If you are not prepared to do your dream alchemy practice you will have a pile of beautiful, philosophical insights. And while that is something awesome to treasure, it's when you put the elements of alchemy into practice, following the formulae presented by your dream insights, that real magic begins.

You have the base metal of your waking life and the Philosophers' Stone insights of your dreams. You are, and always have been, a Dream Alchemist. Awaken and go to it.

Dreams we all share –
our common dreams

Break the mould to reveal the gold.

Keyword index
for 41 common dreams

1: I'm flying

The dream

You are flying, floating or hovering in the air, either unaided or with a bizarre prop.

To rise above a situation, release your hold. The world cannot benefit from your talents unless you unfold your wings.

In your dream perhaps ...

♦ You are floating above a group of people, encouraging them to join you.

♦ You are flying so high that you get a bird's-eye view of the landscape below.

♦ You are trying to fly higher, but the power lines are in your way.

♦ You are flying to escape something or someone chasing you.

♦ You are travelling a metre or so above the landscape, perhaps following a road or track, perhaps in a flow of cars or pedestrians.

♦ You are performing acrobatic flying tricks for an admiring crowd.

♦ You are floating against your will.

♦ You are sitting on or using a cushion, piece of wood or other bizarre prop to keep yourself in the air.

♦ You are not flying alone.

How do you feel in your dream?

Elated. Amazed. Awed. Empowered. A sense of wonder. Ecstatic. Limitless. Relaxed. Released. A sense of achievement. Inspired. Motivated. In control. Controlled. Fearful. Insecure. A sense of danger. Surprised. A sense of disbelief. A sense of belief. A sense of faith. Confident. Not confident. Supported. Frustrated.

How does your dream end?
Positive changes are on the way if ...
- ◆ You experience only positive emotions.
- ◆ You overcome difficulties or fear and end the dream on a high note.
- ◆ You succeed in encouraging other people to fly with you.
- ◆ You see a view, when you look down, that inspires or enlightens you.

It's time for a new approach if ...
- ◆ You can't fly above the power lines.
- ◆ You can't escape the person or thing that is chasing you.
- ◆ You don't overcome the fear of flying or floating.
- ◆ You fall or have a flying accident.
- ◆ You can't find your way back to the ground again.

What your dream means
Your way forward may be blocked by ...
Not having enough faith in your own ability. Needing to rise above a situation. Being too close to a situation to see a higher view. Escaping instead of facing a situation. Fear of letting go. Fear of power.

Moving forward
Practise letting go. Give yourself permission to use and develop your talents to their full potential. Take time out to get your bearings and form an overview of your situation. Focus on feeling free through self-empowerment rather than restricted by control.

◆

Superman does it for us. Angels do it for us. So do fairies. We have invested power, mystery and magic in these winged beings because they can go where we can't. Well, not without planes, helicopters, hot-air balloons or hang gliders anyway — except in dreams.

Oh for the power to fly, to go beyond your physical limits, to leave the everyday solid ground behind you and to feel the lightness and freedom of flying! No bonds, no limits ... nothing to pull you down; nothing to restrict or control your self-expression! When you fly in dreams you are exploring powers, mystery and magic beyond your everyday restrictions and limitations.

We are creatures of habit, generally sticking with what we know, moving within our personal comfort zones — believing there are physical, mental, emotional and spiritual limits beyond which we cannot go. But in our dreams we feel no limitations; instead, we feel the enormity of our unconscious mind and our potential to do or be anything we wish.

Your flying dreams help you to see your limitless horizons. Just when you think you know where your horizons are, your dream pops up to beckon you further ... and further. So, what's stopping you? Fear? Insecurity? Lack of faith? Not being ready to let go? Do you prefer to stay 'in control'?

The very common dream of feeling frustrated because you cannot fly above the power lines is often said to prove that we fly out of the body when we dream. But take a close look at the landscape around your home. There are many more likely obstacles than overhead power lines, so why do so many people still dream of getting entangled in them? Dreams play with puns. Power lines may be dream code for power. If your power lines prevent you from flying higher, then consider how much power gets in your way in your waking life. You probably feel that more powerful people seem to be in your way at work or at home. Turn around your thinking and ask yourself if you have let power become a big issue for you. Who is doing the controlling — and of whom?

The power of flying should be a positive feeling of personal empowerment and freedom. For many people, power is not about freedom but about using power over other people: being in control and controlling others. And when we need to control others we are far from being free!

The other common flying dream is the one where you find yourself urging a group of admiring or disbelieving supporters on the ground to join you in the air. There you are, achieving and doing; and there they are, lacking faith and wishing they could do what you can obviously do so well. Other people in your dreams stand for your own various and conflicting beliefs. This kind of dream shows you that you *can* raise yourself to a higher potential. It also shows you that you lack faith in your ability. It's time to ignore those niggling, dissenting feelings and rise above them.

We dream-fly in the air. The invisible air may represent the invisible mind and thoughts. All manmade things in the world started as an invisible thought. From the invisible we create the visible material world. When you dream-fly you are exploring the incredibly powerful invisible parts of your being — those powerful enough to create anything you wish.

In dreams, you can look down from way up and see the landscape. When you are on the ground you can see only the territory around you — maybe a desert, a broken car and no water. From up high you can see the bigger picture — maybe the oasis just over the next sand dune, or the car already driving to your rescue. You fly high in dreams at times when you need to get an overview of a problem. Your dreams put your problems in perspective and offer you solutions.

Sometimes we dream-fly to escape something that is bothering us, something we should be facing instead of escaping. The upside of this is that flying gives you the opportunity to look down on the problem and see it from a different perspective. The downside is that dreams of escaping are usually too panicky for you to find the time to look. It's always true that unless you face your fears they chase you forever.

Let your flying dreams help you to keep your life in balance. When you pluck a great idea from the air, use it! Create something! Otherwise you'll fly so high you might end up way 'off the planet' and you know what happens when you fly too close to the sun, don't you? Your wings burn up and you crash to earth.

In your life this could be about ...
- An unused or unrecognised talent.
- A situation you are too enmeshed in to see other options.
- A power struggle with a work supervisor, colleague or partner.
- That idea you haven't acted on yet.

- That thing you'd love to do but feel you lack the confidence to try.
- The 'real you' that you keep hidden to keep other people happy.

Your unique dream contains personal clues only you may recognise

- If you're using a prop for flying, what is it and what message could this be giving you?
- Look at any people you know in the dream: people from work may signal work issues, or perhaps there are people who represent a talent or ability that could be yours.
- Do you say something when you're flying? Apply this message to yourself.
- What clues could your flying clothes be giving you?
- Are there any clues in the landscape you're flying over?

Why has this dream come up for you now?

Your answers to these questions will reveal the reason:

- What feelings and emotions did you experience in your dream?
- Which situation in your life now do these feelings remind you of?
- Which area of your life feels stuck, grounded or restricted?
- Have you been feeling frustrated that others do not recognise your abilities?
- Have you been making excuses and rationalising why you cannot do or achieve something close to your heart?
- Imagine doing or achieving this thing. What feelings does this give you?

Your answer to the last question may reveal the reason your dream has come up for you now. You may be too close to your situation to see the way forward, or you may be holding yourself back for fear of making the change.

Dream alchemy practice
Starting the inner work

This is what to *do* if you hope to see dramatic transformations in your life.

A. Take a large piece of paper and some coloured pencils or crayons. Imagine you are five years old (so it's okay if you're not the world's best artist). Now imagine you are dream-flying and looking down on the problem you want to solve, or the thing you want to put into action. The lefthand side of the page is the past, the centre is now and the righthand side is the future. Now simply *draw* your bird's-eye view of how it was (on the left), where you're at (in the centre) and where you're going to from this moment forward (on the right). As you draw, *feel* all the good feelings coming into your life as you move your hand across the page from left to right. Look at your dream alchemy picture every day, always moving your eyes from left to right until the drawn outcome manifests.

B. If you dream of not being able to fly above the power lines, here's an affirmation for you:
I feel the positive power from the power lines energise
my wings as I fly beyond the lines that once held me
back. I am now free to be whatever I choose to be
and to fly wherever I choose to fly.

C. Blow up ten balloons and write on nine of them, 'To fly higher I simply let go.' On the tenth write, 'My *talent* is my gift to the world. I unfold my wings and let my light shine.' (Where it says *talent*, write photography, songwriting, teaching, gardening … name your talent.) Then go to a wide open space, a high rooftop or a beach and release your balloons, finishing with the tenth. (If any burst or get stuck, repeat the process until all ten balloons are flying high.)

Glimmers of gold
In your dreams
When your recurring dream changes to embrace a happier ending, you are making good progress. Look out for the positive dream changes listed under 'How does your dream end?'

Taking others flying with you is a sign of success, and seeing a positive change in the landscape while flying is another.

Some symbols from your dream alchemy practice may appear in your dreams. For example, you may find yourself in the righthand page landscape of your flying picture, or you may find a balloon bearing an important message or insight. You may dream of going up in a hot-air balloon yourself.

If you are letting go of control or of feeling controlled, you may experience some dreams of struggling free from restrictions, or of intense anger or frustration at being tied down or stuck. These are excellent signs of success as you are letting go of old feelings that once protected you from your fear of being free and empowered. Think of these as letting go of silent screams from old pressures. Letting go ... going ... gone.

Look out for dreams of finding gold, gems or treasures as these are likely symbols of discovering the value of your talents and showing these to the world.

In your waking life
You experience a sense of lightness and freedom.

You are more insightful, seeing ahead with clarity and a sense of assurance.

Over the weeks you begin to feel more confidence in your abilities — feeling more empowered and willing to show your talents to the world.

You notice other people living below their potential, and feel increased respect for their freedom to go at their own pace. You feel more at peace 'walking your talk', or flying your sky regardless of what anyone else does or thinks of you.

2: Dead body discovered

Dead body

(Also see 41: Death and murder)

The dream

A body that has been dead and hidden is discovered
or is about to be discovered. You feel guilty or
responsible for the death.

*Bittersweet fruit emerges from the long darkness as fine
vintage wine.*

In your dream perhaps ...

◆ The dead body is revealed by natural events. These
could be flooding, beaching, the thawing of snow, the
draining of a lake, a mud slide, an earthquake or the set-
tling of the land.

◆ The dead body surfaces when work is done on the land.
This could be farming, earthworks, road construction,
digging, demolishing a building or renovating a house.

◆ The dead body is still hidden but you feel threatened
by its imminent discovery by police, detectives or other
people.

◆ You are shocked to remember that you killed the person
long ago. How could you have forgotten this dreadful
act?

How do you feel in your dream?

Guilty. Remorseful. A sense of grief. Responsible. A sense of
loss. Fearful. Threatened. Amazed. A sense of disbelief.
Shocked. Reunited. Surprised. Relieved. Joyful. A sense of
denial.

How does your dream end?

Positive changes are on the way if ...

◆ You admit the crime.

- You feel sad, cry in the dream or wake with a feeling of grief.
- You embrace, hug or kiss the dead body.
- The dead body comes to life in a positive way.

It's time for a new approach if ...
- You are accused of the crime but you deny it.
- The body remains hidden and you feel intensely threatened.
- The police or authorities are on their way and you are fearful.
- You run away from the scene or try to run away.
- You escape or try to escape.
- You hide or try to hide.

What your dream means
Your way forward may be blocked by ...
Past regrets, denial of old feelings, unexpressed grief, guilt, fear of responsibility or fear of facing past issues.

Moving forward
Look back, give thanks for what your past has taught you, then let it go. Forgive yourself and others. Know that from this day forward you have free choice. The past is past and today is a new day.

♦

Dead bodies from the past often symbolise things that you have previously allowed to die within yourself. They surface from burial when you need to deal with the loss because it is holding you back in some way. Usually this dream comes up because you are facing a similar dilemma now.

We're very good at killing off and trying to bury the positive as well as the negative. The dream reveals feelings of guilt about committing the crime of killing positive qualities or about long-buried thoughts, feelings and attitudes that you felt at the time were inappropriate. We are also very good at being our own judge and jury. We're brilliant at hiding what we don't want to face — until our dreams remind us about it.

These dream images come up when it's time to reconsider what we have tried to bury and why. The dream reminds you that it is better to heal issues in your life rather than bury them unresolved, or that it is better to seek whole expression of yourself rather than hide vital positive qualities.

People who are out of touch with expressing their emotions commonly dream of a long-buried female body resurfacing. People working in routine or non-creative jobs with little spare time to add creative balance into their lives can dream this too. Women in our dreams often symbolise our creativity, emotions, intuition and spirituality. They represent our right-brain qualities or Yin essence. If you repress these qualities in your life, it is as if you have killed a vital part of yourself. This dream typically occurs as a wake-up call when life has become too left-brained and logical.

The intense guilt you probably feel in this dream is your personal judgement about your past. It is not about the future, so it needs to be released. If you allow your feelings about the past to convict you, then you will never be truly free.

When you feel guilt in a dream, welcome it and allow yourself the luxury of acknowledging your past, of forgiving yourself and seeing the experience in a new light. Value your past for how it has shaped the experienced person you are today and the person you are becoming, and then let go of the judgement and walk free.

And what of the fear of discovery this dream delivers? Put simply, when you have invested years in hiding something, then naturally you are going to feel a bit shaky about making a change. The good news is that the place in your life where you feel most stuck is the very place that is going to shift into fast forward once you discover the gold in what you have tried so hard to hide.

In your life this could be about ...
+ A study course you left unfinished.
+ A buried but unresolved relationship.
+ An old debt (financial or emotional) that you have pushed to the back of your mind.
+ An old, unfulfilled wish or dream.
+ A talent you have abandoned.

- Grief and sadness you have tried to hold back.
- An old attitude you want to forget.
- A past event you want to forget.

Your unique dream contains personal clues only you may recognise

Your dream may have time clues to help you identify this situation by indicating a date when you first buried it. Look for these clues:

- People from a certain time.
- A dream place (house, city or building) that reminds you of a time.
- An object, song or other symbol that can be dated or linked to your past.
- If there is a child, how old is he or she? If the child is, for example, seven, you might have originally tried to bury this issue seven years ago, or you might have buried it when you were seven years old. The time reference may also be seven months, or July (the seventh month), or seven weeks, or it may indicate the duration of the buried issue (a seven-year marriage, a seven-year job or course of study).

Why has this dream come up for you now?

Your answers to these questions will reveal the reason:

- What feelings and emotions did you experience in your dream?
- Which situation in your life now do these feelings remind you of?
- If you have identified the situation you tried to bury in your past, is there a similar situation occurring in your life now?
- Which area of your life feels unsatisfactory for you now? If you could move forward in this situation, what would you fear most or feel threatened by?

Your answer to the last question may reveal the reason your dream has come up for you now. You want things to improve in this area of your life but you fear facing or repeating past experiences and regrets.

Dream alchemy practice
Starting the inner work

This is what to *do* if you hope to see dramatic transformations in your life.

A. If you have already identified when you first tried to bury the past issue, write a letter to yourself as you were at that age. In the letter describe your older and wiser thoughts on looking back. Finish the letter by choosing words to express your love and forgiveness for that young, naïve person sitting reading your letter so far in your past. Wait a few days and then imagine yourself back then, replying to your letter. Write that reply.

B. If there were people in your dream, write down their names. Spend some time thinking about what would be the best gifts you could give them. Choose a different present for each person. Write the gift beside each name. Now close your eyes and visualise giving everyone their gift, one at a time. Repeat this dream alchemy visualisation for as many days or weeks as it takes until you have only positive and loving feelings for each person.

C. If your dream had an unhappy or unresolved ending, create a better one. Running away or escaping is not a suitable ending, however. The best ending for this dream is the one where everyone in the dream ends up happy and where there is no conflict. Once you have your new, improved dream ending, decide on an uplifting emotion or an inspiring song as the theme for your dream-movie credits. Visualise the new dream story as you summon up the new uplifting emotion and hear the new dream-movie song. Better still, play the song you've chosen at the end of your visualisation. Repeat this dream alchemy practice regularly.

Glimmers of gold
In your dreams

When your recurring dream stops or changes to embrace a happier ending, you are making good progress. Look out for the positive dream changes listed under 'How does your dream end?'

Some symbols from your dream alchemy practice may appear in your dreams. For example, you may read a dream letter, receive the visualised gifts yourself, or welcome people from the old dream bearing different gifts for you.

If you experience some dreams of grief and shock, waking up feeling teary but lighter, you are making good progress too. These are all positive releasing steps and great indicators of successful magic. Any grief is transitionary — let it evaporate with your tears.

Look out for dreams of opening cupboards, doors and boxes, symbolically releasing issues, thoughts and feelings you have kept hidden and locked away.

In your waking life
You experience a sense of release and movement in at least one area of your life.

Over the weeks you begin to feel lighter and, possibly, less harsh towards yourself.

You feel less judgemental towards others, or freer to make choices in areas of your life which have seemed restricted before.

You feel more expansive about your life and your future.

3: Teeth falling out

Teeth

> **The dream**
>
> One or more of your teeth start falling out.

After the tumbling and crumbling of uncertain words, contemplate your hesitation to be heard.

In your dream perhaps ...

♦ You are trying to speak to someone when your teeth start falling out.

♦ You are trying to speak to someone but you spit out teeth instead.

♦ You can feel your mouth filling up with loose teeth.

♦ You look in a mirror and see gaps in your teeth.

♦ You find teeth and realise they're yours — they must have fallen out at some time.

How do you feel in your dream?

Embarrassed. Horrified. Awkward. Frustrated. Hesitant. Irritated. Weak. Incapacitated. Silenced. Vulnerable. Restricted. Choked. Blocked. Fearful. Self-conscious. Over-powered. Silly. Inconsequential. Unimportant. Not Confident. Belittled. Inadequate. Insecure. A sense of inequality.

How does your dream end?

Positive changes are on the way if ...

♦ You overcome difficulties or fear and end the dream on a high note.

♦ You communicate your message and are heard and respected.

♦ Your teeth grow back or you grow new (better) ones.

♦ You gather your lost teeth and arrange for them to be put back in place.

♦ You find lost teeth and the dream ends happily.

- You receive a reward for a fallen tooth — think of the 'tooth fairy'.

It's time for a new approach if ...
- You can't communicate your message, or no one listens properly.
- The person you are speaking to is disrespectful to you.
- You swallow a tooth and it hurts, or you choke on it.
- Your teeth keep falling out.
- You get false teeth to replace the lost ones.

What your dream means
Your way forward may be blocked by ...
Feelings of insecurity and inequality, making it difficult for you to speak up and get your message heard. Feeling pressured to agree with others. Giving up your personal power for someone else's benefit. Losing faith in your spiritual beliefs. Fear of being belittled.

Moving forward
Know that you are entitled to walk this Earth and breathe the air — you are equal to all others. You deserve equal respect to express yourself according to your beliefs and to be heard. Know it, feel it, walk it, breathe it, be it.

◆

Remember the excitement of losing your first 'baby' tooth? Your gummy gap showed you were leaving your baby years behind you, and you were proud of it. Even better, the tooth fairy would bless your initiation into the world of big people by leaving a little reward under your pillow. Then reality hit. Well, maybe the tooth fairy lived up to your expectations but you hadn't counted on being the butt of big people's jokes every time you opened your mouth and lisped. Were they listening to you or were they lining up the, 'All I want for Christmas is my two front teeth' retort? All you wanted was to be heard and taken seriously, like a grown-up.

Is it any wonder that when you feel you're not being heard, or not being treated as an equal with something valuable to say, your dream chooses the symbol of your teeth falling out? As a gap-toothed child you might have felt hurt, disrespected and, perhaps, patronised. When you're not getting your message across to someone today you may feel the same, so your dream searches your memory bank for feelings and comes up with the teeth falling out scenario. Basically your dream is saying, 'You deserve to get your message across and you deserve to be listened to, but when you try to communicate with so-and-so you feel the same as when you were a child losing your teeth.'

When you dream that you are trying to communicate but are being hindered by falling teeth, you'll know the issues you're struggling with are those of feeling disrespected or, perhaps, put down. Deeper than this, your dream is really pointing out that you are struggling with reactions to authority where you feel as if you are a child, undeserving of serious attention. It's time to increase your assertiveness and self-esteem — to be heard and to know you're worth every word.

A dream of losing teeth might also take you back to an event or memory connected with a time you were losing teeth. If you dream of losing three teeth, for example, the dream could be reminding you of those months when you were missing three teeth (and something that happened for you then that is affecting life for you now).

Apart from losing your milk teeth, and perhaps a few more due to decay, accident or old age, the shape and size of your smile is basically with you for life. Longer, really. Think of a skeleton. Your teeth and bones form your basic hard structure, the part that all the soft bits of you hang from. In dreams, your teeth and bones may symbolise your solid beliefs about life, the beliefs you then hang everything else on. So losing teeth in a dream may reflect deep issues of questioning your once solid beliefs about life.

When you are going through a crisis of spiritual faith, or feeling a shift in your basic beliefs about life, you may dream about losing teeth. The gaps in your mouth are the gaps in your beliefs, and your difficulties in communicating are based on the uncertainty of your beliefs. When things are shifting and changing for you, you speak with less certainty, with a shaky voice. You are not sure. And so you dream of trying to communicate but failing through lack of conviction. What plays out in your dreams can also play out in your waking life. Have you ever noticed that you need to visit the dentist at times when your basic beliefs about life are under threat or changing?

'Spit it out,' orders a rude, inconsiderate, impatient person, wanting you to get to the bottom line without the joy of telling your story. Immediately your story evaporates and you lose confidence. You are a child again, vulnerable and exposed. So you dream of spitting teeth. You may even 'swallow your own words' and that hurts, especially in a dream, when it's teeth that you're swallowing! Or you may regret something you've said, unable to take your words (teeth) back.

Now, what would false teeth in a dream mean, do you think? Get your teeth into that one.

In your life this could be about ...
- Not getting your message across to an employer or someone you work with.
- Holding back your views to keep a parent or in-law happy.
- Not being able to get a word in when talking with a friend or partner.
- Beginning to question your religion or spiritual understanding of life.
- Not feeling respected by a person in authority.

Your unique dream contains personal clues only you may recognise
- Does anyone in your dream represent work, family, church, study or social life?
- How many teeth fall out? The number may be the clue to how many years this situation has been bothering you, or how many times the difficulty has come up.
- What are you trying to say in your dream? Who would you like to say this to in your waking life?

Why has this dream come up for you now?
Your answers to these questions will reveal the reason:
- What feelings and emotions did you experience in your dream?

- Which situation in your life now do these feelings remind you of?
- Have you recently tried to be more expressive than usual and not been heard?
- Where is there a gap in your life?
- If this gap were filled, what new concerns do you feel this would bring up for you?
- What would happen in your life if you spoke up and were heard?

Your answers to the last two questions may reveal the reason your dream has come up for you now. You may be holding back from expressing yourself fully for fear of the changes this may bring.

Dream alchemy practice
Starting the inner work

This is what to *do* if you hope to see dramatic transformations in your life.

A. Here's an affirmation for you:

> My teeth are strong and white, and my words are
> firm and powerful. I say what I need to say with
> love, knowing I am respected and equal to all people.
> I am at peace with the positive changes that flow into
> my life when I speak.

B. For this dream alchemy practice start by making a 'Spit it out' list. Imagine spitting out all the things you want to say. Write them down as a list: Spit 1, Spit 2 and so on. Put the list to one side for three days while you focus on doing your affirmation. Then get the list and, starting with Spit 1, change the title to Story 1. Get comfortable in a private space where you cannot be overheard, and imagine you have the person you need to talk to in front of you. Imagine they are all ears. You have all the time in the world. Tell your story and make it long. Express everything you need to say at a leisurely pace. Enjoy telling your story. Imagine a huge audience now filling the room and enjoying it too. Make the end of your story positive. Turn each spit into a long story in this way.

C. Use lipstick or crayon to write 'Respect' on your bathroom mirror. Keep it there for a week. Every time you look in the mirror say, 'I am equal to all others and receive respect for what I say.'

Glimmers of gold
In your dreams

When your recurring dream changes to embrace a happier ending, you are making good progress. Look out for the positive dream changes listed under 'How does your dream end?'

Some symbols from your dream alchemy practice may appear in your dreams. For example, you may find yourself telling stories to an attentive audience or reading empowered lipstick messages.

You may release some strong emotions in your dreams, expressing yourself way beyond the gentle but firm words needed in waking life. This is good. It is your dream's way of releasing your pent-up feelings. With these out of the way you are free to state things clearly, lovingly and effectively.

Look out for dreams featuring flowing, opening and releasing, showing your readiness for moving forward in an empowered, equal and respected way.

In your waking life

You experience a sense of equality and power. Your voice may become slightly deeper and more resonant as your words carry more strength.

You feel more comfortable about expressing a view that is different to someone else's.

You notice most people giving you more respect, while others disappear from your life altogether.

Your sense of spiritual connection and understanding about life may increase.

4: Tidal waves and tsunamis

Tidal waves

> ## The dream
> You see a huge tidal wave or tsunami rolling towards
> you or flooding an area.

Tame the waves before they tame you.

In your dream perhaps ...

- You are on the shore when you see the tidal wave coming. You try to run but cannot move.
- You are on the shore when you see the tidal wave coming. You manage to run or drive to higher ground, but the tidal wave could still reach you.
- You face the tidal wave and it disappears.
- You face the tidal wave and ride on top of it.
- You face the tidal wave and it washes over you.
- The tidal wave remains a threat on the horizon.
- You see the tidal wave flood an area. You are on higher ground or in a building.
- You watch several returns of the tidal wave. Each time the flood level gets higher.
- You watch several returns of the tidal wave. Each time the flood level gets lower.
- You return to a place previously flooded by a tidal wave.

How do you feel in your dream?
Fearful. Threatened. Devastated. Overwhelmed. Pressured. A sense of dread. Trapped. Stuck. Cornered. Doomed. In control. Detached. Amazed. Fragile. Awed. Exhilarated. Surprised. Relieved. Accepting. Acknowledging.

How does your dream end?
Positive changes are on the way if ...
- You watch the tidal wave recede.

- You are comfortably out of range of the tidal wave and you have no fear.
- You face the wave.
- You ride the wave.
- You return to the site of an area once flooded by a tidal wave.

It's time for a new approach if ...

- You try to run away but cannot move.
- The tidal wave seems to chase you.
- The dream ends in fear and dread.
- The ground seems unstable.
- The tidal wave remains a threat on the horizon.

What your dream means

Your way forward may be blocked by ...

Ignoring or denying an overwhelming feeling or emotion. Staying too cool. Avoiding a situation that needs your attention. Storing up problems to deal with later. Putting yourself under too much pressure. Running away from your true feelings. Doing the 'right thing' by others instead of the 'right thing' by yourself. Fear.

Moving forward

Admit your true feelings. Stop playing cool and start playing real. Face your fear. Take the pressure off for a while. Start dealing with problems one by one.

◆

Faced with a twenty-metre wave rolling towards you, you don't really have much chance, do you? Or do you? The amazing thing about dreams is that you *can* change them. You can turn dream tides and stop tsunamis dead. Imagine having that kind of power in your waking life! You might not want to stand in front of a tsunami willing it to freeze, but you *can* overcome life's emotional tidal waves and this kind of dream shows you how. Think *emotional* tidal waves — it is the key to understanding this dream.

Isn't it strange that you can be born into a land and culture that has never experienced a tidal wave, yet dream, along with millions of others, this very common dream?

Clearly tidal-wave dreams are not about predicting tsunami disasters or we'd all have been washed away long before. But these dreams are everything about predicting possible emotional disasters. Dreams give you the warnings. It's up to you to act on them.

Water mostly symbolises your emotions — your unconscious ones as well as the ones you know about. You might be ultra cool on the surface about something, but seething underneath. You might know about your seething, or you might push it so far into your unconscious that it bubbles away while you cope with life all cool, calm and collected. Aha! But only for a short while!

Imagine trying to press water into a small space. What happens? You can squeeze it in and then put it under pressure, then contain the pressure while it steams then ... well, next thing the pressure cooker blows and scalding water sprays everywhere. The same thing happens to emotions you push away — or into yourself when you're under too much pressure. The solution? Look at the situation. Deal with it. Face it. Release the pressure before it's too late. Stop playing cool and start playing real. Say, 'This is how I feel and this is what I can do about it.'

Your tidal-wave emotions might be anger, jealousy and resentment and you might be holding these at arm's length. If you keep on running nothing's going to change. That tidal wave will chase you until it breaks. The only way to address feelings you're not comfortable with is to face them and say, 'Yes. Okay. This is true. I do have these feelings. Now, why is that?'

Your tidal-wave emotions might be passion, love and excitement. You can dismiss the best of emotions in the name of living up to the expectations of others or doing 'the right thing'. Turn around, own the feelings and ride the crest of that wave.

Does your tidal wave dream leave you frozen with fear? Are you pushing something you fear away from you? Is your dream warning you that you need to face the fear because it is freezing your forward progress in life? If you turn around and face a tidal wave in a dream it usually disappears — or the danger does. And so it is in waking life — face your fears and they disappear.

In your life this could be about ...

- Something you're not expressing in your relationship.
- Feeling pressured by work or by someone.
- Something that feels too big to handle.
- A situation you cannot work out how to deal with.
- A feeling you think it's 'not nice' to have, such as anger or jealousy.
- An unexpressed love or passion.

Your unique dream contains personal clues only you may recognise

- The person you are feeling pressured by may be in your dream.
- A building or person that reminds you of a time in the past gives you a clue about the first time this feeling or pressure came up for you.
- The number of tidal waves may indicate the number of times this situation has come up before, the number of years or months ago the pressure first started or the number of pressured situations you need to face and deal with.
- Certain people or animals in your dream may remind you of feelings, emotions or instincts. These give you clues about what you are ignoring or using to cover your true feelings.

Why has this dream come up for you now?

Your answers to these questions will reveal the reason:

- What feelings and emotions did you experience in your dream?
- Which situation in your life now do these feelings remind you of?
- Where do you feel most pressure in your life now? If you could wave a magic wand and remove the pressure forever, how would you feel in your new situation? Do you picture this change bringing a new worry or challenge?

Your answer to the last question may reveal the reason your dream has come up for you now. You may be hiding your true feelings and keeping yourself under pressure to avoid this next step in your life.

Dream alchemy practice
Starting the inner work
This is what to *do* if you hope to see dramatic transformations in your life.

A. Do this visualisation regularly:

Imagine yourself facing a huge wave. Make it stop, then change it from water into a golden light. Feel yourself walking into the golden light and swimming in the wave. It is warm and a feeling of love seeps into every pore of your body. As you swim and float, see the wave relax into a smooth sea. Hear it sigh as it relaxes. Now swim back to the shore and walk up the beach feeling the power of a golden sun gently warming your back.

B. This dream alchemy practice is for you if you have identified a physical situation that feels too difficult to sort out (a project too big to handle, a desk piled too high, an unsuitable job you feel burdened with). You may need someone to help you with this one. With your helper, write out a step-by-step practical plan to reduce the pressure. Add a manageable time frame for each step. Then name a reward you get for achieving each step. Ask your helper to phone you regularly to check your progress and make sure you carry out each step in the given time. Celebrate each step with your rewards.

C. With your left hand if you are righthanded, or with your right if you are lefthanded, write a ten-minute poem titled, 'Unexpressed'. No need for rhyming or anything clever. Just let the words spill out onto the page. When you have read your poem as many times as you wish, go back and write, 'This feeling is now released. Love is now free to grow.'

Glimmers of gold
In your dreams
When your recurring dream stops or changes to embrace a happier ending, you are making good progress. Look out for the positive dream changes listed under 'How does your dream end?'

Some symbols from your dream alchemy practice may appear in your dreams. For example, you may dream of swimming in golden light, or of clearing that pressured situation, or enjoying your chosen rewards.

If you experience some dreams of grief, shock or anger, waking up feeling teary but lighter, you are making perfect progress too. These are all positive releasing steps and great indicators of successful magic. Any grief is transitionary — let it evaporate with your tears.

Dreams of watching calm water, enjoying uncluttered spaces, and building on firm foundations are also signs of successful dream alchemy.

In your waking life
You experience a sense of release and movement in at least one area of your life.

You notice more sensitivity to your feelings and may have memory flashbacks to the past. Let yourself fully feel and then let the past go.

You find life easier to manage, especially in practical areas that previously seemed overwhelming. Simple solutions to previously impossible problems suddenly surprise you.

You notice more balance in your life. Something that used to take up a lot of time and attention may seem less important, or require less energy to achieve. There is more space in your life for new things and positive feelings.

5: Naked in public

Naked

(Also see 15: I had sex with ...!)

The dream

You are surprised to discover you are naked or semi-naked in public.

When they know you as you truly are, you truly are.

In your dream perhaps ...

- You are embarrassed and try to hide yourself or your nakedness.
- No matter what you do to try to hide, you become more naked.
- You feel comfortable with being naked.
- You feel proud of being naked.
- The dream feels sexual.
- The dream has no sexual content.

How do you feel in your dream?

Surprised. Embarrassed. Vulnerable. Exposed. Uncomfortable. Comfortable. A sense of ease. Proud. Sexy. Fearful. A sense of danger. Natural. Relieved. Unmasked. Peaceful.

How does your dream end?

Positive changes are on the way if ...

- You feel comfortable with being naked and stay naked.
- You feel comfortable with being naked but find clothes that you like and wear these.
- You have an enjoyable sexual encounter.

It's time for a new approach if ...

- You are still embarrassed at the end of the dream.
- You become more exposed as the dream continues, and still feel uncomfortable with this.

- People take advantage of your nakedness in the dream, or they make fun of you.
- You end up hiding or running away.
- You find clothes to cover your body, but you don't like them.
- You end up wrapped in a cover but still feeling uncomfortable about your position.
- You have an uncomfortable sexual encounter.

What your dream means

Your way forward may be blocked by ...

Trying to hide your true self from other people. Not feeling comfortable with who you really are deep down inside. Feeling vulnerable to being judged by others.

Moving forward

Let go of the facade. Let your true light shine. If others judge you that's their problem. Judgement is in the eye of the beholder and has nothing to do with who you really are.

◆

So there you are, in the middle of a dream, about to impress someone with your verve and savvy when you look down and catch a glimpse of ... your nakedness. As you blush red hot, your poise, confidence and composure go into rapid meltdown. Scurrying for non-existent cover you have to face facts: you are exposed. There's no hiding behind a facade of carefully chosen clothing now. This is the real you and you are way out of your comfort zone and feeling vulnerable.

Cut! Take two. So there you are, in the middle of a dream, about to impress someone with your verve and savvy when you look down and catch a glimpse of ... your nakedness. You strike a pose to make the most of what you've got. This is the real you and they can love it or leave it. Who needs a comfort zone?

And that's it, basically. This very common dream is all about how comfortable you do or don't feel with showing and being your real self. It's got nothing to do with how you feel about the shape of your body or your sexuality, and everything to do with how you feel about who you are underneath it all. Below the surface, under the skin, deeper than your nakedness, at the core of your heart and soul — the Authentic Self: the real you.

This dream mostly comes up when you're feeling vulnerable about something or someone. The details of your dream reveal why you feel uncomfortable and why you try to hide. How you handle this information from here on is your choice, in your waking life as well as in your dreams.

And if the dream takes a sexual turn? The rule of thumb is that good dream-sex reflects positive personal growth and not so good dream-sex shows work is still needed.

In your life this could be about ...

* A job involving presenting yourself or your work to the public.
* A relationship where you are pretending to be someone you are not.
* You living beyond your financial means.
* An exam you are about to take — you feel your performance will not live up to other people's expectations.
* A job interview you are about to attend or speech you are about to give.
* A situation where you are being two-faced.
* A secret you have been keeping.

Your unique dream contains personal clues only you may recognise

* Which part of your body is exposed? The back of your body may mean you fear your past (what is behind you) being exposed. The front of your body may mean you fear your future plans (what is in front of you) being discovered.
* What clothes do you lose? If these are clothes you own or have owned, they may give you a clue to the situation or year when this matter first started.
* What clothes are you left wearing? These may give you a clue about what you are hanging onto as an inadequate cover-up.
* What is the location of your nakedness? Being outdoors may show what you are already bringing out into the

open or are ready to show, while being inside may show a deeper feeling of vulnerability. Does the street or house give a clue about your waking life situation?

Why has this dream come up for you now?

Your answers to these questions will reveal the reason:

◆ What feelings and emotions did you experience in your dream?

◆ Which situation in your life now do these feelings remind you of?

◆ Have you recently felt challenged to reveal something about yourself?

◆ Have you recently felt threatened by someone's questioning or expectation of you?

◆ If you were to reveal your true self in the situation you are thinking about right now, what would change in your life?

Your answer to the last question may reveal the reason your dream has come up for you now. You are struggling between being your natural self and facing your fear of the changes that this may bring.

Dream alchemy practice
Starting the inner work

This is what to *do* if you hope to see dramatic transformations in your life.

A. Here's the fun one. Go out and buy yourself something to wear that reveals a little more of your true self. You can spend big on a whole new outfit or choose something smaller — a watch strap, a tie, a different shade of make-up, a scarf in a more-you colour or a piece of fun jewellery. Wear this dream alchemy practice and *feel* it.

B. Buy a book about a subject that is very you, or featuring a character that is very much like you. Read it, enjoy it, then pass it on to your friends and colleagues, recommending it as a great read. What you are doing is subtly giving them a glimpse of the real you — doors will open as they relate to you and you feel more comfortable with people knowing more about what makes you tick and what turns you on.

C. Imagine yourself as an older person — add forty years to your present age. Now give your older self the freedom to be a bit eccentric, to be proud to be an individual in a cheeky, happy, fulfilling way.

Glimmers of gold
In your dreams
When your recurring dream changes to embrace a happier ending, you are making good progress. Look out for the positive dream changes listed under 'How does your dream end?'

Some symbols from your dream alchemy practice may appear in your dreams. For example, you may dream you are an eccentric older person or dream of meeting an extraordinary older person enjoying life.

You may release some strong emotions in your dreams such as guilt or fear, or you may find yourself being judged and sentenced. This is your dream's way of releasing the feelings you have tried to keep hidden from the world. Let them go.

Look out for dreams of fighting your way out from under heavy blankets or freeing yourself from some other kind of cover. You may also dream of wearing clothes that express the real you clearly.

In your waking life
You experience a sense of your own presence and power.

You feel more comfortable with being yourself in all areas of your life.

You concern yourself less and less with what other people think about you.

You may feel a need to toss out your clothes and buy new ones that more adequately reflect how you feel.

You notice people responding more positively to you, more energetically. People tell you they feel inspired by you. You realise that showing your light is helping others to see their way out from under cover.

6: Lifts and crazy stairs

Stairs and lifts

(Also see 21: I've lost my way)

The dream

You are trying to get to a floor or level in a building, but there is a problem with the lift or the stairs.

The destination is yours. How long do you wish to journey?

In your dream perhaps ...

♦ You know where you want to go but you can't get there.
♦ You don't know where you want to go and you feel lost.
♦ The lift or stair exit to your floor seems to be missing or inaccessible.
♦ The lifts or stairs go up when you want to go down, or down when you want to go up.
♦ You always end up at a certain level or floor, for example, Floor 7.
♦ The stairs are like an M. C. Escher drawing: you turn to go up the next flight of stairs but find yourself trying to walk on the underside of the steps. You can't work out how to get onto the top of the steps.

How do you feel in your dream?

Frustrated. Lost. Inadequate. Out of control. Confused. Unentitled. Blocked. Discriminated against. Powerless. Denied.

How does your dream end?

Positive changes are on the way if ...

♦ You finally arrive at your chosen destination.
♦ You suddenly see a way past an obstacle or difficulty.
♦ The lift or stairs take you to a better place than where you were heading.
♦ You lead others to a positive destination.
♦ The dream has a positive ending.

It's time for a new approach if ...

♦ You are as lost at the end of the dream as you are at the beginning.

♦ The lifts and stairs increase in complexity in the dream, or from dream to dream.

What your dream means

Your way forward may be blocked by ...

Avoidance. Going the long way around a problem. Fear of success. Not feeling entitled to succeed. Feeling life was meant to be hard or complicated. Something you've lost touch with and are avoiding facing.

Moving forward

Know that it's part of life's learning process to make errors or to fail. Know that life doesn't have to be tough to be worthwhile, and know that you can be rewarded for working smart rather than working hard. Know that you are as entitled as everyone else is to succeed. When you find yourself hesitating, ask yourself what you are avoiding.

♦

All these ups and downs have one thing in common: you can't access the floor you want. You know it's there somewhere. You're in the lift and you know Floor 7 is there. You know no one's wiped out a whole floor overnight, so why can't you get there?

You want to go up, so why does the lift go down? You want to go down but the thing has a life of its own and takes you up. Or you're trotting happily up a perfectly normal staircase when it rearranges itself.

The connection between these dreams is that there is *no* connection! Translated into waking life, your dream is showing you that you're not in touch with an important connection. The number of the floor you want is a key. If you're looking for Floor 7, think age seven, or seven years ago, or the seventh chakra (the yoga energy point for spiritual connection) — the list goes on.

No one has wiped out your memories of being seven, or the events of seven years ago, but your dream shows that you are blocking your own access to those memory banks or feelings. When you want to know who's in control of the dream lift or who rearranged the whole dream staircase the answer is always: *you*. Now, what would be your vested interest in blocking yourself? You want to get somewhere and you don't want to get somewhere. What could you possibly fear?

This kind of dream shows that you are hesitating to access memories or feelings that hold the key to solving an issue in your life. You are choosing the long way round which may never get you there at all. This is avoidance. The short way to success is to let go of the hesitation and allow yourself to explore your fears. What would you rather do?

In your life this could be about ...
- A course or project you are spinning out to make it last.
- A relationship past its use-by date.
- Your as yet unfulfilled search for the perfect relationship.
- Your job, if you are overworked and under-appreciated.
- The talent you are avoiding using.
- The reward or success that you feel is well overdue.

Your unique dream contains personal clues only you may recognise
- The type of building in your dream may give you a clue about the area of life that you are endlessly trapped in.
- Any props you are carrying may be clues to what is keeping you trudging in your endless journey.
- Any objects or people you are looking for may give you a clue about your missing connection.
- Anyone or anything you avoid in your dream may be a clue to what you need to face in waking life.
- The floor number you can't get to may be a clue to the age you were when this avoidance problem began.

Why has this dream come up for you now?
Your answers to these questions will reveal the reason:
- What feelings and emotions did you experience in your dream?
- Which situation in your life now do these feelings remind you of?

♦ Has there been a movement forward recently, a glimpse of resolving this situation or a decision to stay in it?

Your answer to the last question may reveal the reason your dream has come up for you now. You are likely to be entering maximum avoidance, so your unconscious will be alerting you to this pointless game of avoiding success.

Dream alchemy practice
Starting the inner work

This is what to *do* if you hope to see dramatic transformations in your life.

A. Do this dream alchemy visualisation regularly:

Imagine yourself back in your dream faced with the staircase or lift that leads nowhere. Now change the dream. Feel yourself stepping off the last stair or from the lift into a happy and fulfilling feeling. It's best not to visualise a precise scene. There may be a better outcome for you than the one you think is best. Focus on summoning up the feeling of total fulfilment and let the universe provide the right situation for you.

B. Take ten minutes only to write a poem, with no attention to rhyme or reason. Keep it simple and give it the title: 'When the long way round is the wrong way round.'

C. For this dream alchemy practice draw a tall building with as many floors as your age. Number the floors with arrows. By each arrow write one word to describe the feeling of that year of your life — one feeling for each year only! See what comes up. If you cannot find words for some arrows take some time to explore whether you are avoiding anything from those years. Keep asking your heart for answers until all the arrows are labelled. When your drawing is complete, imagine walking up from the ground floor, feeling each feeling as you go through a floor and then letting it evaporate behind you as you ascend to the next level. At the top of the building, take a deep breath and let the past go.

Glimmers of gold
In your dreams
When your recurring dream changes to embrace a happier ending, you are making good progress. Look out for the positive dream changes listed under 'How does your dream end?'

Some symbols from your dream alchemy practice may appear in your dreams. For example, you may dream you are climbing a tall building, moving easily from one level to the next, or stopping to explore feelings about one particular floor.

Your dreams may bring up people, memories and feelings you have been avoiding, or grief and feelings of exhaustion connected with the long, hard trials you have put yourself through in life. This is your dream's way of allowing you to acknowledge your past so that you can move forward, or of releasing old wishes and plans that are no longer suitable to allow for better outcomes to flow into your life.

Look out for dreams of sudden positive changes of scene and possibly for death and birth dreams that show your old ways ending so that new ways can begin.

In your waking life
You are more comfortable with memories from the past and with looking at feelings and situations you have avoided. You are surprised that you once found this difficult to do.

You see short cuts and easier ways of doing things in many areas of your life. You are surprised to see better quality results compared with doing things the original, longer way.

Success in at least one area of your life comes easier and you don't mind being seen to make mistakes along the way.

You notice other people being laborious and paying too much attention to jobs that could be completed in less time producing better quality results.

Life may seem to speed up or present more opportunities.

7: Losing or forgetting the baby or child

Baby, lost or forgotten

(Also see 34: On the cliff edge — or falling; 41: Death and murder)

The dream
You lose your child or a dream child, or you keep forgetting that you have a child or baby to look after.

Why is it that as your heart reaches out to another, you forget what is in your heart? All hearts beat with the same longing.

In your dream perhaps ...
- Your baby or child slips down the drain in a bath or down a stormwater drain and disappears.
- Your child is lost at sea or in a body of water.
- Suddenly you cannot find your child or baby.
- You keep forgetting that you have a baby to feed.
- You keep forgetting to change your baby's nappy.
- Your child falls from a window or off a cliff.

How do you feel in your dream?
Shocked. A sense of grief. A sense of loss. Lost. Devastated. Powerless. Fearful. A sense of dread. Inadequate. Guilty. Responsible. Horrified. Forgetful. Ashamed.

How does your dream end?
Positive changes are on the way if ...
- You are reunited with your child or baby.
- You successfully feed the baby or change the nappy and everyone is happy. No damage has been done by the forgetfulness.
- You grieve for the loss and find some form of resolution.

♦   After the shock the dream changes and delivers a positive feeling.
♦   You feel teary for a few days and then feel much clearer.

It's time for a new approach if ...
♦   You wake up devastated.
♦   The baby or child is suffering from lack of attention.
♦   The dream ends with a sense of loss.

What your dream means
Your way forward may be blocked by ...
Losing touch with something once precious in your life. Lack of self-nurturing. An unresolved hurt or grief you experienced as a child.
Moving forward
Love and care for yourself as you would love and care for your own children. Give yourself space and time to attend to your personal needs, feelings and dreams. Find room in your heart to hear the cry of the child you once were and reassure your child-self that all is now well.

♦

It's in your genes — round face, big innocent eyes with toes and fingers that curl and squirm in sheer delight. No, that's not you. That's a baby. You're the one with the genes built to respond to these cues, to nurture and protect. Ordered by instinct, whether you're male or female.

It's a pity the instinct doesn't always stretch to nurturing and protecting yourself. Once upon a time you were a baby and, hopefully, someone cradled you and provided for your needs. As adult you cradle and provide for others, maybe for your own children or maybe for the needs of other adults. Are you caring for your own needs too?

When you dream of forgetting to feed a baby, or forgetting to change the baby's nappy, you are probably forgetting to attend to your own needs. Your dream conjures up a soulful baby image to eat away at those nurturing genes of yours. When you dream of forgetting that you have a baby at all, you can be sure there is a hungry voice inside your soul crying out for help.

You've heard all about the 'child within' or the 'inner child'. Well, this is it, only when it's a baby it's the 'baby within' or the 'inner baby'. As you go through life you encounter emotional wounds and hurts. Some hurts are bigger than others but the unconscious remembers them all. When hurts are not healed, the cry for help lives on in your feeling and memory banks. Sometimes, in your dreams, you hear the cry of the three-year-old inner child — the you that is still waiting to be cuddled and forgiven, or cuddled and reassured, or cuddled and loved.

When a dream reminds you of a forgotten baby or child who needs attention, it may well be you. 'Ah,' you argue, 'But the child in my dream doesn't look like me. He looks just like my son when he was three.' Dreams are like that. Dreaming of your own three-year-old in need is going to have a bigger impact on you than dreaming of yourself as a three-year-old. And what you will do for your own child, you must also consider doing for yourself.

There is an economy about dreams, or a budget. They like to double up on symbols sometimes. Dreaming of your own child plucks at your heartstrings and demands your attention — so your dreaming mind uses this same symbol for something else. You may find your son as a three-year-old turning up in a dream that's about something that's been in your life for three years — a job, perhaps. Or your dreaming mind will pop in your daughter as a baby crying to be fed to remind you of a new project in your life that is crying out to be fed.

One of the most shocking dreams is the very common one where you're bathing your baby and he or she drowns or disappears down the plug hole. A variation is the horror dream where your child falls into a stormwater drain and is washed away, never to be seen again. Rest assured that if this dream were a premonition the world would be desperately underpopulated.

So what would the plug hole or stormwater drain mean in a dream and why the need for such a strong shock rating? It would be trite to say this is the anxiety dream of a new parent. Superficially all dreams are anxiety dreams, but it's what lies below the anxiety that is helpful in making life-changing choices. All anxiety says is, 'I'm not feeling comfortable with this.' The deeper question is, 'Why not?' Dreams show you what you're not comfortable with and how to smooth your path.

When you dream of your child drowning or slipping down a drain, you are dreaming a feeling of shocking loss, of emptiness. Something incredibly precious has been lost or drained away from you. Whenever a baby is born, no matter how precious and fulfilling for you, something is also lost. Perhaps you have left a career or a job. Maybe your contact with the outside world has temporarily suffered. Or do you feel, as you hold new life with all its potential in your arms, that your own potential has slipped away? Perhaps, busily caring for your baby's every need, you see your creative ideas and dreams fading away. What are you afraid of losing touch with? What seems to be slipping away from you?

Whether it's a bath plug hole or a stormwater drain, the dream connection is water and water usually symbolises emotions. These are deep emotional issues.

It's *so* important to remember that your dream children are *not* your children. They are your memories of yourself as a child or something new in your life. They are *your* beliefs and feelings, given the faces of your children to draw your emotional response. Boy babies and girl babies symbolise different things, even when the babies look like your own children. Boys usually represent the 'outer world' (Yang), or the qualities of your left brain (logic and rational thinking, assertiveness, intellect, competitiveness, doing rather than being, relating to the world of work). Girls usually represent the 'inner world' (Yin), or the qualities of your right brain (intuition, holistic thinking, nurturing, creativity, being rather than doing, relating to the inner world and spirituality). Be guided by the sex of the child in your dream. Are you losing touch with something in your outer world or your inner world?

Feeling intense shock in a dream comes either when you have buried a shock in the past because you weren't ready to deal with it, or because you have tried to bury a feeling or thought that you felt would be too shocking to admit. Shock needs to be soothed and smoothed away, not buried.

In your life this could be about ...

- Losing touch with the creative side of life because of overwork.
- Having to be serious much of the time and losing touch with fun, laughter and being playful.
- An overwhelming sense of responsibility that is a drain on you.
- A deep memory of being a child and feeling hurt or rejected, which is perhaps triggered by having children of your own.
- Something you are neglecting to attend to or nurture.

Your unique dream contains personal clues only you may recognise

- A girl baby often represents your Yin or inner world including your creativity, emotions, spirituality and need for being in the moment. Are you losing touch with these?
- A boy baby often represents your Yang or outer world including your work, career, intellect and need for action. Are you losing touch with these?
- The age of the baby or child may give you a clue about the number of years something new has been in your life.
- The age of your dream baby may remind you of a loss you felt when you were that age.

Why has this dream come up for you now?

Your answers to these questions will reveal the reason:

- What feelings and emotions did you experience in your dream?
- Which situation in your life now do these feelings remind you of?
- Has something happened recently to cause you to neglect your needs or dreams?
- Have you been questioning the way you were brought up and how your parents and other carers treated you?

♦ Have you felt that you are missing out on something recently?

Your answer to the last question may reveal the reason your dream has come up for you now.

Dream alchemy practice
Starting the inner work

This is what to *do* if you hope to see dramatic transformations in your life.

A. Find a photo of yourself as a baby. Frame it as it is or enlarged, or cut it out and make a collage picture, surrounding your photo with symbols of nurturing and love. Keep your photo somewhere you will see it many times a day — on your desk, by the kettle, by the bathroom mirror or next to your bed. Study your baby face and get to know it so well that you can imagine yourself as a living baby nestled in your adult arms. Now, imagine carrying your baby self around with you everywhere you go. Whenever anyone asks you to do something, consider making your decision for your baby. Whenever your baby needs love and care, give that love and care to yourself as an adult. Whenever your baby needs to sleep, to eat, to dream or to be heard, allow these needs to be met for you as an adult.

B. Make a list of the activities and dreams you are losing touch with. Talk these over with someone special and ask them to help you see how to reintroduce these things into your life. Ask that person to be your life coach, your motivator, your co-alchemist. Offer to do the same in return. Contact each other according to an agreed schedule to check on each other's progress, perhaps daily to start with, then weekly. Celebrate each other's progress.

C. If you can identify a time, as a child, when you felt hurt, and you feel your inner child is still hurting, it's time to go back and make things right by 'giving back the belief'. Here's an example of how this dream alchemy works:

A little boy was taught that 'boys don't cry' and 'fathers don't hug their sons'. Of course this little one desperately needed to cry or be hugged along the way, but he grew up to hold back his tears and keep an emotional distance from those he loved. On the surface all was cool, but deep inside the little boy lived on, still crying rejected, unloved tears. He took on the beliefs of his father and suffered as a result.

To perform his dream alchemy practice this man imagines going back to meet himself as a little child and hugs this child. He tells him that he can now give his father back this belief that boys don't cry and fathers don't hug because it belongs to the father, not to the child. The grown man helps the child to do this, in this visualisation, and sees the father agree to take back the belief. In its place, the grown man must give the child a new belief to replace the old. He chooses to give the belief, 'It's good for boys and men to cry when they need to and to hug and express their feelings.'

Alter this visualisation to suit your circumstances and give back that belief!

Glimmers of gold
In your dreams
When your recurring dream changes to embrace a happier ending, you are making good progress. Look out for the positive dream changes listed under 'How does your dream end?'

Some symbols from your dream alchemy practice may appear in your dreams. For example, you may dream you meet yourself as a child or a baby.

Your dreams may bring up old grief that you have held back, or a sense of shock at what you have been through or at how successfully you have 'drowned' your feelings — in the same way as the baby drowned in your dream. This is your dream's way of releasing the emotions that have been stopping you from finding what you have lost.

Look out for dreams of giving birth to new babies; of finding precious stones or jewellery; of discovering new talents such as singing, dancing or psychic powers. Also look for dreams of plants growing strong and tall, of flowers blossoming or fruit trees maturing to bear fruit.

In your waking life

You begin to see your childhood in a more positive light. You see your parents, teachers and society back then as the products of their upbringing. You feel forgiveness for any hurts. You feel separate and mature, able to walk your path freely without carrying other people's beliefs that were once hurtful to you and without feeling answerable to them.

You feel more responsible for your own wellbeing and find it easy to make the time and space to attend to your needs. You do things you haven't done for a long time, and wonder why it took you so long to do them.

You feel fulfilled. Your life becomes more balanced. Suddenly and miraculously there *is* time for everything.

8: Who's driving this car?

Driving

The dream

The dream features a car journey. You are either the driver or a passenger.

Whose soul is this? Whose life to behold?

In your dream perhaps ...

- Your dream car is one you have driven in the past.
- You have never driven a car like this one before.
- Things start to go wrong with the car.
- The driver loses control of the car or struggles with it.
- You are driving easily and you arrive at your destination.
- Someone else is driving and you are comfortable with this.
- Someone else is driving and you are not comfortable with this.
- You are in the back seat and feeling uncomfortable.
- You are driving but do not arrive at your destination.
- The car is involved in an accident.
- You park the car but cannot find it later.

How do you feel in your dream?

A sense of ease. Joyful. Elated. Free. Motivated. Inspired. Rewarded. Pampered. Frustrated. Angry. Irritated. Stuck. Overpowered. Restricted. Not confident. Confident. Successful. Awkward. Suffocated.

How does your dream end?

Positive changes are on the way if ...

- You arrive at your destination.
- The dream has a positive outcome.
- As the passenger you have a good relationship with the driver.
- As the passenger you take over the driving from a driver

who was causing you discomfort and you drive the car successfully to your destination.

- You work out how to avoid an accident.
- After an accident, you suddenly see something insightful.
- You mend the car or get it fixed easily.
- You find your lost car.

It's time for a new approach if ...

- You do not reach your destination and the dream does not end positively.
- You do not feel comfortable with the driver and the dream ends without this changing.
- Someone is hurt in an accident.
- You never find your car after parking it.
- You cannot fix your car.
- Your car is out of control.
- You feel overpowered by the wishes of others in the car.
- You and the car are in danger at the end of the dream.

What your dream means

Your way forward may be blocked by ...

Being driven and motivated by beliefs that are not serving you well. Driving yourself to suit other people's expectations, not your own. Not being in touch with the best driving force to get you to the best destination. Exerting too much or too little control over your life, either way being too extreme to get you far.

Moving forward

If things are not working well for you, it's time to change your approach. Look to your driving dreams for specific guidance on how to handle your situation to achieve a better outcome. Get into the driving seat of your life, but don't grab the wheel too tightly or you'll miss out on life's best surprises!

◆

Think of a dream car as your drive. A car gets you from *a* to *b*, and your mental drive gets you from *a* to *b*, or it should do, when your ignition's on and you're all fired up. This is assuming that *b* is the best destination for you.

The car image is perfect because it gets you in touch with who's driving your life. Who or what is the driving force behind a particular issue in your life, and is this really getting you to the best place?

If you're the one behind the wheel of your dream car, look at where it's taking you. How does the dream journey pan out? What does this tell you about how you're driving yourself?

If you're not the one behind the wheel, things get really interesting. Your father's driving you? Easy: you are being driven by your father's expectations or you are approaching an issue as your father would. 'Not me!' you proclaim, wildly. 'I'm not like my dad!' The thing is, your unconscious holds thoughts and beliefs that are often different — perhaps even opposite — to your conscious thoughts. We all do it. As children we listen to our parents and think they are gods. What they say is right. Everything they say goes deep into the unconscious, programming us to believe this or act in a certain way. Then we spend the rest of our lives questioning our programming but often being unable to shake free of it.

This is where dream work is so powerful! Your dreams show you how your unconscious mind thinks and what it believes. They then show you how this conflicts with your conscious thoughts and beliefs and how this conflict is making your waking life a bit rough. Best of all, when you use your dream to create an affirmation, you undo the old program and create a new one. With your unconscious beliefs in line with your conscious beliefs it's easy riding!

Alongside those unreasonable beliefs cluttering up your unconscious are some brilliant sleepy ones that just need a bit of waking up. If you're not paying attention to your intuition your dream might show you a beautiful, mysterious woman or cat (cats are a great favourite dream symbol for intuition) driving your car, taking you smoothly and easily to a perfect place.

Be guided by the reaction of your dream car to whoever's driving. If your car reverses every time you try to drive it forward and if things get worse the more you try to grip the wheel and take control, then stop and think. Maybe there's something in life you're trying to control and your dream is showing you exactly where this is not getting you. Loosen your grip, give up trying to control things, let things and people be. Your next dream will probably show you feeling free — speeding along with great ease, hands lightly touching the wheel.

In your life this could be about ...

- Your motives for choosing the course you are studying.
- Why you have chosen certain goals in life.
- How you handle your money.
- The disciplines or routines you follow at home or at work.
- A relationship in which you have given up your power to the other person.
- A relationship in which you are trying to control the other person's behaviour.
- An addiction.
- A personal quest or plan you are following.

Your unique dream contains personal clues only you may recognise

- If your dream car is one you owned in the past, those years hold the clue to the beginning of this driving-force attitude.
- If the dream car is a type owned or once owned by someone you know, then the personality of that person or their beliefs may hold something for you to explore and question in your own life.
- The name or image of the dream car may be a clue: a convertible meaning 'be adaptable'; a racing car implying speed; a rust-bucket implying you may be driving yourself so hard that you're falling apart, or not putting quality into your life. Where in your life would this make sense?

Why has this dream come up for you now?

Your answers to these questions will reveal the reason:

♦ What feelings and emotions did you experience in your dream?

♦ Which situation in your life now do these feelings remind you of?

♦ What would you have to do, in the dream, to achieve a successful outcome?

♦ What is the mirror of this in your waking life — what would you have to do to achieve a successful outcome?

♦ If your dream-car journey had a successful outcome, what would you have to do in your waking life to emulate this?

♦ If you were to make these waking-life changes, what fear or challenge does this bring up for you, or what other part of your life do you feel would be threatened?

Your answer to the last question may reveal the reason your dream has come up for you now. You want to achieve a more successful outcome but you are concerned about how this may change other areas of your life.

Dream alchemy practice
Starting the inner work
This is what to *do* if you hope to see dramatic transformations in your life.

A. After you have looked at your dream and worked out what you really want to achieve on your life's journey and which attitudes and beliefs are the best ones to take you there, choose a car to symbolise all of this. No, you don't have to buy it! Choose the type and colour and then visualise yourself driving your dream alchemy practice car. How would it make you feel? How will achieving your successful outcome make you feel? Now repeat this visualisation, accentuating these desired feelings.

B. Here's an affirmation for you:
I am the sole and soul driver of my car. I am peaceful, unhurried and relaxed, holding the wheel firmly enough to choose or change my direction and loosely enough to be guided by my intuition. We are all free to choose our destinations and our journeys.

C. Write a list of all the main people whose beliefs have driven you throughout your life. Write a short 'thank you' letter or card to each one, naming the belief you followed and thanking them for being a life-shaping force. To the people whose driving beliefs were positive, thank them for their gift. To the people whose driving beliefs were inappropriate for you, thank them for the lessons you learned along the way and give them back their belief. Tell them what new belief you now have and suggest they might like to try it. You may wish to send some of the letters or cards (perhaps to those whose driving beliefs were positive), but this is not necessary for the dream alchemy to work. Burn the letters you do not send, knowing that new and vibrant life will spring from the ashes.

Glimmers of gold
In your dreams
When your recurring dream changes to embrace a happier ending, you are making good progress. Look out for the positive dream changes listed under 'How does your dream end?'

Some symbols from your dream alchemy practice may appear in your dreams. For example, you may dream of driving that dream alchemy car.

Your dreams may bring up old anger that you have held back, or exhaustion if you have been driving yourself too hard. This is your dream's way of releasing the emotions and energy that have been stopping you from reaching a more appropriate destination.

Look out for dreams of driving a range of cars, of breaking through barriers into a less restricted space, of flying with ease, of being carried forward in a positive way by unseen forces or being given guidance and support by loving strangers.

In your waking life
You feel freer and are aware of more options. The obstacles that seemed to lie before you disappear. You feel less

driven and more in the flow of achieving your goals and living your life.

You feel more powerful in the choices you make and in seeing things pan out the way you wish. Any concerns you had about keeping things or people in control evaporate as you discover how to use your power for yourself and release others to make their own choices.

Your life becomes more balanced as your road ahead becomes clear and easy to navigate.

9: Late for the appointment

Late

(Also see 16: Slo mo running or walking)

The dream

You are running late for a meeting, appointment, train, boat or plane.

Between perfect words lie infinite spaces.

In your dream perhaps ...

♦ You are trying to get to the meeting but you keep coming up against obstacles.
♦ You realise the plane is going to take off without you.
♦ You arrive at the train station but you can't get a ticket in time.
♦ You are almost there and then realise you have forgotten your notes or cases.

How do you feel in your dream?

Frustrated. A sense of panic. Forgetful. Weighed down. Disappointed with yourself. Embarrassed. Concerned. A sense of urgency.

How does your dream end?

Positive changes are on the way if ...

♦ You finally make the appointment.
♦ You catch the plane, boat or train.
♦ You decide you don't need your cases and let them go.
♦ You get tickets easily or discover you've had them in your pocket all along.
♦ You phone to say you're not coming to the meeting and you feel happy with this outcome.
♦ You phone to set a new appointment time that is more suitable for you and you know you will be able to make this.

It's time for a new approach if ...

* The journey gets more complicated during the dream or from dream to dream.
* Your cases or bags get heavier.
* You see the train, boat or plane leave without you.
* You feel a sense of urgency you cannot overcome.

What your dream means

Your way forward may be blocked by ...

A fear of success because of a fear of failure. Perfectionism. Needing approval. Needing to get things 'right'. Needing to be seen to perform well. A belief that success is hard-won. Too much focus on one area of your life at the expense of another.

Moving forward

Allow yourself the freedom to make mistakes, knowing that the best insights and new ideas often spring from so-called mistakes. Know that you will never be approved of or loved by everyone — many people will judge you but that is their burden, not yours. Know that there are many shades of right, and many inspiring colours ranged between black and white. Focus equally on all areas of your life.

◆

Don't tell me, I know ... this never happens to you in waking life? You're aware of time, you allow time, you prepare well and it takes a major drama to make you late for an appointment. You never lose your ticket and you always catch your plane.

Perfect. This dream's a classic from the perfectionist's portfolio. It's also a classic for workaholics and people who are considerate of others to the extreme. Quite a diverse lot, really. So what have they all got in common? A need to perform, to get things right; being driven by a fear of getting things wrong.

The dream shows you as wanting to catch the plane but throwing up obstacles along your way to delay facing the fear of success. Or is that the fear of failure? Remember, everything that goes wrong in a dream, every delay, reveals your unconscious mind busily sabotaging the outcome. When you examine the details of the dream obstacles you get a handle on the negative beliefs and thoughts programmed into your unconscious mind. These can help you to understand why you fear getting things wrong so much that you'll move mountains to make life difficult for yourself, but you'll *always* make that plane, or not hurt that person's feelings. You'll create an enormous number of appointments, ensure that you have to work extremely hard to prove you're good enough and throw in a bit of a doormat attitude so as not to fail in your need to be perfect and loved by everyone.

So, you make life hard for yourself but you get there anyway, right? Wrong! If you're a workaholic you may be catching planes for work appointments but you're sure to be missing those otherwise destined for relationships, relaxation and personal development. If you're a perfectionist you may be creating perfect work in perfect time, but probably at an enormous cost to other areas of your life. Can you work smarter rather than harder? Can you delegate? Can you release yourself to catch life's other planes?

All the while you are missing planes in dreams you can be sure that your unconscious is crying out because something is missing in your life and you're not giving yourself permission to have it.

In your life this could be about ...
+ Your work performance.
+ Your feelings about how things should be done.
+ Your addiction to work.
+ The time you don't give to your family or to yourself.
+ A project or idea you talk about but don't do.
+ An unused talent.
+ A past failure that bugs you.
+ A past success that you feel you can't live up to.

Your unique dream contains personal clues only you may recognise
+ If you recognise the location of the airport, meeting or station from sometime in your past, this gives you a clue about the time this situation started or escalated.

◆ The props you carry provide clues. That saxophone may take you back to learning to play and all the issues that you have carried with you about those experiences, or it may give you a clue about realising that you are not allowing time to enjoy your musical talents.

◆ Look at any times mentioned in your dream: the 2.30 departure or the 8.00 meeting. These numbers may give you a clue about the age you were (23, 8) when this issue started or when there were significant changes. The numbers may also give you a clue about months (23 months ago or 2.3 months ago) or to house numbers that help to pinpoint a year. The 7.40 plane might take you back to 1974. Your dreaming mind thinks laterally when it comes to numbers and is often precisely accurate — once you've worked out the clue!

Why has this dream come up for you now?

Your answers to these questions will reveal the reason:

◆ What feelings and emotions did you experience in your dream?

◆ Which situation in your current life do these feelings remind you of?

◆ Which area of your life are you most proud of?

◆ What challenges would you have to face if you lost everything you have gained in this area?

Your answer to the last question may reveal the reason your dream has come up for you now. This dream comes up when you feel insecure about the possibility of having to face these challenges one day.

Dream alchemy practice
Starting the inner work

This is what to *do* if you hope to see dramatic transformations in your life.

A. Take twenty minutes to write a story. Just let it flow, no clever words or plots. The title of the story is, 'Whatever happened to the boy who missed the plane?' or 'Whatever happened to the girl who missed the meeting?' (Alter the title to suit you and your dream.)

B. Put the story away for a week then look at it again. How much of your life is in this story? If it had an unhappy ending, rewrite it now with a different ending. For powerful dream-alchemy punch, don't let the boy or girl simply catch the plane or make the meeting. Add in what he or she learned about life from missing out the first time.

C. Here's an affirmation for you.

> I feel the beauty and light of the many colours that shine between black and white. I am the colour and energy of life. I walk the path of maximum colour, shrugging my shoulders at those who choose to live in the colder extremes of black or white.

Glimmers of gold

In your dreams

When your recurring dream changes to embrace a happier ending, you are making good progress. Look out for the positive dream changes listed under 'How does your dream end?'

Some symbols from your dream alchemy practice may appear in your dreams. For example, you may dream of wearing many colours.

Your dreams may bring up a range of strong emotions and images from past situations where you felt under pressure to perform. Some of the emotions may be directed, in your dreams, towards the people who influenced you back then. This is your dream's way of releasing emotions and beliefs that have narrowed your focus or shaped your need for approval.

Look out for dreams of arriving at meetings or airports ahead of time, of planes falling out of the sky (see common dream 40: Plane crash) and of curves, circles and round shapes (as opposed to rectangles and straight lines).

In your waking life

You see easier solutions and simpler ways of doing things.

You begin to think more laterally, in curves rather than in straight lines.

The more serious areas of your life start to loosen up. You see more of the funny side of situations and develop more of an urge to play to liven things up. You may feel attracted to wearing more vibrant colours or decorating in strong colours.

You want to spend more time doing things you had less time for previously. You see that there are many ways to skin a cat and many ways to let the cat go free.

What people think of you becomes less important than what you think of yourself. Life breathes more easily.

10: Unprepared for exam

Exam

(Also see 9: Late for the appointment; 11: Back at school)

The dream

You are about to sit an exam or give a lecture or presentation and you realise you are totally unprepared for it.

By whose measure do you succeed or fail?

In your dream perhaps ...

- You are back at school or university, about to sit an exam that you are unprepared for. When you wake up, you are puzzled because this is an exam you passed in waking life years ago.
- You are about to sit an exam in a subject unrelated to anything you have studied before, either in the dream or in waking life. You feel unprepared.
- You have no idea about the subject of the exam. You cannot read or understand the questions.
- Although you feel unprepared for the exam, you start to answer the questions and realise you do know the answers.
- Although you feel unprepared for the exam and do not know the answers, you start to answer them creatively and you're pleased with the results.
- You walk into a lecture theatre or conference room to give a presentation and see the attentive audience. You suddenly realise that you have not prepared adequately for this and you feel you're going to let yourself and the audience down.
- You are about to sit an exam or give a presentation that you are about to face in waking life. You feel unprepared in the dream but you are surprised, when you wake up, because you feel you have prepared very well for the actual event.

How do you feel in your dream?

Unprepared. Inadequate. Vulnerable. Shocked. Anxious. A sense of panic. Fraudulent. Embarrassed. Surprised. Resourceful. Empowered. Enlightened. Dismayed. Remiss. A sense of shame. Guilty. Unburdened.

How does your dream end?

Positive changes are on the way if ...

* You find creative answers to the exam questions or creative ways of delivering your presentation that you know are good ones.
* You realise you can only do your best in the given situation and apply yourself to doing exactly that.
* You discover a new talent.
* You realise that passing this exam or giving this presentation is no longer important to you, so you leave.
* You help someone else to pass the exam or inspire someone in the audience.

It's time for a new approach if ...

* Things are still not going well by the end of the dream.
* Your audience walks out on you.

What your dream means

Your way forward may be blocked by ...

Feeling tested in one area of your waking life and reacting according to the kind of beliefs and attitudes you had at school or college. These beliefs might include issues about authority, performance, proving yourself to others and pleasing or displeasing a parent or teacher. Feeling judged or judging yourself harshly. Living and thinking according to old-fashioned values and methods learned at school that are no longer appropriate for you today.

Moving forward

Know that you are equal to all adults and to people in authority. You have no need to prove your worth to satisfy another's judgement. There are many right solutions to a problem or situation. Know that you are forever both student and teacher, and that testing situations are opportunities to change your approach or invent new ground.

◆

When you find yourself at a dream school sitting exams, you are probably feeling tested in waking life, perhaps at work, perhaps in a relationship, and you are responding as if you are still the school child or student you once were.

Your old attitudes and beliefs often live on, like comfortable old habits, ready to surface and take you by surprise when something in life resonates with your old memories. You find yourself in a testing situation and up pop the old school child fears. You're out there in an adult world, sporting an adult body, stumbling along like a child.

As a child or student, did you want to win your parents' approval by doing well in exams, or to prove something to yourself or those in authority by performing well? Or did you want to draw attention to your needs by failing exams? Did you study to avoid emotional issues in your family? Are these things still important to you or can you let these old habits go now?

The dream audience represents your own judgement of your abilities. In dreams you are the presenter and the audience, the teacher and the student. If a dream teacher is authoritarian then you can be sure you carry strong beliefs about authority. If your dream audience boos your delivery, then you can be sure you carry strong beliefs about performance excellence. Your dreams look at extremes of thought and feeling so that you can find a balance between the two.

Emotional issues aside, we easily become creatures of habit. At school we are taught certain ways of thinking and doing — especially left-brain analytical ways. There are often better ways to solve problems or find creative solutions and school-exam dreams can sometimes be showing you just this: the old ways have left you unprepared for life today, so why not adopt a different approach?

Are you unprepared in your dream but always prepared in your waking life, never missing a beat? Read common dream 9: Late for the appointment.

In your life this could be about ...
◆ A friend who is questioning the way you do something.

- A new skill you are developing or practising.
- A criticism or judgement someone has just levelled at you.
- A competitive sport you are involved in.
- A teamwork situation or committee you belong to.
- Your religion: the authority figures, the disciplines, the sermons or your expected behaviour.
- Your relationship with a work superior, parent or critical partner.
- Meeting someone you want to impress.

Your unique dream contains personal clues only you may recognise

- Look for clues in dream puns: for example, dreaming of sitting an exam in clay-modelling may give you a clue about a waking-life situation that is testing your skills as a role model.
- The score you achieve for your dream exam may give you a clue about a year (77 per cent representing 1977, perhaps) or an age (28 per cent as age 28) significant to your feelings of being tested.
- The place where you are being tested may be a clue. That exam held in a church hall may be about your religion and how it tests you, rather than a throwback to sitting exams in draughty church halls.

Why has this dream come up for you now?

Your answers to the questions will reveal the reason:

- What feelings and emotions did you experience in your dream?
- Which situation in your life now do these feelings remind you of?
- Have you recently noticed yourself using language or expressions from your school days, or reacting more like a child than an adult?
- Have you recently felt insecure during a communication with someone or questioned your abilities?

Your answers to the last two questions may reveal the reason your dream has come up for you now.

Dream alchemy practice
Starting the inner work

This is what to *do* if you hope to see dramatic transformations in your life.

A. Who was the teacher you most feared when you were at school? How old do you think he or she was? Imagine going back, at the age you are now, to talk with the teacher. If you wish, you can make yourself older than you are now and, if it feels good, much taller. Now, ask your old teacher what she feared most about working with your class. Discover her weak points and what made her the scary authority figure she felt she needed to be. Tell her some of the things you've learned about life and then teach her about new developments in the world that she would have known nothing about back then — the Internet, perhaps. Think up a suitable gift for her and then let her give a gift to you. Write this dream alchemy practice up as a story.

B. When you notice yourself feeling tested by someone, imagine him or her as a little child. Continue the rest of your interaction as the adult you are, talking to him or her with complete respect and equality but seeing the child he or she once was standing before you.

C. Do this dream alchemy visualisation twenty times a day for a week, then ten times a day for the second week, then twice a day for the next month. Imagine yourself back in your dream, about to sit the exam or give the presentation. Now imagine the feeling of finding creative and brilliant answers to the exam questions, or the feeling of delivering a stunning presentation to rapturous applause. (You don't need to think about what your answers are, or about what you present. The dream alchemy practice works purely by summoning up the *feeling* of approaching your testing situation with a natural brilliance and with an astounding result. Focus on the feeling.)

Glimmers of gold
In your dreams
When your recurring dream changes to embrace a happier ending, you are making good progress. Look out for the positive dream changes listed under 'How does your dream end?'

Some symbols from your dream alchemy practice may appear in your dreams. For example, you may dream of delivering that presentation or chatting with the old school teacher.

Your dreams may bring up a range of strong emotions and images from past situations where you felt you were being tested or judged. Some of the emotions may be directed, in your dreams, towards the people who judged you back then. This is your dream's way of releasing emotions and beliefs that might have channelled your creativity towards proving yourself to others rather than enjoying a full range of creative expression.

Look out for dreams of driving a new car smoothly to your dream destination, discovering treasures or enjoying doing your own thing.

In your waking life
You feel wiser and freer. You see your school or college education in a different light: an introduction to the basics to equip you to make your own way, rather than a black and white 'how to' manual.

You are more relaxed and able to prepare for any situation with minimal anxiety. You feel more inclined to prepare well rather than to prepare thoroughly as you discover the value of leaving spaces in your work and life to explore new ground spontaneously. You are more creative — your sudden insights surprise you.

You relate more as an equal to other adults. You see their shortcomings as easily as you see your own and you value these as the springboard to new ways of thinking or approaching problems.

11: Back at school

School

(Also see 10: Unprepared for exam)

The dream

You're either at your old school or at a dream school.

Break the mould to reveal the gold.

In your dream perhaps ...

- You're at your old school, as a student with your old teachers.
- You're at your old school, as a student, sitting an exam.
- You're at a dream school as a student.
- You're at a dream school, unsure whether you're a student or a teacher.
- You're at a dream school as a teacher.
- You're at school, at your present age, even though the other students are all school age.
- You know you've been away from school and you've come back to finish a course.
- You've had enough and you leave school.

How do you feel in your dream?

Free. Restricted. Childish. Authoritative. Subordinated. Guilty. Reminiscing. Longing. Playful. Wise. Adaptable. Confined. Ordered. Tested. Disciplined. Corrected. Judged. Excluded. Included. Adolescent. Hopeful. Successful. A sense of failure. Remorseful. Angry. Frustrated. Revengeful.

How does your dream end?

Positive changes are on the way if ...

- You become the teacher.
- You make friends with an old enemy, whether student or teacher.
- You have an insight in the dream from the teacher's point of view.

- You have an insight in the dream about another student.
- You have an insight in the dream about a teacher or about the way the school is run.
- You pass a test, solve an argument or resolve a situation.
- You express intense anger at an old 'enemy' or at a teacher who had made life difficult for you.
- You express intense grief for an old student or teacher who had been abused or disrespected.
- You suddenly remember you are an adult and do not need to be at school so you leave.

It's time for a new approach if ...

- You suffer at the hands of a teacher or student without resolve.
- You feel restricted, hurt or punished by a teacher or student.
- You express yourself in childish or adolescent ways.

What your dream means

Your way forward may be blocked by ...

A life lesson you need to learn. Reacting to something or someone as if you were still at school. Grief, anger or other strong emotions from school days that you have not yet expressed or healed.

Moving forward

Know that learning is a lifelong process and that you are forever both student and teacher. Free yourself from childhood beliefs and hurts so that you can grow towards being a wise elder, helping others along your way.

◆

If your dream takes you back to school you can be sure that something in your life is reminding you of how you felt in those days. You can be certain that somewhere, deep within, you live on as that school child with beliefs, attitudes, emotions and concerns belonging to the child you were back then.

And *that's* the key! Your old school day worries were important to you at that time but they shouldn't be important to you now. There's no place for the child you were in the life you lead now, is there? Or is there ...?

When dreams go back in time they reveal some of your beliefs that are stuck in those days. Your dream shows you how those beliefs are still operating in your life now, hampering your progress. You go back to understand, to let go of beliefs that were once important but are not important for you now. Along with the beliefs go the emotions that were tangled up with them: usually anger and grief.

Perhaps you battled with authority figures, felt like one of the crowd or like an outsider, worked hard to please people through good behaviour or by passing exams, bullied or were bullied, or struggled to relate to people from backgrounds different from your own. As a child you learned how to act and react to survive the school and playground jungles. As an adult playing big people's games in a work or relationship jungle it's easy to fall into the old survival tactics. But the attitudes that saved and protected you way back then are not going to serve you well now.

If you meet a fantastically inspiring teacher in your dream, this is your own wisdom — pay attention! While the little school child may live on deep within you, the wise elder is already taking form and gathering life's wisdoms to help you through.

If you're the teacher in the dream you may be experiencing old issues with authority from the opposite perspective or, if you sense a touch of magic, you may be trying out those wise elder's shoes to see how you might best walk in them.

What is your dream school teaching you about yourself and about life?

In your life this could be about ...
+ Someone who treats you as a child.
+ A working environment heavily controlled by rules.
+ A relationship where you are feeling bullied.
+ A course or task that you are learning.
+ A problem you feel you cannot solve.

◆ A 'friend' or relation who manipulates you.

Your unique dream contains personal clues only you may recognise

◆ If the dream school is the school you went to, try to estimate the year from the school friends or teachers in your dream. This gives you a clue about the beginning of an attitude you took on, or a hurt that you have not yet expressed and released.

◆ Someone you know today in your dream may be a clue to the area of your waking life under question.

◆ Look at whether the action takes place in the classroom (and for what subject?), in the playground, in the gym changing rooms or in the dining hall. These are clues. For example, childish attitudes in the dining hall may be about nurturing in your relationship, and a dream set in the playground may be about teamwork at work or being bullied by a so-called friend.

Why has this dream come up for you now?

Your answers to these questions will reveal the reason:

◆ What feelings and emotions did you experience in your dream?

◆ Which situation in your life now do these feelings remind you of?

◆ If someone you know is at the dream school, write down three words to describe their attitude to life. Now write down the opposites to these three words (for example: polite, rude). Where, in your waking life, are you being confronted by these attitudes, for example being too polite or dealing with people who seem unable to get the balance right?

◆ If this problem were to disappear, what would be your next challenge?

Your answer to the last question may reveal the reason your dream has come up for you now. You want things to improve in this area of your life but your old schoolchild attitudes or hurts would make it difficult for you to move on to the next challenge without change. It's time to change!

Dream alchemy practice
Starting the inner work
This is what to *do* if you hope to see dramatic transformations in your life.

A. Write a conversation between yourself as a child (pick an age from the clues in your dream) and yourself at the age you are now. Arrange the conversation like a script on your page. (This dream alchemy practice is called a dialogue.) Don't think — just let the words flow out. Look at what comes up.

B. Look for the kind of things kids collect: butterfly wings, petals, pieces of bark, birthday ribbons, magazine pictures, beads or sweet wrappers. Now make a collage or sculpture from your bits and pieces. This is a farewell monument to any old schoolchild beliefs or hurts you have been carrying. Find a way to express the new adult beliefs that you decide to replace the childhood ones with in your piece of art so that the work shows your transformation into full adulthood.

C. Here's an affirmation for you.

I am forever the student and the teacher, so I am
forever moving forward in my understanding of life.
I feel a sense of peace and freedom with every day
that I grow in wisdom. I feel uplifted by the release
change brings.

Glimmers of gold
In your dreams
When your recurring dream changes to embrace a happier ending, you are making good progress. Look out for the positive dream changes listed under 'How does your dream end?'

Some symbols from your dream alchemy practice may appear in your dreams. For example, you may dream of sculpting an amazing monument or counselling a child.

Your dreams may bring up a range of strong emotions

and images from your school days and childhood. This is your dream's way of releasing emotions you have not yet expressed or healed. This dream release is your healing. Watch these emotions, feel them, understand them and let them go.

Look out for dreams of flying, planes crashing (see common dream 40: Plane crash) and deaths and births, showing that you are letting old attitudes die and giving birth to new ones. (See common dream 41: Death and murder).

In your waking life
You are more aware of life's continual learning process and more confident to take the role of teacher or counsellor to others.

You feel more at peace with yourself, more settled and wiser. You may be surprised to notice other people acting in childish ways.

You will embrace change in your life and be surprised at how quickly opportunities for change come up and at how smoothly they happen when you make your choices.

You may find yourself dressing in a different style or changing your hair cut or colour.

12: Intruders

Intruders

(Also see 33: Trapped and under attack; 36: Paralysed — can't move, can't shout!)

The dream

People are trying to break into your house, or you may wake up thinking there really are strangers in your home.

Breathe to be seen and you will be seen to breathe.

In your dream perhaps ...

♦ You hear intruders inside your house and you try to hide from them.

♦ Intruders are trying to break in and you are locking doors and windows.

♦ You are trying to phone the emergency services because someone has broken in.

♦ You think there are intruders in your house but you cannot see them.

♦ You come face to face with intruders all of a sudden.

♦ There are intruders and someone has been taken hostage.

♦ Intruders are damaging something or stealing something.

How do you feel in your dream?

Fearful. A sense of panic. Paralysed. Angry. Frustrated. Inadequate. Vulnerable. Weak. Defensive. Sad. A sense of grief. Disrespected. Ignored. Trampled upon. Hurt.

How does your dream end?

Positive changes are on the way if ...

♦ You confront the intruders.

♦ The intruders retreat or disappear.

♦ The intruder turns out to be unthreatening: a gentle bird or a friend bringing you a gift perhaps.

- ◆ You realise there is a guardian in the house looking after you.

It's time for a new approach if ...
- ◆ You remain scared at the end of the dream.
- ◆ You come face to face with the intruders but you cannot speak or breathe.
- ◆ The intruders hurt you.
- ◆ You cannot get through to emergency services on the phone.
- ◆ The intruders are damaging or stealing things.

What your dream means
Your way forward may be blocked by ...
Your difficulties in securing your own private thinking and emotional space. Being too defensive and closed towards others *or* too vulnerable and available to others. Your personal barriers or your complete lack of personal boundaries.

Moving forward
Find a balance between locking the world out and welcoming the whole world in. Discover your personal boundaries (no defensive barriers or walls are needed) that mark where other people end and you begin. Emerge from behind your wall or become visible to those who abuse your welcome because they do not see you.

◆

Think of a dream house or building as your body, or your mind, or your self. The outside is what the public sees, but the inside is the real you.

You should be able to feel comfortable and secure within yourself, able to state who or what may enter your house or be invited to know the real you. You shouldn't need strong locks and burglar alarm systems to feel safe inside your house or your body. But a permanently open front door does not secure your privacy and personal space when you need it. Whether it's your house, your body or your mind, the trick is to achieve a balance between locking the world out (being defensive) and welcoming the world to invade your personal space at its own whim (being a doormat).

The secret, and the point of this dream, is to find a balance between these two extremes, having personal boundaries that mark where other people end and where you begin, rather than having barriers that keep the world out or having no choice over your personal space.

Barriers lock other people out but they also lock you in and isolate you. They weigh you down and obscure your view of the world. They stop all the good things getting to you: experiences, fun, kindness, support and love, just for a start.

Your boundary is the shape of your house, body, mind or self. When your boundary is clear, people can see you and respect you. They feel welcome but they would not over-run your space or place their demands on you. Boundaries give you personal power.

When you dream there are intruders in your house or trying to break into your house, your personal boundaries are not in place. If you dream of trying to lock or fortify your house, then your dream suggests you may be erecting barriers and personal defences because you feel vulnerable. The dream shows you that when you try to defend your house, body or mind, people still break in. When you build barriers you are trying to solve difficult issues by keeping them out, but you know, and your dreams know, that the only way to solve issues is to resolve them — to confront them and embrace them. Make friends with your invaders, resolve issues and then show them the way out.

If you are trying to phone emergency services in your dream, you are calling for 'help' in a big way. Dreams love playing with words. See 'emergence' in 'emergency'? When you face a crisis or an issue you may face pain, you may feel hurt, you may need healing, you may need rescuing, but after all of this you emerge a better person.

Sometimes this dream comes up a few days before you get sick. This is because your dreaming mind detects the invasion of a virus or bacteria before it gains enough strength to make you sick. The intruders are the bugs and the house is your body. When you think of sickness or disease (dis-ease) as an uneasiness of the mind that affects the body, you can look at the invasion of your body by a bug as being like the invasion of your body or mind by other people and issues. Dreams can be great indicators of forthcoming disease or sickness; if you look at the emotional issues your dream is bringing up and address these, you may prevent the physical disease or sickness from developing at all.

Take down your barriers to reveal the power of your boundaries.

In your life this could be about ...
♦ Not having time and space to yourself at home.
♦ A relationship in which you constantly give, and receive little in return.
♦ A past sexual hurt that needs healing.
♦ A sickness or disease.
♦ A person or situation you feel threatened by.
♦ Someone who has recently criticised you, leaving you feeling hurt.
♦ A rapidly dwindling bank balance or a fear of losing money.
♦ A situation that has exhausted you.

Your unique dream contains personal clues only you may recognise
♦ What you are wearing or carrying in your dream may be clues about your defences or lack of them.
♦ What the intruders are wearing or carrying are clues to what you feel threatened by.
♦ The number of intruders may be a clue about the number of people or situations that are a problem for you, or to the number of times this issue has come up.

Why has this dream come up for you now?
Your answers to these questions will reveal the reason:
♦ What feelings and emotions did you experience in your dream?
♦ Which situation in your life now do these feelings remind you of?

♦ When you think about your waking life, which situation makes your body feel stiff and on-guard? (A sign of feeling defensive.) Which situation makes you feel drained of power? (A sign of having no personal boundaries.) Has either of these two situations become more challenging recently?

Your answer to the last question may reveal the reason your dream has come up for you now. You are ready to define your boundaries or to let go of your walls, but you feel anxious about the changes and new challenges that this may bring.

Dream alchemy practice
Starting the inner work

This is what to *do* if you hope to see dramatic transformations in your life.

A. Do this visualisation regularly. (This practice is good to do whether you think you are too defensive or too open. This dream alchemy practice works by showing you the balance point between the two extremes.)

Imagine yourself encircled by a barrier made of stone or barbed wire. See yourself inside the barrier as a blurred form with no visible boundary to mark your shape. Now let the barrier dissolve and, at the same time, let a white light sparkle around your form until a clear and naturally strong body shape emerges. Feel the power of the white light and the freedom of being able to see beyond the old barriers. Feel the utter safety of your personal boundary showing the world your true and natural strength.

B. Choose a name for yourself that gives you the feeling of having an awesome personal boundary that others can see, while not needing any barriers to defend yourself. For a few weeks, as you go about your life, think of yourself by this name. Draw your energy from the name. This is a powerful dream alchemy practice that you can use for as long as you wish, or return to whenever you feel the need for a boost.

C. Write a conversation on paper (arrange this dream alchemy dialogue like a script) between a butterfly hidden inside its chrysalis just before it emerges, and a little child who is watching and waiting for it to come out into the light. See what unfolds — apart from the butterfly's wings!

Glimmers of gold
In your dreams

When your recurring dream changes to embrace a happier ending, you are making good progress. Look out for the positive dream changes listed under 'How does your dream end?'

Some symbols from your dream alchemy practice may appear in your dreams. For example, you may dream of being a butterfly emerging from your chrysalis.

Your dreams may release the huge anger or hurt that you shut in when you erected barriers to defend yourself against further pain. They may release grief that you have gulped back behind a welcoming smile as you tried to help everyone except yourself, leaving the grief raw and unhealed. Go with this positive, life-changing dream alchemy. It is your dream's way of releasing what you would not release because of fear before now, because you were not ready to.

Look out for dreams of building a beautiful new house, of moving to a more spacious and suitable home or of looking at grand sweeping views through windows or from verandahs.

In your waking life

You feel lighter yet stronger and more powerful than ever before. You explore new talents or develop new skills. You are surprised to feel so expansive and full of potential that you know you will gradually fulfil.

You notice other people noticing you. You realise you have a greater presence than you did before.

You may lose so-called friends or acquaintances who now feel uncomfortable because you are no longer always available for their selfish needs and wants, or who once enjoyed sparring with you across your barrier. You accept this as part of the clearing process and as part of restoring your own energy to contribute to others without exhausting what you have to give.

You gain new friends as you welcome positive change in your life.

Your energy levels rise dramatically, yet you feel quietly at peace.

13: In a wheelchair

Wheelchair

The dream

You find yourself in a wheelchair because you are
unable to walk in your dream.

*Who calls your steps? When you are pushed, stand, sniff
the wind and walk.*

In your dream perhaps ...

◆ A friendly helper is pushing you in your wheelchair.
◆ You are uncomfortable about the person who is pushing
   you in your wheelchair.
◆ The person pushing your wheelchair is in control, taking
   you somewhere contrary to your wishes.
◆ You are moving your own chair, or it is motorised, or flying.
◆ You have legs but cannot move them.
◆ You have one or both legs in a plaster cast.
◆ You have no legs, or one leg is missing.

How do you feel in your dream?

Passive. Accepting. Relaxed. Released. Supported. Controlled.
Manipulated. Frustrated. Angry. Peaceful. Incapacitated.
Weak. Lost. Aimless. Uninterested. Uninvolved. Indecisive.
Unsure. Unheard. Dismissed. Overlooked. Overpowered.

How does your dream end?
Positive changes are on the way if ...

◆ You get out of the wheelchair and stand or walk.
◆ You express anger or grief in the dream.
◆ You use the wheelchair to fly or get somewhere faster
   than you can by walking.
◆ You learn something insightful from the person who is
   pushing your chair.
◆ You see an inspiring view.
◆ You arrive at an inspiring place.

It's time for a new approach if ...

- ◆ You feel pushed against your will.
- ◆ You still feel uncomfortable at the end of the dream.
- ◆ You are abandoned in your chair and do not have the power to move it yourself.
- ◆ You sense a loss of power, or feel overpowered by another person.
- ◆ You are not listened to or heard.
- ◆ Your feelings and needs are dismissed by others.

What your dream means

Your way forward may be blocked by ...

Not 'standing on your own two feet' about something or allowing yourself to be pushed around by someone or by a certain belief in life.

Moving forward

Let your dream show you what beliefs you hold, consciously or unconsciously, that are draining your personal power. Then let them go, stand on your own two feet and make your own empowered choices.

◆

Feeling pushed around? Unable to 'stand on your own two feet' about an issue in your life right now? Feeling like you 'haven't got a leg to stand on' in a situation? Dreams take the stuff of your expressions and play them back for you to see. They take your feelings and spin them into a picture to deliver a more poignant statement of where you're at.

Dreams speak your many beliefs. You know and understand your conscious beliefs. Dreams remind you, however, of your unconscious beliefs. When you dream of being pushed around in a wheelchair you can take it for granted that somewhere, consciously or unconsciously, you have a belief that it is not right to stand up for how you want to go about your life.

You may be able to identify with this straight up and say, 'Yes! My boss is pushing me to work extra hours and I can't get out of it'. Well, there *are* ways to get out of it and your dream shows you how. But the *big* thing to remember about dreams — their most powerful magic — is that all the people in a dream are connected with your own beliefs. That person pushing your wheelchair is a belief you hold. You are being pushed around by no one but yourself!

The same applies to your waking life. Your boss doesn't and cannot push you around unless you let him or her do so. In this example, your life situation is more about you giving in to your belief that it is acceptable to be pushed around by an authority or power. It's time to prove that miracles do happen! Stand up and walk!

There are times in life when you need a push, a bit of friendly encouragement, an almighty kick in the pants or a global crisis or two to make you sit up and take notice. Dreams of being pushed would fit in here, especially if you feel you are making better progress in a speedy wheelchair with a helping hand than you would be plodding along on exhausted legs. There are times for being carried or pushed so that you can get back on your feet with renewed energy and passion.

Again, take note! Turn around in that dream wheelchair and have a close look at the helper pushing you forward. He or she, after all, is connected with one of your beliefs — probably one you've been ignoring for quite some time. He or she might be a singer. (Haven't you always believed you could sing for your supper but done nothing about it?) He or she might be someone you know from waking life, a laid-back, easygoing person (haven't you been working so hard for months that you've ground to an exhausted halt?).

With or without the wheelchair, it's time for you to stand up in a new way, with real power.

In your life this could be about ...

♦ That great business idea you are putting off.
♦ That special talent that you lack confidence to get up and use.
♦ Living according to your partner's or parent's wishes and goals instead of your own.
♦ Believing people who tell you you're not good enough to do whatever it is you would love to do in your heart.

♦ That argument you lost even though you knew your feelings were valid and needed to be acknowledged.
♦ The friend or relation you always give in to.
♦ That person who always undermines what you say or think.
♦ Your lack of confidence in expressing ideas, opinions or arguments.

Your unique dream contains personal clues only you may recognise

♦ Do you know the person who is pushing your chair? If so, write down three words to describe their attitude in waking life. Now write down the opposites to these three words, for example arrogant, humble. These extremes are all clues to the beliefs *you* have about life. For example, you may have a conscious or unconscious belief that standing up for yourself in a situation is arrogant. Or that it is good to be humble, even if it means you're not heard.
♦ Look for prop clues. What are you carrying, or what is out of your reach in the dream because you are sitting in the chair at the whim of the person pushing you?
♦ Look for dream puns. Your 'pusher' (of your chair) might be a clue about a reliance on a drug, for example.

Why has this dream come up for you now?

Your answers to these questions will reveal the reason:

♦ What feelings and emotions did you experience in your dream?
♦ Which situation in your life now do these feelings remind you of?
♦ If you have identified what it is you need to stand up for, imagine yourself doing this. What feeling does it bring up? In how many ways would your life change if you did this?

Your answer to the last question may reveal the reason your dream has come up for you now. You are ready to make a stand but you fear the challenges ahead of you. Let your dreams show you how to face those challenges and come out on top.

Dream alchemy practice
Starting the inner work

This is what to *do* if you hope to see dramatic transformations in your life.

A. Play! Get some modelling-clay or papier-mâché and spend contemplative time making a model of yourself standing strong. If your artistic skills are not up to making a look-alike, any face and body shape will do as long as you can relate to the model as yourself, standing strong. You might want to add fabric as clothing for a sense of vibrant colour, or give your model a significant prop to hold. As you take your time moulding your figure, imagine the powerful feeling of standing on your own two feet whenever you need to or want to. Keep the model somewhere so you'll see it every day until you do whatever you want or need to do!

B. Do this simple dream alchemy practice frequently:

Stand with your feet hip-width apart and imagine a beam of light on the crown of your head. The light beam runs through your spine, straightening your posture. Feel yourself standing tall and then focus on the solid strength of the ground beneath your feet. Centre your weight equally between both feet. Stand for one minute feeling the uplifting power of standing on your own two feet.

C. If you have identified the belief that is pushing you around, write it down beside its opposite. For example, a need to be humble or a need to be arrogant. Now take a piece of chalk and draw a line a few metres wide on the ground. (Or use a piece of masking tape, a string or a line of pebbles.) Now draw a second line at right angles to the first, crossing in the middle so you now have a big cross marked out on the ground. Stand on the centre of the cross. Look along the line extending to your left (the 'west' arm). At the very end of that line is 'humble'. (You can imagine this or write it on the ground.) At the other end of that line, to your right (the 'east' arm), is the other extreme, 'arrogant'. Stand there and *feel* humble when you look at *humble* and then *feel* arrogant when you look at *arrogant*. Now *feel* what it is like to stand halfway between the two — neither humble nor arrogant but with all the positive power of the potent mix of these two elements. Now turn around and walk along the line (with 'north' behind you, towards south) as you feel the combined power of walking the middle path *and* standing on your own two feet. Know that you can never easily be pushed around again.

In dreams, 'north' sometimes represents your head (thinking) and 'south' your heart (feeling). By walking 'south' in this powerful dream alchemy practice you are consolidating the new belief from your head into your heart and feelings. This evokes the same change in your unconscious.

Glimmers of gold
In your dreams
When your recurring dream changes to embrace a happier ending, you are making good progress. Look out for the positive dream changes listed under 'How does your dream end?'

Some symbols from your dream alchemy practice may appear in your dreams. For example, you may dream of walking that middle path.

Your dreams may release anger towards people you felt pushed around by in the past. This is okay. Remember the people in your dreams are *not* themselves. They are your dream's way of representing your beliefs. Get as angry as you want with your own beliefs if they haven't served you well! This is your dream's way of clearing your unexpressed emotions so you can walk forward, free and strong.

Look out for dreams of tall strong towers, earthworks and new landscaping as you create new solid ground beneath your feet.

In your waking life
You feel taller and stronger. You feel the solidity of the ground beneath your feet. You feel grounded as you make decisions and you make those decisions easily and with conviction, as if making up for lost time.

Your voice may get slightly deeper as you breathe more fully and speak from your diaphragm and not from your throat.

People who used to push you around either change or disappear from your life. Don't let this concern you. When you work with dream alchemy you are achieving positive personal and spiritual change. You move on to better relationships and better ways of being. The old trials are no longer required.

14: Bags, baggage and cases

Bags and cases

> **The dream**
>
> You are carrying or responsible for bags, baggage or cases. Your progress is made difficult or delayed because of this.

Whose journey is this anyway?

In your dream perhaps ...

* The bags or cases are yours.
* The bags or cases belong to someone else who is travelling with you.
* The bags or cases belong to someone who is not travelling with you.
* You keep forgetting where you put your baggage, or losing it.
* The amount or weight of your baggage keeps increasing.
* Things are falling out of the baggage, or you have to keep opening it to repack things.
* You are pushing a heavy case in front of you.
* You are increasingly delayed in your travels.

How do you feel in your dream?

Responsible. Burdened. Over-burdened. Weighed down. Delayed. Held back. Used. Needed. Dismissed. Depended upon. Dependable. Reliable. Forgetful. Lost. A sense of missing out. Unprepared. Subservient. Caring. Useful. Frustrated. Angry. Helpful. Unsatisfied. Confused. Cluttered. Disappointed. Let down. Abused. Unappreciated. Insufficient. Unable to help.

How does your dream end?
Positive changes are on the way if ...

* You set the baggage down and travel on without it.
* You take some items out to make the baggage lighter.

- You give the baggage to someone else to carry.
- You express anger.
- You open the case or bags and learn something insightful from the contents.
- You discover that the baggage, or some of it, belongs to someone else, not to you.
- The case you are pushing disappears and you are at ease with this.

It's time for a new approach if ...

- The baggage gets heavier and your progress gets more and more delayed.
- Other people give you more baggage to carry.
- You are unable to close the over-packed cases.

What your dream means

Your way forward may be blocked by ...

Hanging onto emotional burdens and hurts from the past. Being weighed down by old beliefs no longer appropriate to you. Carrying the weight of other people. Pushing your case or cause without reward.

Moving forward

Lighten your load. Heal and release old emotional hurts; exchange old beliefs that weigh you down for new beliefs that are more empowering. Help other people to lighten their own loads instead of bearing them for them.

◆

Yes, this is the emotional baggage dream. As in, 'Don't get involved with him! He's still carrying a lot of old issues from his marriage break-up.' Same thing: old issues, emotional baggage — hurt and pain from your past that you should have put down ages ago but you can't quite let go of.

Emotional baggage weighs you down just as the baggage does in your dream. You are better to resolve or let go of the past rather than to keep on carrying it around with you. This applies especially if that dream baggage is unopened and hauled from *a* to *b* without being looked at or without having a useful function.

You might dream of carrying someone else's baggage

while they skip along light and free. You might feel that's how your life is — carrying other people's problems and bearing their weight for them. Is this virtuous? It can be. But there's always another way to help someone and your dream is showing the toll that being virtuous is having on you.

As always, remember the magical dream formula! Those people in your dream are not who they appear to be. They represent your own beliefs, thoughts, feelings and memories. So, what if in your dream you're lugging things for a hypochondriac? Well, perhaps you have a belief about needing to be sick to gain attention from others and your dream is showing you just how much this need is weighing you down, preventing you from making real progress in your life. Maybe in your dream you're hauling tonnes of baggage for a tough mountaineer. Perhaps the reason you strive to get on top of things or to achieve difficult things is that you are carrying a rather large chunk of emotional baggage (a need to prove yourself or a need to do it tough?) that is only making things even tougher than they already are.

Of course if it's only a very small bag you're slinging to carry some precious stuff around then you're not dreaming in the emotional baggage league. You're dreaming about what you are taking on your journey, or what you hold precious. If you've lost that little bag, see common dream 35: I've lost my handbag, wallet, jewellery or …

Are you carrying cases rather than bags in your dream? What case are you carrying or pushing in your life now? ('Case' as in *cause*.)

The bottom line is, if there's nothing in those dream bags you're using, you're burning up a lot of energy and weighing yourself down over nothing that's of any use to you. Find a way to lighten your load or simply let it go.

In your life this could be about …
♦ An old financial or emotional debt.
♦ A choice you made in the past that is weighing heavily on you now.
♦ Something or someone you feel guilty about.
♦ The demands placed on you by a needy relative.

- The demands placed on you by a voluntary job, organisation or campaign you committed to in the past when you thought you had more time or didn't know how big the job would get.

- Hurt, anger or grief from an old relationship that is affecting your current relationship or fears about new relationships.

- That shoulder you keep offering to people to cry on.

- Those emotional work issues and conflicts you bring home that get in the way of family life.

- The demands you place on yourself because you have high expectations or wish to impress someone else.

Your unique dream contains personal clues only you may recognise

- Your destination in your dream may be a clue to what you are *not* able to do easily because you are burdened. For example, if you are sightseeing in a foreign country but can't get around because of all the baggage, then perhaps you are trying to see something new and foreign to you but you can't. What new and foreign thing are you involved in?

- Look at the number of bags you are carrying as a clue to the number of burdens or issues weighing you down, or to the number of years since you took on the burden, or to the age you were when you first started overloading yourself.

- Look at the emotions you experience in your dream. If you feel rejected by the touring group because you are the one left to stay with the baggage, then rejection might be a clue to the unhealed, heavy issue. When have you been rejected?

Why has this dream come up for you now?

Your answers to these questions will reveal the reason:

- What feelings and emotions did you experience in your dream?

- Which situation in your life now do these feelings remind you of?

- Has your patience or generosity been tested severely recently?
- Has someone you care for just dumped an extra burden on your shoulders?
- What is the thing you would love to do 'if only' you had more time or were freer? What challenges would this freedom bring you?

Your answers to the last questions may reveal the reason your dream has come up for you now. You are approaching overload in what you are carrying for others or in what you choose not to deal with or heal from your past. You would love to be free to do your own thing, but you fear that freedom more than you yearn for it, so you hang on to those burdens as a good excuse. It's time to face your fears!

Dream alchemy practice
Starting the inner work

This is what to *do* if you hope to see dramatic transformations in your life.

A. Here's an affirmation for you:

> I feel free and light as I put down all the unnecessary baggage I have been carrying. I take forward only that which is needed for my personal and spiritual journey. I step forward to do what I must do. My hands are now free to … (insert here what it is that you want to do).

B. Make a list of all the people whose baggage you have been carrying. Some of them may still be in your life, but remember that most emotional baggage belongs to the past, so include in your list people from your unresolved relationships and business that have left you with a feeling of burden or hurt. For example, a teacher who gave you the belief that your accent was to be pitied and left you carrying the weight of having little or no confidence about speaking in public. Or an ex-wife who wanted your support, but was never there to console you through your own grief or fears, leaving you feeling you had to be emotionally strong in any subsequent relationships.

Now collect some little boxes (matchboxes will do) — one for each person whose beliefs you have carried unnecessarily. Each little box is an item of baggage. Label each box with the name of the person. You can take this dream alchemy practice further and decorate each little box to look like a suitcase or symbol of the particular baggage. Finally, cut out some pieces of paper, each small enough to be folded and individually placed inside a baggage box. On each piece of paper write a belief that you have carried and that you now wish to return to the person. Here's your template: 'I return to you your belief that my accent was not publicly acceptable. I thank you for what I have learned from this. I no longer need it now.' Put the right pieces of paper in the right boxes and burn or destroy them all safely.

C. Celebrate the above ritual with a 'Return to Sender' party. Invite good friends (but not those named on the boxes!) and toast your new life.

Glimmers of gold
In your dreams

When your recurring dream changes to embrace a happier ending, you are making good progress. Look out for the positive dream changes listed under 'How does your dream end?'

Some symbols from your dream alchemy practice may appear in your dreams. For example, you may dream of dumping a pile of bags at a Lost Property office.

You may dream of opening bags, boxes and cupboards and you may dream such strong emotions as shock when you see what's inside. These dreams are clearing out the emotions that you had kept locked away — seeing and feeling only the weight, not the real issues. If you have been in denial about your reasons for hanging onto baggage, you may feel shock as your dreams present the evidence for you to confront, once and for all. This is your dream's way of making you acknowledge what you have done so that you can let it all go.

113

Look out for dreams of having the freedom to use your hands and arms to create, embrace, give and receive, as well as dreams of speedy movement or flying.

In your waking life
You feel freer, lighter and, possibly, younger. You feel released, as if you have walked out of a jail you didn't know you were in. It feels as if a great weight has been lifted from your shoulders.

You see what you have been missing in life. You feel in need of nurturing, attention, love and care. You feel entitled to receive these things so you receive them. People appear in your life offering you precisely these things.

You spend less time thinking about the past, re-running old conversations and holding onto hurts (you did, before, didn't you!). You spend less time worrying about other people and whether they need you to look after them. You spend more time enjoying being in the present.

When people come to you for help, you find easy ways of showing them how to help themselves. When they leave your house they leave no baggage behind because they know that you no longer accept it. Those who do not care to solve their problems disappear from your life. New friends who know how to give as well as receive come into your life.

15: I had sex with ...!

Sex

The dream

You have sex with someone other than your partner.

From fusion: awareness. From awareness: fusion.

In your dream perhaps ...

- You enjoy the sex.
- You invite or encourage the dream partner but the sex turns out to be repulsive to you.
- The sex is repulsive or you are raped.
- Your dream partner is unknown to you in waking life.
- Your dream partner is someone you know but you are not attracted to in waking life.
- Your dream partner is someone you find sexually attractive in waking life.
- Sex with this person is socially or ethically questionable: for example, sex with your boss, a client or a relation.
- Your partner is of a different sex than your usual preference.
- You discover that you are of the opposite sex, or that some of your body parts are.
- You have an orgasm in the dream.

How do you feel in your dream?

Joyful. Ecstatic. Loved. Loving. Passionate. A sense of oneness. United. Strong. Powerful. Fulfilled. Surprised. A sense of wonder. Close. A sense of warmth. Supported. Embraced. Safe. Repulsed. Uncomfortable. Uneasy. Unwilling. Used. Abused. Hurt. Overpowered. Dismissed. Dismissive. Angry. Fearful. Guilty. Secretive. Mysterious. Adventurous. Conspiring. Uplifted. Released. Relaxed. Open. Vulnerable.

How does your dream end?

Positive changes are on the way if ...

- The sex felt good, no matter who the dream partner was.

- Your feelings in the dream were positive, no matter how you felt when you reviewed the dream on waking.
- You communicated with an undesirable sex partner or rapist and felt empowered by what you said and by their reaction.
- You expressed anger or grief.
- You felt shocked in the dream.

It's time for a new approach if ...
- You went along with undesirable sex.
- You felt used or abused by the end of the dream.

What your dream means
Your way forward may be blocked by ...
A new approach to life that is not working well for you *or* an approach that has been missing for you and you are just beginning to see this.

Moving forward
Let the details of your dream show you which approach to let go of or which to take on board. Either way, be prepared to change.

◆

Let's deal with the physical side first. Yes, your sex hormones can play a part in directing your dream drama in the same way that a headache might wheedle its way into your dream as a head-rack torture device, or a ringing alarm might transform into a wailing dream fire-engine siren. But just as the headache and the ringing alarm are transformed in a dream, so your hormones can write their way into a number of different dream scenarios.

When a bodily or external sensation makes its way into your dream, the choices your dream makes in decoding the sensation into dream language are revealing. Given the huge range of possibilities, how *your* dream deals with your sex drive is about *you*. After all, you may have dream sex with someone you fancy from the office, but why would you have dream sex with someone you are not in the least bit attracted to? And even if the dream sex *is* with someone you fancy, what does the attraction say about you?

There's no place for guilt here. With or without a physiological reason for dreaming sex, and with or without a real orgasm, your dream is meaningful, healthy and normal.

In dreams, as in waking life, there is good sex, great sex, average sex and bad sex — even rape and abuse. In dreams and in waking life, good sex is about sharing intimacy. Great sex is about fusing on a physical, mental, emotional and spiritual level with your partner. Average sex lacks deep intimacy. There is no intimacy in bad sex. Bad sex is about lack of respect, lack of consideration and lack of communication. Bad sex can also be about vulnerability, intrusion, pain, harm and abuse on a physical, mental, emotional and spiritual level.

Sex in dreams is about what you are bringing into your life, what you are fusing and integrating with. The 'what' is symbolised by the 'who' in your dream.

So, in your dream you're having sex with Peter, someone you regard as being emotionally unstable. Your dream suggests you feel you are accepting emotional instability into your life, and if the sex with Peter is bad, then your dream is revealing your discomfort with the situation. You are embarking on something that may be quite harmful to you. In another dream you're ecstatically entangled with Frank, a dream character. Remember how dreams love to throw in something cryptic. Here is Frank — a frank person. Great dream sex with Frank suggests there may be great personal value to be gained by being more frank and open.

What if your dream sex partner is no one you know in waking life and doesn't sport a dream-clue name? Well, you met the person in your dream, so ask yourself what kind of personality they had. How would this person approach life? Your answers will reveal the key qualities that your dream shows you blending into your life, for good or for bad.

What about the tall, dark, handsome man or the mysterious, magical, beautiful woman inviting or shunning sexual union with you in your dream? They are your Yang and your Yin. It sounds sexist, but we are stuck with the way our dreams play this scene. Unknown men (or your male life partner) so often represent your Yang, your left brain functions or your outer world. Unknown women (or your female life partner) just as often represent your Yin, your right brain functions or your inner world. These dreams are about your union, or lack of it, with your Yang or Yin, your left or right brain, your outer or inner world. When sex is shunned or chased to no avail, you are missing that Yin or Yang balance in your life. When the dream union takes place you're doing something right in your world and your dream is reflecting your great move.

What if you're heterosexual and you dream of having sex with a same sex partner? Is your dream showing repressed homosexual desire? Most likely not, as such a big issue would usually come up in a symbolic rather than literal dream. If you're a woman dreaming of having sex with a woman, your dream is about how you are blending with your Yin or right brain functions. Or, if you know the woman, apply the 'Peter or Frank' dream-name or 'Peter' personal qualities approach described before. The same applies if you're a man with a male dream sex partner.

What if you're a woman but dream you are a man or a man dreaming you are a woman? You are dreaming about the Yin or Yang of yourself first hand, instead of seeing these qualities in a separate dream partner.

Everything here applies whether you are homosexual or heterosexual because sexy dreams are less about sex and more about yourself and what you are bringing into your life. Sex is simply a perfect symbol of deep union and, when the dream sex is good, it's a great way to communicate with your unconscious!

In your life this could be about ...

♦ Any area of your life where you are on the verge of changing your approach or where you are trying out a different way of being.
♦ Any area of your life that has recently changed which requires you to act in a different and uncomfortable way.
♦ Any area of your life where you know something is missing.

Your unique dream contains personal clues only you may recognise

◆ If your dream partner is someone you know, write down three words to describe their approach to life. One of these may give you a clue to the new approach to life you have been contemplating or need (represented by good dream sex) or don't need (represented by bad dream sex).

◆ If your dream partner is someone you know, write down three words to describe their personality. One of these words may give you a clue to a personality quality you have been developing recently, that you fear developing or that you need to develop to balance what is missing.

◆ Who else is in your dream? If someone in your dream is from your past, this may give you a clue to a past approach that is coming up for you again. Sex with an ex-partner, for example, might give you a clue that you are approaching life in a similar way to how you did back then.

Why has this dream come up for you now?

Your answers to these questions will reveal the reason:

◆ What feelings and emotions did you experience in your dream?

◆ Which situation in your life now do these feelings remind you of?

◆ If you could change this situation for a better outcome, what challenge would this bring up for you?

Your answer to the last question may reveal the reason your dream has come up for you now. You are ready to make a change and to grow in some way, but you fear the challenges that you imagine this change may bring.

Dream alchemy practice
Starting the inner work

This is what to *do* if you hope to see dramatic transformations in your life.

A. Write a conversation between your dream partner and yourself. Arrange the conversation like a script on your page. Start the conversation with you asking the partner:

'What attracts you to me?' Write fast without time for thought. Just let the words flow and see what comes up.

B. If your dream sex was good, start this dream alchemy practice by writing a list of the approaches and qualities of your dream partner that you feel would be good for you. If your dream sex was not good, write a list of the *opposites* to all the approaches and qualities demonstrated by your dream partner. Now you have a list of only good qualities.

In dreams, circles can be symbols for integrating qualities into your life, of union or completion. A mandala is a painting or collage in the shape of a circle, like a whole universe. Your dream alchemy practice is to create a mandala (painting, drawing or collage) to symbolise your new life, incorporating all the good qualities and approaches from your list. For example, if one of the qualities on your list is 'prepared to take risks' you might symbolise this with someone parachuting from a plane; or if one of the qualities is 'witty' you might symbolise this with a witty cartoon or saying. You can make your mandala as simple or as complex as you wish. When it is finished, put it in a place where you will see it every day. For the next week set aside five minutes every day to rest in front of your mandala, summoning up the *feeling* of each quality in turn as you look at your symbols. At the end of the five minutes, bring all those feelings into the centre of your heart and take them with you as you journey through your day.

C. Here's an affirmation for you.

I am whole and complete. My life is in perfect
balance. I am the Yin and Yang of perfect union,
the mother and father of all my days from
this day forward.

Glimmers of gold
In your dreams
When your recurring dream changes to embrace a happier ending, you are making good progress. Look out for

the positive dream changes listed under 'How does your dream end?'

Some symbols from your dream alchemy practice may appear in your dreams. For example, you may dream of finding perfect symbols for your mandala.

You may dream strong emotions such as grief (as you acknowledge what has been missing in your life) or anger (with yourself for sticking with approaches to life that haven't served you well). This is your dream's way of releasing you from the past to embrace the new.

Look out for dreams of births, seedlings growing into mature plants and some really great practical and creative ideas ready for you to make happen.

In your waking life
You feel more complete and balanced. You begin to see an 'old' you — the person who once was — as quite distinct from the 'new' you.

You feel as if a storm has passed and that you have seen new light.

You feel fulfilled and purposeful, creative, confident and empowered.

You especially notice a balance in your life between doing and being. You feel more at peace with yourself and with the world.

16: Slo mo running or walking

Running and walking
(Also see 9: Late for the appointment)

The dream

You are running or walking in slow motion as if with gluey feet. Every step is hard. You feel as if you are moving against a huge resistance, putting in a huge effort but achieving little progress.

The stone weighs as heavy as your doubt and as light as your faith.

In your dream perhaps ...

♦ You are running or walking on level ground, but making minimal progress.

♦ You are running or walking up a steep slope, which gets steeper and more impossible as the dream progresses.

♦ The going is so tough that you end up on your hands and knees, or using your hands in an effort to pull your-self forward.

♦ A strong wind is holding you back.

♦ Someone is with you, talking you through or guiding you.

♦ You particularly notice that everyone else in the dream moves with ease.

♦ Other people are moving in the same direction as you, but with ease.

♦ Other people are coming towards you and passing you, all with ease.

How do you feel in your dream?

Patient. Impatient. Frustrated. Weighed down. Penalised. Confused. Martyred. Denied. Restricted. Driven. Determined. Insistent. Battered. Exhausted. Burnt out. Striving. Thwarted. Discriminated against. Winning. Struggling. Hopeful. Inspired. Released. Insightful. Freed. Rewarded. Competitive. Strong. Weak. Pressured. Stuck.

How does your dream end?
Positive changes are on the way if ...
* The resistance disappears and you run or walk normally.
* You discover a new and efficient way of moving.
* You take an easier path, road or surface.
* You say (or someone else says) something insightful.

It's time for a new approach if ...
* The resistance stays the same or increases.

What your dream means
Your way forward may be blocked by ...
Self-doubt. Hesitation. Fear of success or fear of change. Lack of trust in the future.
Moving forward
Give yourself permission to succeed and know that you can handle the changes success brings. Stop resisting and start flowing. Let change take you to a better place. Trust.

◆

Just how hard can it be to get from *a* to *b*? You can normally walk with ease — not even thinking about how you put one foot in front of the other. Yet here you are and the simplest task in the world is impossible. You struggle on despite the huge resistance, but unless something changes all that happens is that you get totally exhausted or the terrain gets even harder. Everything seems to be against you, but still you labour on.

What is it in your life that should be so simple but is proving to be so hard? What resistance do you feel you are meeting? What don't you trust? The interpretation of this dream is this simple, but the secret it holds is a treasure. The secret is that no matter how much you think someone or something is resisting your efforts or making life tough for you, the reality is that the greatest resistance is coming from you!

Everything that moves, shakes, rattles, rolls or gets stuck in your dream is dream poetry for your feelings, thoughts and beliefs. Every atom of every dream picture is about you. People and circumstances around you have their power and sway but nothing can overpower you. Successful outcomes come down to how *you* handle people and situations. Okay, so it's easier said than done, perhaps, but there are ways to solve those too-tough situations. You can leave a relationship that is too hard for you, apply for a better job or become self-employed, or negotiate a more rewarding way of caring for a grumpy older relative.

But your dream is more about what you *don't* know than what you do know. You don't really need to dream about what you already know — your conscious thoughts and beliefs. Your dream looks at the conflicts between your conscious beliefs and your unconscious beliefs. You know you want to get somewhere or achieve something important to you. You know you're feeling under pressure and things are tough. You feel you are meeting resistance, though you know you could lessen or change some of that by making some clear decisions and acting on them. What you *don't* know is that you have unconscious beliefs that are keeping the going tough. You don't know it, but your dream does. Top of the list is hesitation and doubt. For example, your conscious mind may think 'I want this relationship to succeed', but your unconscious mind may believe 'I will lose my valued independence in this relationship.'

If you're in 'slo-mo no-go', something needs to change before you freeze-frame out of life altogether. That change is in your hands. Until you blast that unconscious resistance out of existence you'll continue to get nowhere fast.

In your life this could be about ...

- The unexpected delays that keep postponing the start of a new project.
- The money, promised to you weeks ago, that has not yet arrived.
- The job that seemed so straightforward when you started it, but has become complex.
- The way your partner or someone else just can't seem to get the message no matter how you put it.

- The employer who keeps demanding more of you: longer hours, less pay or additional responsibilities without acknowledgement.
- The way you keep doing more, hoping to be noticed or rewarded.
- A past failure or letdown that is making it hard for you to trust that all will be well.
- The bank balance that stays the same no matter how hard you work or how much you earn.
- The weight you can't lose or the cigarettes you can't give up.
- Your pattern of being in unfulfilling relationships.

Your unique dream contains personal clues only you may recognise

- Who are the people coming towards you in your dream? Get a feel for their approach to life. The clue might be in their personalities (if they are people you know), in their dress or in the way they move. In your dream you are going against the tide represented by these people. What you are resisting in your dream is a clue to what you are resisting in your waking life, or to the situation that is feeling so slow for you.
- Where are you trying to get to in your dream? Your dream destination gives you a clue to the waking life goal that you are resisting.
- A location from your past may be a clue to when your resistance pattern started.

Why has this dream come up for you now?

Your answers to these questions will reveal the reason:

- What feelings and emotions did you experience in your dream?
- Which situation in your life now do these feelings remind you of?
- Have you recently felt delayed over something?
- Have you recently moved closer to achieving a goal you have been wanting for a long time?
- Imagine yourself achieving that goal. What would change in your life if you achieved this success?

Your answer to the last question may reveal the reason your dream has come up for you now. You want to achieve a goal but you resist it because of the changes you imagine it will bring.

Dream alchemy practice
Starting the inner work

This is what to *do* if you hope to see dramatic transformations in your life.

A. Do this dream alchemy visualisation regularly:

Imagine yourself back in the dream but make the run or walk easy. Feel how light, elated, free and joyful the run now is. Feel how easy the air is to breathe and how effortless the run is. Summon up the feeling of trusting the run to take you to a better place. Bathe in the joy of your successful arrival.

B. Write a conversation between yourself in your dream where you are running in slo-mo and the ground, which seems sticky. Arrange the conversation like a script on your page. Start the conversation with the ground asking you, 'Where are you going?' Don't think — just let the words flow out and see what happens.

C. Identify a small task around your home that you've been meaning to do for ages. (Yes, you have at least one of these tasks, and yes, you have been resisting it no matter what other excuses you can come up with!) Do it without any more delays. You must not introduce complications or make the task more elaborate — remember these are signs of resistance. While doing the task, summon up the same feelings you are focusing on in your visualisation.

Glimmers of gold
In your dreams

When your recurring dream changes to embrace a happier ending, you are making good progress. Look out for the positive dream changes listed under 'How does your dream end?'

Some symbols from your dream alchemy practice may appear in your dreams. For example, you may dream of running with ease.

You may dream strong emotions such as fear (the fear that has held you back) or grief (as you acknowledge how hard you have worked to deprive yourself of reward). This is your dream's way of releasing you to trust the future and have it too.

Look out for dreams of release such as taking off heavy clothing, putting down heavy bags, seeds bursting open, animals being released from cages or fences being taken down.

In your waking life
You feel more trusting and begin to wonder why you suffered self doubt or mistrust before.

Life's tasks look much simpler. Hesitation is a thing of the past. You feel more as if you are experiencing life's flow.

You complete some of those old must-do jobs but the rest are done by other people or suddenly become obsolete. You wonder why some of these tasks were on your list so long because you can no longer see any importance in them.

At least one area of your life is released into fast-forward, making up for lost 'slo-mo' time. At least one goal is achieved 'out of the blue'.

Greater changes than you had expected may occur. You are aware of the old fears you once held about these changes, but you move beyond them and find yourself in a much better situation.

17: Aliens and UFOs

Aliens

The dream

There are aliens, or UFOs are around — seen or unseen.

For successful alchemy, precipitate the invisible and amalgamate the indivisible.

In your dream perhaps ...

◆ You sense the presence of a UFO on its way to Earth, although you cannot see it or communicate with it.

◆ You sense the presence of a UFO and, although you cannot see it, you are in telepathic communication with it or the aliens inside it.

◆ You see a UFO in the sky, or landing.

◆ You feel the presence of unseen aliens.

◆ You meet aliens and communicate with them: you are frightened or wary.

◆ You meet aliens and communicate with them: you feel a sense of union and belonging.

◆ You are not on Earth. All your dream action takes place on another planet or on a space station.

How do you feel in your dream?

Amazed. Awed. Surprised. Shocked. Wary. Frightened. Fearful. Rewarded. Excited. Special. Favoured. Chosen. United. Reunited. Hurt. A sense of belonging. Privileged. Invaded. Overpowered. Weak. Unsafe. Threatened. Defensive. Adventurous. Distanced. Detached. Supported. Spaced out. Weird. Manipulated. Welcomed. Welcoming. Dubious. Unsure. Cautious. Pushed away. Pulled towards. Enlightened. A sense of home-coming. Recognised. Unrecognised.

How does your dream end?
Positive changes are on the way if ...

- There is a reunion or sense of unity with the aliens.
- Some of the aliens introduce themselves by name.
- You embrace an alien and feel good about this.
- You experience grief.
- You experience relief.
- You or your body feels more powerful or bigger, when you wake up.
- When the UFO lands, you feel a sense of home-coming.
- If you are on another planet or space station, you finish the dream back on Earth.

It's time for a new approach if ...

- There is a war, fight or conflict that is not resolved by the end of the dream.
- You are abducted onto the ship or another planet.
- You feel manipulated or hurt and do not have the power to express your feelings about this or to communicate with the aliens about it.
- The aliens are withholding information or feelings from you.
- You or your body feels drained or smaller when you wake up.

What your dream means
Your way forward may be blocked by ...

Thoughts, feelings, experiences and beliefs that belong to you but that you deny so forcibly that you do not recognise them. Feeling alienated or isolated. Fear of some of your beliefs or experiences, often springing from a strict religious or judgemental upbringing. Not being grounded — being 'spacey'.

Moving forward

Ground yourself by bringing more physical pursuits into your life. Know that it is okay to have a range of feelings and that there are plenty of people who can understand how you feel or what you have been through. Know that there are many different ways to view the world and that it is always right to question your religion or upbringing. Be ready to let go of some of the rules or beliefs you were taught to fear or judge as a child or to let go of some of the promises you made in the past. Be ready to feel any pain or feelings you have covered up, knowing that this is your liberation.

◆

Are you star-trekking in your dream universe, boldly going where you have never been before, or are you quaking in fear as the alien spacecraft opens its doors before you? In the inside-out, upside-down land of dreams, it may come as no surprise to you that you have explored the outer reaches of the universe before. The universe in your dream is your whole self — from the very centre of your being to the outer edges of your mind. So, if your dream universe is you, who are the aliens and why might you be scared of meeting them?

There are things about you that you value and are happy to show the world. Then there are things that you prefer to share only with people close to you. Orbiting out in the next level of your private universe are the things you accept about yourself, but that you haven't yet shared with anyone: sensitive personal information or your ability to dream accurately of the future. Further out still are things that you accept about yourself but want to keep private forever. Beyond this, at the far-flung edges of your universe, are the thoughts, beliefs and experiences that have caused you so much distress that you have pushed them away — so far away that you believe they no longer belong to you. You have disowned them.

How terrible does something have to be to disown it? Remember, what is terrible for one person is okay for another. Strict religious people striving to be 'good' often disown any thoughts they have been taught to believe are 'bad'. These sins are then bundled up and pushed so far away from the person that they take on a separate identity. You might disown grief, emotional pain, love or anger. What you push away and disown in your waking life, however, can come up in a dream as aliens living at the edge of the universe or beyond. You have alienated your beliefs, thoughts or experiences. They are now foreign to you and you are scared of them. Your dream seeks to boldly take you back to where you have been before, to embrace what you have pushed away and to invite it back 'on board'.

If you are the alien in your dream, or if you are living among aliens, the dream is exploring your feelings of alienation. Some part of you feels it is on another planet, or ungrounded.

UFOs represent the thoughts, feelings and beliefs you no longer identify with. When your dreams show you UFOs, or UFOs landing, then you are preparing to unite and identify with these once again. You are ready to face the fear that made you push them away in the beginning. You are ready to heal the hurt and be whole again.

In your life this could be about ...

♦ Your struggle to live according to a set of beliefs: your religion, your family beliefs, the society or class you were born into.

♦ A traumatic event or experience in the past.

♦ Migrating to a new country or being a war refugee and feeling like a complete outsider.

♦ Moving to a new city, changing jobs or leaving home to go to university and feeling isolated or like an outsider.

♦ A sudden change in your beliefs, or suddenly seeing your whole life in a completely different way and hardly recognising yourself.

♦ Feeling outcast by others in your school, workplace or town.

Your unique dream contains personal clues only you may recognise

♦ The age of an alien, the number of aliens or the number of UFOs in your dream may be clues for any of the following: how old you were when this situation first came up for you; how many years ago it happened; how many times it happened; how many different issues of alienation you feel.

♦ If other people you know are in the dream, find three words to describe each person's approach to life and three words to describe each person's personality. This list gives you further clues to the feelings you disown and to the ways you use to deny them.

◆ An object, song, symbol, book or article of clothing in the dream gives you clues to the situation in your waking life where you feel alienated or to a situation in your past that triggered this.

Why has this dream come up for you now?

Your answers to these questions will reveal the reason:

◆ What feelings and emotions did you experience in your dream?

◆ Which situation in your life now do these feelings remind you of?

◆ Have you recently felt challenged about your beliefs, or found yourself vehemently defending them?

◆ Has someone recently told you about a traumatic situation they have endured, or have you seen a movie or news item that touched upon a difficult experience in your life?

◆ What would you describe as your best personality points? Which three emotions or feelings do you show that people usually admire in you? Now name the opposites to all the words on your two lists. Somewhere on this list of opposites is a feeling that you have disowned until now and are now ready to deal with. (It may be one word on your list or it may be more.) For each word on your list, imagine expressing that feeling in your life now. What fear does this bring up for you?

Your answer to the last question may reveal the reason your dream has come up for you now. It is time to face your fears and become more whole as a result.

Dream alchemy practice
Starting the inner work

This is what to *do* if you hope to see dramatic transformations in your life.

A. Do this dream alchemy regularly:

Imagine watching the aliens or UFOs from your dream coming in to land. As they land, a loving white light surrounds them. Soft, spiritual music fills the air. Someone you trust from your waking life is standing behind you, holding you in loving protection and support. He or she tells you that you are completely safe now because the white light has ensured that what is about to emerge from the UFOs or what the aliens are about to give you is for your healing. Feel the healing light entering your body, along with a sense of peace. Feel your body stretching and yawning as you relax properly for the first time in years. Just breathe, knowing you are now entirely safe.

B. How much physical exercise do you do? If your answer is 'none' or 'very little', get started today. Go for a walk or swim three times a week or join a yoga class or take out a gym membership. This dream alchemy practice is about getting physical and getting grounded.

C. Write a story — a page or two only. Write quickly without regard for how well written the story is. The more it seems to be written by a child, the better! You may even wish to write your story with your left hand if you are right handed, or vice versa. (Writing with your non-dominant hand puts you in touch with the side of your brain that holds deep feelings and memories.) The title of your story is, 'From way out here', and it is in the words of a person living on another planet 'way out there'. See what comes up, then put your story away for one week.

At the end of the week, re-read your story and then add a second part. In this part the person decides to move back to planet Earth. You are standing waiting to help the person settle back in.

Glimmers of gold
In your dreams
When your recurring dream changes to embrace a happier ending, you are making good progress. Look out for

the positive dream changes listed under 'How does your dream end?'

Some symbols from your dream alchemy practice may appear in your dreams. For example, you may dream of being embraced by a loving white light.

You may dream a range of strong emotions — the ones you have not yet been ready to face and feel. Let your dreams rage and scream, laugh and cry, knowing that they are safely venting your emotions and memories to free you to move on with your life without leaving part of yourself in hiding.

Look out for dreams of becoming bigger (more whole) or blending. You might dream of groups of people coming together into a circle or of many birds coming home to nest in one big tree.

In your waking life
You feel more whole and life seems to be more diverse and embracing. You are more aware of a greater variety of people and situations around you. You see people and situations in many colourful shades — no more black and white.

You are more open to other people's feelings and more at ease with sharing yours.

Your spiritual values or religious beliefs may strengthen or may change completely — either way this will be the result of you facing your uncertainties.

You are surprised at the depth and range of feelings that come up and you feel strengthened through this process.

You feel more solid, more connected with the ground. You feel as if your eyes are newly opened and you have now seen yourself for the first time. You know this is the real you and you feel really good about this — at last.

18: Beautiful stranger

Stranger

> ### The dream
> You meet a very beautiful stranger, male or female.
> You feel totally beguiled and enlightened in the
> stranger's presence. It is as if you have known this
> person forever.

When love calls, surrender.

In your dream perhaps ...

♦ The stranger is in the distance. You may hear her singing, or feel his presence before you see the person. You are entranced and follow the voice or sense.

♦ The stranger gets further away, so you keep following.

♦ You meet eye to eye and may embrace, soulfully, sexually or platonically.

♦ The stranger offers you wisdom or guides you in some way.

How do you feel in your dream?

Ecstasy. Enlightenment. United. Reunited. Beguiled. Entranced. Amazed. Awed. Loved. Loving. Sexy. Guided. Soulful. Recognised. Helped. Inspired. Opened. A sense of timelessness. A sense of oneness. Passionate. Embraced. Included. Lost. Overlooked. A sense of something missing. Abandoned. Alone. Isolated.

How does your dream end?
Positive changes are on the way if ...

♦ You are embraced by the stranger.

♦ You are inspired or receive some wisdom from the stranger.

♦ A message is communicated when you look into the stranger's eyes.

135

- The stranger presents you with a gift.
- You acquire a new skill from the stranger.

It's time for a new approach if ...
- You never catch up with the stranger.
- You feel alone at the end of the dream.
- You feel that something is missing from your life at the end of the dream.

What your dream means
Your way forward may be blocked by ...

Trying to fit in with the norm instead of being yourself. Hiding your true beauty and talents from the world — or from yourself. Fear of showing your light to the world. Not being in touch with your inner beauty, inborn talents and other special qualities.

Moving forward

Open your heart to feel your inner beauty. Allow yourself to shake off the ugly duckling you thought you were and become the beautiful swan you were all along. Know that it is safe for you to shine your light in the world and to use your full range of talents. You have all the inner wisdom you need to break the mould.

◆

There once was an ugly duckling because that's what the other ducklings called him. Really he was a swan. How deceived we are by the view of others!

The day before the ugly duckling realised his mistaken identity he felt ugly, isolated and rejected. He watched the other ducklings as they grew into ducks that waddled and quacked with a common sense of purpose that did not come naturally to him. But the swans — oh, the swans. Now they were really something! Theirs was a totally wonderful beauty. They flew with such grace and peace. He was entranced, beguiled and felt an ache in his heart to be at one with them. He was, in the same moment, at one with them and yet a million miles distant.

The beautiful stranger in your dream is your swan-self, calling you to follow, meld and become a swan. The beautiful stranger is your natural amazing self, the light you keep in the shadow for fear of … for fear of what? Why would you hide your inborn talents, wisdom and beauty away from the world?

This dream introduces you to your own inner beauty and implores you to cast off your ill-fitting cloak and shine your light in the world. The reason you feel as if you have known this beautiful dream stranger forever is that you have. He or she is you, always has been and always will be.

You might think that your beautiful dream stranger is your perfect soul mate appearing to you in your dream. You may spend eons searching for such perfection. You may discover your soul mate along the way to realising that the most beautiful relationships are those between people who are in touch with their whole swan-self. Get in touch by looking at your female dream stranger as your Yin or right-brain functions and your male dream stranger as your Yang or left-brain functions.

We are all swans, most of us living in a world requiring us to blend in and be ducks. Go on! Break the mould!

In your life this could be about …

◆ A talent you have been feeling drawn to using or expanding upon.

◆ A situation in which you feel something has been missing and you are beginning to understand what it is and what to do about it.

◆ A study course you are doing that feels too traditional — you know how to add a more meaningful dimension and would love to take the risk and express it.

◆ A relationship that has been too superficial.

◆ A situation you are ready to change or leave because something is changing for the better within you.

◆ Your spiritual path — a new insight that is breaking through for you.

Your unique dream contains personal clues only you may recognise

◆ If the beautiful stranger is female, she probably represents your Yin, your inner world or your right-brain functions, such as creativity, spirituality, a sense of being, intuition, nurturing and being in touch with your feelings. In your life now, where might you need to bring some of these qualities to shine?

◆ If the beautiful stranger is male, he probably represents your Yang, your outer world, or your left-brain functions such as intellect, rational thinking, action, competition and work. In your life now, where might you need to bring some of these qualities to shine?

◆ What were you looking for in your dream before you met the stranger? This may be a clue to what you are looking for in your waking life that will be found when you get in touch with the full beauty of your whole being.

◆ Did the stranger give you a gift or a message? This is your clue to unlocking your talents and letting them flow into the world.

Why has this dream come up for you now?

Your answers to these questions will reveal the reason:

◆ What feelings and emotions did you experience in your dream?

◆ Which situation in your life now do these feelings remind you of?

◆ Have you recently held yourself back from expressing a talent or shining your light fully because you were not sure how it would be received?

◆ Have you recently become aware that you have a valuable skill to offer but are anxious about acting on it?

◆ Imagine yourself showing your fuller self to the world in one of these ways. What challenges do you feel this would bring up for you?

Your answer to the last question may reveal the reason your dream has come up for you now. You are ready to blossom in a new or greater way and you are becoming aware of the changes that this action may bring into your life.

Dream alchemy practice

Starting the inner work

This is what to *do* if you hope to see dramatic transformations in your life.

A. Do this dream alchemy visualisation regularly:

Imagine standing in front of the beautiful stranger in your dream then looking directly into his or her eyes. Look deep and see pure love. Now merge your two bodies so that you become one. Feel the essence of the stranger's beauty and love flowing around your body, filling it up and seeping through your pores. Feel this everlasting light and know that it can flow through your pores and into the world forever. Feel this energy lifting your spirits and tuning your inner wisdom. Breathe deeply and know that you now take this power and feeling with you and can draw on it whenever you wish.

B. Name the quality of your inner beauty that you have yet to show the world — or yet to show in full. Think up a simple symbol to represent this quality — perhaps a rainbow to symbolise your talent with colours, a pair of hands to represent your healing abilities, or a star to symbolise your ability to be a light for people in darkness or to inspire people to look up.

The next step is to incorporate your symbol into a piece of dream alchemy jewellery to wear around your neck so that you are constantly in touch with your inner beauty and in touch with the feeling of communicating it. (You speak from your throat — your neck is a symbol of communication.) You might choose to draw your symbol and take it to a jewellery designer to make up for you, or to craft as a piece to hang on a neck-chain. Or you might choose to draw your symbol on a tiny piece of paper and put it inside a locket around your neck. Wear your symbol, feel it, draw upon it.

C. Choose a colour to represent the beautiful stranger you met in your dream. Paint a piece of paper this colour, or find a piece of fabric that has the right hue. Hang this above your front door, on the inside. Whenever you leave your house, touch the colour and take its essence out into the world with you.

139

Glimmers of gold
In your dreams
When your recurring dream changes to embrace a happier ending, you are making good progress. Look out for the positive dream changes listed under 'How does your dream end?'

Some symbols from your dream alchemy practice may appear in your dreams. For example, you may design your necklace symbol in a dream.

Your dreams may release old self-doubts and hesitations, perhaps bringing up symbols or reminders of times when you felt hurt or rejected and less than beautiful within yourself. This is your dream's way of flushing out the feelings that are no longer relevant so that you can move forward uncluttered.

Look out for dreams of finding treasures, gems and gifts or of discovering new paths and reading signs. You may also receive some great creative ideas in your dreams to help you as you spread your wings.

In your waking life
You walk taller, smile more and actually feel more beautiful. Other people will tell you that you are looking younger, happier or especially beautiful — they are seeing your inner beauty as well as seeing how it makes you feel and how it empowers you to be.

You feel freer and wonder why other people believe themselves to be locked into situations or ways of being.

You feel like a round peg in a world of square peg holes, yet you know you have found your home in the world. You understand this paradox.

The judgement of others is less important to you.

You know you are breaking the mould and you love the feeling of reaching beyond the old limits.

19: A scary presence in the room

Ghost

(Also see 17: Aliens and UFOs; 36: Paralysed — can't move,
can't shout!)

> ### The dream
>
> A scary presence is in the shadows or hanging over
> your bed. You may wake up feeling the presence is
> still there. Often the figure appears dark and hooded.

When fear calls, love.

In your dream perhaps ...

♦ The figure is standing next to you as you sleep, its face
  invisible.
♦ The figure is floating over you as you sleep, its face
  invisible.
♦ All you see is a dark cloak and hood.
♦ The figure reminds you of the Grim Reaper.
♦ You feel that the presence is a ghost from the past.
♦ You feel your body being lifted up by the presence.
♦ You want to move but you feel paralysed, and you want
  to scream but you can't.
♦ Instead of dreaming you are asleep, you meet the pres-
  ence in another scary setting, like a graveyard or mortu-
  ary for example.

How do you feel in your dream?

Scared. Fearful. Frightened. Paralysed. Manipulated. A
sense of evil. A sense of death. Frozen. Powerless. A sense of
dread or doom.

How does your dream end?
Positive changes are on the way if ...

♦ You see the face of the presence and you are able to look
  it in the eye.

* You do something to send the presence away.
* The presence transforms into something peaceful: think of a wicked witch becoming a beautiful princess, or an ugly toad becoming a handsome prince.
* The dream becomes filled with light and peace.

It's time for a new approach if ...

* You wake up, still paralysed with fear, and are unable to get back to sleep.
* You wake up and feel the presence is still there — no longer part of your dream.
* You feel your body lifting up beyond your control and you wake up scared.

What your dream means

Your way forward may be blocked by ...

Your own fears that you are not facing. Thoughts and feelings that you judge as dark or evil so you push them so far away that you do not recognise them as your own. Your own negativity. Possibly the negativity of others projected towards you and felt by you, but far more likely your fears about other people's negativity affecting you.

Moving forward

Face your fears. Be ready and willing to see that the darkness and negativity you feel around you is not coming from an outside force but is the sum of your own dark fears and harsh judgements. Be ready and willing to see that it is whole and healthy to experience a range of feelings and thoughts. Be ready to see your own negativity and not to blame others or circumstances for what you are feeling.

◆

The two keys to getting a grip on this extremely scary common dream are 'faceless' and 'dark hood or cloak'. If your scary presence is invisible it still conveys a sense of darkness and facelessness.

This dream can be so scary that you wake up with adrenaline pumping frantically and the feeling that a dark force was present in your room. You may even feel that you weren't dreaming, deciding that you felt a sense of spookiness and opened your eyes to see the dark, hooded form hanging over you. You may be quite certain that your eyes were open and quite certain that the form was visible in front of you. This experience can leave you very frightened.

So what does it mean? Is this a dream, a scary spirit experience or a manifestation of someone's evil thoughts projecting towards you?

The route to sanity and breathing easy is to remember that dreams are all about you. But don't panic! There's nothing evil within you. Here's what's likely to be happening.

Firstly, let's talk about this as a dream experience.

People in your dreams are facets of yourself. They are your beliefs about life, your thoughts, your memories and your feelings. Usually dream people have faces that help you to identify them. For example, Uncle Joe in your dream stands for the beliefs you have about Uncle Joe. When your dream shows you a faceless character it can stand for a belief you cannot face about yourself or something you cannot face in your life.

What kind of beliefs or experiences might be terrifying to face? Sadly there are many terrifying experiences common to humankind that people struggle with in their dreams. Just as common, though, is the situation where you have been brought up to believe that something is evil, or that certain thoughts you have are evil. If you have been brought up within a religion that sees things as either good or evil, then you may dream of all your 'non-good' beliefs or experiences being summoned as a devil or dark evil force. If you feel rage about something but have been taught that it is bad to express anger, then your angry energy may confront you in a dream. It's like saying, 'You can't ignore your anger. You can't pretend to be all sweet and good when you feel rage. You are not facing or owning your real feelings!'

The dream figure is dark because it is your dark side, or what you keep dark and hidden from yourself. What you will not face when you are awake, your dreams will vent while you sleep. All the time you are not facing up to a fear you are living less than a full life, trapped by your own fear.

Your dream asks you to confront experiences, feelings, thoughts or beliefs that you have not faced. When you can say, 'Okay. I admit it. This is how I feel,' you are on the road to being whole and to seeing that dark, fearful form dispersing.

Many people use the word 'presence' to describe their dream. There are two explanations for this. The first is that the things you don't want to face are often pushed so far away that they not only are faceless in your dreams but also appear as non-human in form. They are so much rejected by you that they might have come up in previous dreams as aliens living on another planet or as UFOs. (See common dream 17: Aliens and UFOs.) As you get closer to acknowledging the dark fear you have been rejecting, the alienated fears approach closer in your dreams — they come right into your dream room, right into your presence or present. That's precisely why you *feel* the fear. When your fear was pushed beyond the realms of your being, you could not feel it. The final contact is up to you — acknowledge, accept the whole self that is you and move on.

The second explanation for describing this terrifying feeling as a presence is that you woke, opened your eyes and saw the dark form in front of you. However, this doesn't mean there was anything there. If you open your eyes while dreaming (a common reaction to shock or terror), your brain gets confused, not knowing how to relate the images to the fact that your eyes are open. It solves this by 'seeing' the dream images superimposed on your bedroom scene. You really *do* see the presence in your room because your brain has come to this conclusion. But it isn't there at all: it's a dream image only.

The paralysing cold shivers and racing heart you feel are due to the adrenaline rushing through your body. (See common dream 36: Paralysed — can't move, can't shout!)

The feeling that your body is being lifted up by a negative force against your will is a common experience during times of fear when you are not facing your own negativity. You are being controlled by your own negativity even though you cannot relate to it.

It is sometimes possible to tune into the thoughts and feelings of people close to you, and this is heightened when you are asleep. This is why you may see elements of what is happening for someone close to you appearing in your dream. Typically you will be dreaming a dream and then an odd bit will occur — something that doesn't quite fit into the storyline. These odd bits may be the telepathic thoughts that come in and mingle with the dream. They can become slightly distorted as your dreaming mind tries to fit them into the current dream storyline but you will recognise them when you learn later of the event you were tuning into. If someone is thinking negatively about you, feeling anger or wishing you harm, then it is possible for you to tune into this negativity while you sleep, weaving the feeling into your dream. The way to approach this is twofold:

Step one: As you fall asleep visualise a positive energy surrounding you and totally protecting you. This may be your god, angels, loving spirit, a white light — whatever feels right to you. As you take this energy into sleep, nothing negative can touch you. Combine this with asking your dreams to help you to understand what you need to know through gentler dreams. *Step two:* Return to looking at the presence as being the close proximity of your own fears. Face what you have chosen to keep faceless. The most valuable personal and spiritual rewards are often those gained through facing fear.

Remember that the dark, hooded figure is more likely to be the shape of your own negative feelings rather than those projected towards you by someone else. As this type of dream is about what you push away and disown, it may be too easy for you to reject this interpretation and decide you are the recipient of someone's negative energy. This is why step one is to protect yourself against receiving negative thoughts in your dreams and step two returns to looking at your own disowned negative thoughts and fears.

In your life this could be about ...
- Your fear of facing something threatening within your relationship.

- Your fear of facing a financial situation that may become a disaster unless you do face it.
- Your fear of facing a bad decision you have made and think you have to live with.
- The guilt you feel about a situation or past event that you fear facing.
- The negative feelings (such as anger, jealousy, rage, resentment and scorn) you have towards your partner or a relation that you dare not face because you judge these feelings as bad or evil.
- Any thought, deed or feeling that your church or upbringing has taught you is evil or wrong that you cannot face up to.
- Any situation where you try to be the 'good guy' or to 'do the right thing' while holding bitterness about it inside.
- That person or situation you blame for making your life hard instead of seeing that it is the negativity you harbour against the person that is the source of your unhappiness.

Your unique dream contains personal clues only you may recognise

- Most people suffer the basic dream and then wake up in fear, leaving little room for dream detail and clues. There's the faceless, dark, hooded, evil presence, the fear, and the waking up. If your dream is so short, it is hard to identify the waking life situation this dream is reflecting. The best thing is to read the 'In your life this could be about ...' list again and ask yourself some serious questions.
- If you can recall the dream leading up to the appearance of the scary presence, find the nearest dream theme in this book and use the personal clues list to discover the fear you have not been facing.

Why has this dream come up for you now?

Your answers to these questions will reveal the reason:
- What feelings and emotions did you experience in your dream?

- Which situation in your life now do these feelings remind you of?
- The two questions above may be hard for you to answer if you recall only the scary part of this dream. The difficult task for you is to identify a situation or feeling that you have been working really hard to deny — possibly for years! This dream leaves you feeling powerless. Have you recently felt powerless in a situation?
- Everyone has negative thoughts from time to time. If you had to guess what your biggest negative thought is, what would it be?
- Now go back and answer that question honestly.

Your answer to the last question may reveal the reason your dream has come up for you now. You are ready to face your biggest fear or your biggest negativity.

Dream alchemy practice
Starting the inner work

This is what to *do* if you hope to see dramatic transformations in your life.

A. Allow yourself thirty minutes to perform this dream alchemy practice. Make sure you have a quiet space for this, with no interruptions!

Open this book at random and write down the first 'negative' feeling word you see. This might be from the 'How do you feel in your dream?' lists, but it may also jump out at you from another page. Spend the first fifteen minutes contemplating this negative feeling. Let your memories of negative feelings you have had seep into your mind, lifting the dark cloaks that you had thrown over them to try to hide them. Remember situations that brought up these feelings. Remember why you held back from communicating your distress or from examining why you felt the feelings.

Spend the second fifteen minutes visualising a broom of white light sweeping these negative memories and feelings from your mind forever. Finish by saying aloud,

'Today I found negative thoughts that I had thought were dark and bad, but when I looked I saw that they were natural and human. I saw that these feelings belonged to my past, so I swept them away. I am free now.' Repeat this dream alchemy several times.

B. Take a piece of paper and draw ten circles, each big enough to represent a featureless face. You may not need all ten circles for this dream alchemy practice, but allow for ten. In the next few days or weeks you will find yourself naming the fears you have not been facing. Each time you are ready to name a fear or a negative thought, give a circle on your paper an appropriate face and then add a name. Continue this dream alchemy practice until you feel it is done. Then move on to the third practice.

C. This dream alchemy practice follows from the one above.

In a visualisation, imagine bringing all your named fears (the people wearing the faces you have drawn) together in a circle. Introduce them to each other. Let any conversation take place and then let them all laugh in joyful release together. As they laugh, visualise them merging together to become a single butterfly that flies away. (A butterfly is a symbol of transformation, the beautiful butterfly emerging from the darkness of the caterpillar's chrysalis, just as you now emerge from the darkness into the true light.)

Glimmers of gold
In your dreams
When your recurring dream changes to embrace a happier ending, you are making good progress. Look out for the positive dream changes listed under 'How does your dream end?'

Some symbols from your dream alchemy practice may appear in your dreams. For example, you may dream of watching a huge butterfly rise up to the heavens.

Your dreams may release softer variations of your fears along with symbols from times past when these fears first began. Expect some grief and some tears of relief. This is your dream's way of releasing old fears so that you can move forward.

Look out for dreams of faces emerging from crowds, happy laughter, seeing the funny side of life and children being deliciously naughty.

In your waking life
You see the funnier side of life and drop some old defences. You are more relaxed and more in touch with your spirit as well as with your spirituality. Your spirituality may emerge in a different form — a more encompassing, personally authentic, individual spirituality.

You are less concerned to judge yourself or others. Blame is a thing of the past. You begin to value personal experience and wisdom more highly than you did before.

You see your past in a different light, and you hardly recognise the life you once led compared with the choices you now make.

You are more empowered.

20: The awesome wild animal

Animal

(Also see 24: Snakes!)

The dream

A wild animal appears larger than life, either in actual size or in presence. It is awesome.

Listen to the call.

In your dream perhaps ...

- You see the wild animal in the distance but feel the power of its presence.
- You feel that the wild animal has seen you, knows about you and has a message to convey to you.
- You feel something positive emanating from the wild animal.
- You feel threatened by the animal or scared of it.
- You feel that the animal is watching to see what you do next.
- The wild animal is about to attack you, or it bites you or causes you pain.
- The wild animal has hold of you and you cannot release yourself.
- You want to step in to help the wild animal.
- You feel the pain, hurt or some other emotion of the wild animal.
- The animal is infinitely wise.
- You run away from the animal.

How do you feel in your dream?

Awed. Inspired. Empowered. Guided. Safe. Unsafe. Threatened. Under attack. Fearful. Hurt. Observed. Observing. Hesitant. Caring. Protective. Protected. Cautious. Free. Strong. Weak. Desirous. Restricted. Confined. Cornered. Trapped. A sense of timelessness. Apprehensive. Scrutinised. A sense of expectation.

How does your dream end?
Positive changes are on the way if ...

- You rise to the expectation of the wild animal in a positive way.
- You receive a message or insight from the animal.
- You are bitten or hurt by the animal but you recover and something wonderful happens.
- You are transformed in a positive way by the animal.
- You feel bigger, more whole, or more fulfilled as a result of your encounter with the wild animal.
- You overcome an attacking or dangerous wild animal in a way that leaves you feeling positive.
- You find a way to co-exist with the wild animal to the advantage of you both.
- You help the animal in some way.

It's time for a new approach if ...

- The dream ends with you feeling threatened or hurt.
- You are frozen or paralysed by your encounter with the wild animal.
- You run away or look for escape from the wild animal.
- You just don't know what to do and are in a stalemate situation or stand-off with the animal.

What your dream means
Your way forward may be blocked by ...

An instinct you are not following (and should be) or an instinct that is a bit too raw for a situation that needs a more calculated response. The way you use or don't use your energies.

Moving forward

Become aware of your instincts and animal energies, and look to your dreams to find the right balance between responding instinctively and responding by calculation.

◆

Walk, swim, fly and roar on the wild side! Your instincts are responding to ensure your survival, to protect and guide you through the jungle, to do battle using physical strength or wit. You sniff the wind for food or predators — you have young to feed, territory to protect and genetic wisdom to guide you. How does a mother bird know how to feed worms to her chick? How does a fox know how to hunt? Is it nature or nurture — or both?

You have learned much about life from your parents, school, society and the media: that's the *nurture* part. You were born with a set of basic survival instincts: that's the *nature* part. But how useful are instincts for a person with many communication skills at hand to negotiate life's barbs and hurdles? Is it in your best interests to scratch and bite your enemy to defend your territory or your mate? Or is it better for everyone concerned to talk the matter through and reach a happy, sensible win–win solution?

Think of the wild animals in your dreams as being your instinctual responses to what you are dealing with in waking life, as well as being descriptions of the kinds of raw energy you are facing. When you are confronted by a snarling wolf in your dream, you may recognise the feeling of being cornered and vulnerable. Or you may be confronting your own snarling, defensive energy — that protective survival instinct that is in your dreams because you're not aware of it while you are awake. Remember, it is yourself you meet in dreams, dressed in whatever form. If it's a dream wolf, ask yourself, 'How am I dealing with wolf energy in my life right now?'

People throughout the world tend to see some animals in the same way. We recognise the strength of the lion; the passionate gallop of the horse; the cheeky playfulness of the monkey; and the all-seeing eye of the eagle. But our own feelings and thoughts about the wild animal in our dreams are more important. Many people see the independent, intuitive power of a cat, but you may think 'lap of luxury' or 'alley cat'. The animal in your dream is a picture of an energy that is playing a part in your life, and by looking at how you see that animal you can name the energy.

The more primitive the animal, the more basic the instinct often is. Your dreams may show great instinctual wisdom about your primitive survival patterns. The back of your brain, near your neck, is the most primitive brain area. It controls your basic survival systems such as your breathing and your hormone balance. It's sometimes called the 'reptilian brain'. It's natural to see crocodiles appear in people's dreams when they are wrestling with basic survival issues or suffering hormonal swings or going through menopause.

Think animal totems and you're halfway to 'getting' your animal dreams. According to the culture of your birth you might have been born to the Deer totem, to the Eagle god or under the sign of Capricorn the Goat. You might wear your animal sign around your neck or as a tattoo. The point of all this, traditionally, is to draw on the gentle energy of the deer, the soaring, far-seeing energy of the eagle or the enduring mountain-climbing energy of the goat. Your totem, your touchstone or your visualisation provide you with an extra burst of help and instinct to draw on in times of need.

It's even more powerful to draw on the whole gamut of animal energies. If you need some graceful inner-beauty, think or dream 'swan'. Do you need to show more passion? Think or dream 'jaguar'. Could you do with a touch more courage? Think or dream 'bear'. When you need to draw on under-utilised powerful instincts and energies, your dreams will often cast animals to put you in touch with your instincts.

Look into a dream and you'll see yourself in a far greater range of guises and disguises than you think you show the world. That's precisely why you see a lion of strength silently standing to attention when you have forgotten to feel your strength. It's also why you can see the strutting peacock; the greedy, chauvinistic pig; or the broken-record caged parrot. Could these traits be yours?

Resist the urge to rush to the nearest bookshop and buy a dream dictionary listing the entire zoological range from 'aardvark' to 'zebra'. Look at what your dream animal means to *you!* You *can* do this. Just close your eyes and let the animal's energy speak to you.

In your life this could be about ...

♦　A work situation where your survival (job) is threatened.
♦　Your ticking biological-clock posing the question of whether to have a baby.

+ Your sexuality and sexual relationships.
+ Your passion, or lack of it, for a project, situation or person.
+ A difficult situation that you don't know how to handle.
+ A communication problem that could be fixed with a little animal magic.

Your unique dream contains personal clues only you may recognise

+ If the animal in your dream had a personality, which three words would you pick to describe it? Which three words would you use to describe this animal's approach to its life? What word would you say summed up this animal's raw energy? Which situation in your life now is either described by these words or by the exact opposite of these words?
+ Was the animal in your dream involved in hunting, looking after babies, mating, eating, nest building or some other instinctual activity? If so, this is a clue to the life situation your dream is addressing.
+ Is there a dream-cliché clue for you, such as the dog that chases its own tail, the parrot that repeats itself incessantly or the tortoise that goes slowly and steadily to win the race? Where can you see that cliché appearing in your life?

Why has this dream come up for you now?

Your answers to these questions will reveal the reason:

+ What feelings and emotions did you experience in your dream?
+ Which situation in your life now do these feelings remind you of?
+ Have you been feeling low in energy or drained from too much mental or physical exertion?
+ Have you been feeling out of touch with your intuition or your gut feeling?
+ Has someone suggested that you have acted too quickly, too emotionally or without measured thought recently?

Your answers to the last two questions may reveal the reason your dream has come up for you now. There is a situation that would be better solved by a more instinctual response *or* by a more calculated response — basically, something is out of balance.

Dream alchemy practice
Starting the inner work

This is what to *do* if you hope to see dramatic transformations in your life.

A. If your dream animal acted in a way that led to a successful and happy dream outcome, then it's time to borrow some of that energy and apply it in your waking life. Close your eyes and imagine the animal standing behind you. Feel its energy radiating into your back in a friendly, supportive way. Now absorb that positive animal energy into your body. Feel it as a wise instinct that is yours to guide you whenever you call upon it. Repeat this dream alchemy practice as often as you care to.

B. If your dream animal acted in a way that led to an unhappy outcome in your dream, then visualise yourself back in the dream and change the drama to produce a better ending. Never kill or trap the animal. Persuade it to act in a more positive or balanced way that influences the possible outcome. Or ask it to tell you why it was in your dream — what message it wanted to deliver to you.

C. Here's where dream alchemy meets the 'cooking pot'. To begin this dream alchemy practice pick three words to sum up the energy you would like to absorb from your dream animal. For example, you might pick 'passion, strength and spirit' to sum up a horse that entranced you as it ran through your dream. Then think up foods, herbs or spices that you feel symbolise these energies. For example, you might pick oysters for passion, spinach for strength and whisky for spirit. Design your new culinary wonder (you can add other ingredients but make these the features), cook it and eat it! If you wish, create a special setting or ritual for your meal. If you feel like sharing, invite three friends and assign one of the energies to each (passion to one, strength to the second and

155

spirit to the third) and ask them to bring a poem or story featuring the energy to share during the feast.

Glimmers of gold
In your dreams
When your recurring dream changes to embrace a happier ending, you are making good progress. Look out for the positive dream changes listed under 'How does your dream end?'

Some symbols from your dream-alchemy practice may appear in your dreams. For example, you may dream of sharing a ritual feast.

Your dreams may release animal energies you have repressed, so you may feel like a cat in a dream or discover an unaccustomed sexual energy or find yourself breast-feeding a dozen babies nuzzling at your many teats.

Look out for dreams with wild and beautiful landscapes or dreams of meeting native people who give you the gift of ancient wisdom or guidance.

In your waking life
You see solutions to problems more easily and feel a sense of wisdom, confidence and balance in applying these.

You find communication easier and negotiate more win–win outcomes.

You feel more in touch with your natural desires and instincts and may feel ready to make decisions about moving in with a partner, having children, returning to work (hunting and providing) or accepting your role as an elder, for example.

You notice your energies in general seem more balanced — you have more playfulness as well as more focus, or you are both stronger and softer in your communications with others.

Your physical and mental energy levels are more highly tuned.

21: I've lost my way

Lost

The dream

You can't find your way through the city, a big building or the countryside. You're lost and you know it.

The way may change but the compass always points true.

In your dream perhaps ...

- You half recognise the place, but streets you used to know don't lead to the same places anymore, hallways you were once familiar with lead elsewhere, and the countryside you knew so well is now all changed.
- You wait for buses or trains but realise you're at the wrong bus stop or train station. You don't know where the right stop or station is.
- Street signs are confusing. They are of no help in directing you.
- You can see where you want to be, or know where you want to be, but you can't fathom how to get there.
- You have no idea where you want to be. You just know you're lost and can't find your way out.

How do you feel in your dream?

Lost. Confused. Puzzled. Unsure. Unconfident. Aimless. Determined. Exhausted. Tired. Frustrated. Deserted. Desolate. Lonely. Abandoned. Unsupported. Incapacitated.

How does your dream end?

Positive changes are on the way if ...

- You find your way to your original destination.
- You find a short-cut to your original destination.
- You end up at a much better place.
- You learn something insightful or discover something interesting instead.

157

- You meet up with someone who helps you find your way.
- You decide on another plan and feel good about it.
- You find the right bus or train station.

It's time for a new approach if ...
- You are still lost at the end of the dream.
- Your confusion in the dream increases.

What your dream means
Your way forward may be blocked by ...
Old approaches or ways of relating that no longer work for you. Inflexibility or difficulty in adapting to changed circumstances. Being out of touch with your intuition or other life skills needed to find your path to where you want to be. Doubt about the goals you have been aiming for.

Moving forward
Be more flexible and open to new ideas and ways of doing things. Know that life is about change (who wants to be stuck?) so be still and watch the way the wind blows. Tune into your inner guidance and reconsider your goals.

◆

There are times in life when the old ways just don't work for you anymore. Things have changed and moved on but you are still expecting the new world to operate in the old, familiar way.

The destination may read the same but the old route has been superseded by a new order. That old boys' or girls' network once useful for getting a good job no longer works; those childish tears no longer bring you the attention you want; playing the underdog has lost its sympathy-pulling power now you are expected to be more mature.

Life isn't a puzzle with a single solution. There is no right answer, no one and only way. Life is more like a kaleidoscope, ever changing, ever reflecting the last move. Today's decision changes tomorrow's path. The map you were handed in childhood is no longer relevant. It's time to find a new way or to change destinations, but first you must change your ways!

In your life this could be about ...

- Preferring to use the work skills you were taught instead of new systems and technologies.
- That job, marriage or house purchase you had set your heart upon seeming to be out of your reach.
- The loss of a partner leaving you to find your own way in the world — something you haven't had to do for a long time.
- The loss of your job and income leaving you feeling lost about how to survive.
- Old ways of relating with family members no longer working.

Your unique dream contains personal clues only you may recognise

- If the streets, bus stops or street signs are from a place you knew in your past, think back to that time. What were your goals then and how were you approaching them? Which of those ways might no longer be working for you?
- What is your destination in your dream? An ocean destination might give you a clue to an emotional goal, a church to a spiritual goal, a restaurant to a self-nurturing goal or a place you once knew to a need to re-evaluate your past.
- Look at your dream clothes or shoes for further clues. For example, high-heeled shoes (perhaps indicating a corporate approach or using your sex appeal) hindering your progress in your dream may give you a clue about the need for a new way of approaching your goal.

Why has this dream come up for you now?

Your answers to these questions will reveal the reason:

- What feelings and emotions did you experience in your dream?
- Which situation in your life now do these feelings remind you of?
- Imagine the best possible outcome for you in this situation. What fears or challenges does achieving this bring up for you?

Your answer to the last question may reveal the reason your dream has come up for you now. You are ready to find new ways to achieve your goals — or to create new goals — but your fears about the changes ahead are causing you to hesitate.

Dream alchemy practice
Starting the inner work
This is what to *do* if you hope to see dramatic transformations in your life.

A. It is the year 2050. Your biographer is preparing her material to write a book about you. She is looking back over the years from 2050 down to where you are today. She has drawn circles over the page and is writing a landmark achievement in each one. Later she will link the circles as stepping stones, showing how you got from where you are now to where you are in 2050. She will use this stepping-stone map as a guide when writing her book. Close your eyes and imagine her doing this — see what she is writing in the circles.

Now take a piece of paper. Write the title '2050: Looking back' on the page. At the top of the page draw a face or stick figure (or cut out a picture from a magazine). This is your biographer. Now draw the circles and put yourself in her shoes as she writes your landmark achievements in them. Don't think too hard — just let this dream alchemy practice flow. Then link the circles up to form a stepping-stone map.

If you like this life story, study it every day for up to three weeks and visualise yourself achieving these goals and the steps between. On the first day of the fourth week decide on your first step and do it.

If you don't like what you see, take a second piece of paper and write the title '2050: The rewrite ...' on it. Rewrite your life from this day forward! Then follow the same dream alchemy practice as above, studying the map every day for three weeks and so on.

B. Here's an affirmation for you:

I look to my left, I look to my right and suddenly I see
a new way. My destination is near and is shining in
the light bathing my path. I feel the surge of energy,
excitement and joy as I set foot on this new way. The
journey is smooth and fast. I feel elated and successful
as I now arrive at my destination.

You can insert the name of your goal instead of the word
'destination' if you wish (for example, 'perfect job').The
dream alchemy will be more powerful if you insert your
dream destination, even if you're unsure of its symbolism.
So, if you were trying to get to the ice-cream shop in your
dream, insert 'ice-cream shop' instead of 'destination'.

C. List three things that you have done in the same way for
at least several years. For example, the route you drive to
work (always the same), the way you do your shopping
(same supermarket after work) or the method you use to
remove weeds from your garden (pull them out). Then
design new ways of doing each of these. For example,
drive a different way to work, or walk or take a bus; learn
how to shop online; grow plants that counteract weeds
(ground covers) or take a permaculture approach.

Glimmers of gold
In your dreams

When your recurring dream stops or changes to embrace
a happier ending, you are making good progress.

Some symbols from your dream alchemy practice may
appear in your dreams. For example, you may pick up
your biography in a futuristic bookshop.

Your dreams may release grief as you let go of old goals
or old ways of doing things. The passing of the old always
needs to be mourned before the birth of the new. This is
a natural and positive process.

Look out for dreams of earthworks, looking down from
a high place to see a pattern or map and, possibly, some
great creative ideas and solutions.

161

In your waking life

Things that used to puzzle you are much clearer. You are surprised to realise that you were stuck in old ways before without really knowing it. Everything looks quite different to you now.

You feel more vitality and energy. You are ready and keen to take risks. Your intuition is sharp.

You feel younger and see your life ahead as one of endless choice, great opportunity and change.

You feel empowered by the range of choices ahead of you, and experience a great sense of achievement and flow as you make those choices and step on those stepping stones.

22: Can't find a suitable toilet!

Toilet

(Also see 25: Cuts, wounds, blood, guts and vomit)

The dream

You are searching for a toilet, but if you do find one it is unsuitable for you to use.

Process to refine.

In your dream perhaps ...

- You are following signs for a public toilet, but you are getting led on a longer and longer route.
- You find a public toilet, but all the toilets are occupied.
- You find a public toilet but there are no walls to mark the stalls. You are unwilling to sit on a toilet next to a stranger.
- You sit on a toilet but then the door opens, or a wall falls down or you realise you have no privacy.
- You find the toilet but it is dirty or overflowing.
- Yes, you find the toilet! But just as you are about to sit down, it changes into a chair, bidet or bed.

How do you feel in your dream?

Frustrated. Delayed. Obstructed. Denied. Vulnerable. Pressed. Embarrassed. Relieved. Patient. Defeated. Disappointed. Prudish. Put out. Exposed.

How does your dream end?
Positive changes are on the way if ...

- You find a toilet and relieve yourself comfortably.
- You find a toilet and relieve yourself despite being on view to others.
- You give up worrying about other people or inadequate toilets and just get on with it — putting your needs first.
- You give up looking for a toilet and choose an open field or other suitable nearby place.

163

It's time for a new approach if ...
◆ You never find relief in your dream and, when you wake up, discover that there is no urgent need for the toilet that your dream could have been alerting you to.

What your dream means
Unless your dream is prompted by a real need to use the bathroom:

Your way forward may be blocked by ...
Not having enough privacy, space and time to process and release feelings, thoughts and beliefs that have been cluttering your mind. Hanging on to toxic or uncomfortable feelings that you don't need in your life anymore.

Moving forward
Find a way to make time for yourself each day to sit and watch your feelings and think about your life. Examine your negative or bitter thoughts and then let them go. Give yourself permission to flow with the changes life brings to you.

◆

You might have had toilet dreams where you have woken up bursting, which explains those dreams. But there have been other times where you have woken from such a dream with no physical need.

Have you been a parent of tiny children who always wanted to follow you to the toilet, or who needed your urgent help the moment you closed the door? If so, you'll be familiar with the theme of just wanting the smallest amount of privacy and peace and not getting even that. The same goes for those jobs where you're alone, expected to be on your feet for hours on end and putting endless queues of customers first no matter what.

When life deprives you of the basic necessity of privacy and space, whether to visit the toilet or to simply take time out on your own to think or breathe, this kind of dream rushes in to illustrate the point. When you have this dream, ask yourself why you're not giving yourself the courtesy, self-respect and grace to have a decent amount of private time. This dream is also about what you do — or don't do — with your private time.

When you empty your bladder you are releasing toxins and other unneeded elements from your body along with all the excess water. In dreams, water usually symbolises your emotions, so dreaming of emptying your bladder is about releasing emotional toxins or emotional issues you have processed but not yet let go of. This dream, however, is more often about *not* finding the space and privacy to let go, isn't it? Are you finding enough time to process your feelings and release them?

When you empty your bowel you are releasing all the indigestible stuff that's left after all the goodness has been extracted to nourish your body. In dreams this equates all the things you don't need in your life anymore. This is a good dream pun — are you hesitant about letting it go?

Next time you have this dream, ask yourself what is annoying you or weighing you down and then find the space and privacy to let it go.

In your life this could be about ...

- The way you jump out of bed, eat breakfast on the run, work, socialise and go to bed with barely a moment to yourself.
- The way every waking moment of your attention is focused on your family's needs.
- The way you have been hanging on to what someone said to you for far too long, feeling more hurt or bitter as time goes by.
- A routine you have been sticking to for too long that is an unnecessary burden — for example, doing all the family ironing when the others are taking time out to relax and you are equally deserving.
- A social relationship that has become an unnecessary duty, fulfilling no one.
- A relationship that is past its use-by date.
- The pain you have chosen to suffer instead of sorting a situation out.

Your unique dream contains personal clues only you may recognise

- Is your dream set in your past: back at school, in your old home town or at a previous workplace, for example? If so, these are clues to other times when you overlooked your need for privacy and may give you a clue about why you're in a similar situation now.
- Does someone else in your dream get to the toilet before you do? How would you describe their approach to life? Where in your life now are you noticing this approach or its exact opposite, either with someone you know or within yourself?
- If you are carrying something in your dream, this is a clue to what you need to contemplate within yourself in privacy.

Why has this dream come up for you now?

Your answers to these questions will reveal the reason:

- What feelings and emotions did you experience in your dream?
- Which situation in your life now do these feelings remind you of?
- Have you recently felt rushed off your feet or talked out by someone with little attention directed towards your needs?
- Have you recently found yourself with time to spare and felt lost or bored so you immediately made yourself busy again or switched on the television or phoned a friend?
- Imagine you have time to sort out one problem in your life. Which one would it be? If this problem was solved, what challenges do you feel this would bring up for you?

Your answer to the last question may reveal the reason your dream has come up for you now. There may be reasons why you keep yourself busy and avoid time to yourself, and why you are stuck.

Dream alchemy practice
Starting the inner work

This is what to *do* if you hope to see dramatic transformations in your life.

A. Buy a small kitchen garbage bin (perhaps a counter-top one) and place it near your back door. Every time you have a negative thought or find yourself feeling uncomfortable about something someone has said to you, write the thought or feeling onto a small piece of paper and then screw it up and place it in your bin. If you find yourself thinking the same thought again, repeat the process. At the end of each day, ceremoniously empty the contents of your bin into the outside bin, ready for the garbage collectors to take away. This dream alchemy practice is about processing and letting go, about cleansing and clearing your personal space.

B. Imagine yourself back in your dream, replaying all the details up to the point where you can't find a suitable toilet. Then change the ending. See yourself finding the toilet quickly and relieving yourself in peace and privacy. Summon up a feeling of relief, peace, quiet contemplation and success.

C. If you don't already have a water-purifying system in your home, invest in one. Each time you pour yourself a glass of water imagine your body and mind being as efficient as the water-purifier, filtering out the toxic thoughts and feelings and nourishing you with a pure and healthy energy. Clean or replace the water filter regularly and, when you do, imagine your body and mind being as timely and efficient at ridding itself of the toxins and wastes that you do not need in your life.

Glimmers of gold
In your dreams
When your recurring dream stops or changes to embrace a happier ending, you are making good progress.

Your dreams may release feelings and images from the past that you have been unhealthily hanging onto. This is the dream's way of clearing your body and mind so you can treat yourself more lovingly from now on.

Look out for dreams of open spaces, freedom and houses with many unused rooms for you to explore.

167

In your waking life

Suddenly you have more time available for yourself. Life gets less frantic and yet you are surprised that everything that really needs to get done still gets done.

You become more comfortable with delegating some tasks and responsibilities.

You look back and wonder why you bothered dedicating time to some tasks, people or situations. You reassess and find you are able to move on to direct your energy along more positive channels.

You are far more positive in your outlook and more interested in moving forward than in hanging on to the past.

23: Revisiting a past home

Home

> ## The dream
>
> You return to a home or neighbourhood where you once lived. Things might or might not have changed.

The past delivers its gifts when you are ready to receive and use them.

In your dream perhaps ...

- Everything is exactly as it was. The people are the age they were when you lived there with them, but now you are visiting them at your present age.
- The house and neighbourhood are the same, but the people are all older now, or they too are revisiting their past with you.
- There have been minor changes to the structure of the old home or neighbourhood.
- There are massive changes. Nothing is as it was.
- You cannot get to the old home because the streets have changed or you have forgotten the way.
- You get to the home but there is something dark or foreboding about it. You don't want to go in.
- You always visit neighbours, never your family.
- Time has moved on and strangers are now living in your old home.

How do you feel in your dream?

Curious. Absorbed. Hesitant. Surprised. Detached. Released. Angry. A sense of grief or loss. Peaceful. Resolute. Embracing. Embraced. Fearful. Childish. Wise. Nostalgic. Lost. Indifferent. Sad. A sense of letting go. Changed. Enlightened. Forgiving. Restricted. Accepting. Guilty. Responsible. Empowered. Powerless.

How does your dream end?

Positive changes are on the way if ...

- You embrace or are embraced by people in the old home.
- The old home is full of light. Perhaps there are bigger windows.
- The house has been extended. There are more rooms and a bigger garden.
- The bathroom, toilet or laundry has been renovated.
- The attic or basement has been cleared or opened up.
- You see the old home and the people in it from a different perspective.
- You understand something about your past in the dream.
- You have bought the house.
- You express anger, grief or other feelings in some way.
- Everything has changed and you feel at peace with the changes.

It's time for a new approach if ...

- The house seems dark or you fear going inside.
- You react to other people as you would have done in the past, as if you have not changed in any way since then.
- Someone or something is buried in the house.
- You cannot find your way to the house.
- You are searching for something or someone in the house without success.

What your dream means

Your way forward may be blocked by ...

Beliefs about the future based on past experiences. Unresolved hurt or unexpressed grief or anger from the past. Remorse, regret or unfinished business from the past.

Moving forward

Know that your memories of the past are yours alone and that everyone experiences the same situation from a different point of view. You can go back at any time to review your past and to release yourself from the experiences you had back then. You can leave past beliefs and hurts in the past and release any emotions that have kept you tied to those times. You are free to move forward and embrace today with new beliefs and a clear heart.

◆

To understand where you are now, and to see your way forward, you sometimes need to understand where you have come from. The past has shaped who you are and can shape who you will become — if you let it. You can choose to make some changes, to look back and see your past through wiser eyes, letting go of beliefs and feelings that belong to another time and place. Dreams that take you back to your old homes, the scenes of your past dramas, help you to put your past in perspective.

Think of an event that happened for you ten years ago. Now think of the other people who were there at that time. Imagine everyone describing the event through their own eyes, their own feelings. Each perspective would be slightly different. We remember some things and forget others; we react to an event according to our previous experiences, our memories and our feelings. Now imagine that same event again, only this time add an extra person — you at your present age, ten years older than you were at the time. Now let that older you describe the event in hindsight. Is it different?

You can rewrite your past simply by seeing it through more experienced eyes. You don't change the original event. You experienced one version of what happened. Other people there experienced other versions and you, looking back now, experience yet another version.

You can live a life and make decisions based on your experiences of an event without seeing it for what it was. With wisdom you can rewrite and 're-right' your past in ways that help you to let go and move forward. Going back to the past in your dreams helps you to go forward in your life.

If your dream takes you back to a house you once lived in and it looks just the same as you remember it, then perhaps you are looking at the beliefs you hold now that have remained unchanged since then. But if the old home looks different in some way then your dream is showing you how your beliefs about the past have changed.

Rooms that deal with water and cleansing (bathrooms, toilet, laundry) can symbolise emotional cleansing because water usually symbolises your emotions. So if you dream of going back to an old home and the bathroom has been modernised and extended, then you can be sure you have cleared some old emotional issues that were holding you back.

If the old home has had a new level added, then perhaps you have acquired a new level of understanding about your past. If the old house has fallen into disrepair, then perhaps you have forgotten to keep alive some of the good memories, hopes and dreams relating to those days.

If you can't get to the old home because the roads have all changed, then it would seem that you have changed your approach to the past so much that you are finding it difficult to access the memories. Sometimes this is because you have buried memories and feelings you couldn't cope with at the time and tried to obliterate any return by changing all access routes. Sometimes this is because your old ways no longer exist.

You may feel and release tremendous grief or anger when you revisit the past in your dreams. This is wonderful progress, no matter how frightening or devastating the release is in the dream. These are emotions that you repressed at the time and that need to be released and acknowledged so that you can move on with your life unencumbered.

In your life this could be about ...

- The state of your bank balance influenced by a past negative experience with money.
- Your attraction to controlling partners influenced by your relationship with a controlling parent when you were a child.
- Your competitive nature influenced by your schooling.
- Your lack of self-esteem influenced by being told you weren't good enough at home.
- Your weight problem influenced by family beliefs about concealing your sexuality.
- Your fear of intimacy stretching back to events in your childhood.

Your unique dream contains personal clues only you may recognise

♦ Let your dream float in your mind's eye until a memory from those days emerges. Follow the memory. If you relax and let this process happen you will usually come up with an event or experience that clearly points to an issue in your life now.

♦ Look for the absurdities in the otherwise familiar past home. Is there a power line outside? Look to issues of power back then and in your life now. Is there a huge shell on your old home instead of a roof? What did you clam up about or retreat into your shell about then, and now?

♦ Is there someone from your life now in your dream? The person might be a clue about the current life situation that this dream is about.

Why has this dream come up for you now?

Your answers to these questions will reveal the reason:

♦ What feelings and emotions did you experience in your dream?

♦ Which situation in your life now do these feelings remind you of?

♦ If you can identify this situation, what better outcome would you choose for yourself? What challenges do you feel this change would bring you?

Your answer to the last question may reveal the reason your dream has come up for you now. You are ready for change and your dream shows you the roots of these challenges.

Dream alchemy practice
Starting the inner work

This is what to *do* if you hope to see dramatic transformations in your life.

A. Write a conversation between yourself and the old home from your dream. Arrange the conversation like a script on your page. Start the conversation with you asking the old home how it feels seeing you back there again. Let the dialogue flow from there.

B. If you have identified the belief from your past that is not working well for you now, here's your dream alchemy practice. You are going to give the belief back to the person you borrowed it from — it was theirs, not yours. See yourself returning, at your present age, to the past home and holding hands with yourself as you were then. Gently explain to your younger self about how the belief belonged to (name that person!) and that it is now time to give it back. Explain that this belief has made life interesting for you and that you have learned a lot from it but that you no longer want it. Tell your younger self about the new belief you now have. (When you remove an old belief always replace it with a better one.) Now help your younger self to give the belief back to the person it belonged to. You, as your older self, are there for moral support, so speak up for both of yourselves! See the person taking back their belief, then hold hands with your younger self and feel the power of the new belief as you share it. Then return to today, knowing all is now well.

C. Take the address of your old home as the title for a quick poem. The title is, 'Farewell to 10 Epiphany Street' (or whatever your address was). Give yourself no longer than ten minutes to write a simple poem. No rhyming is required. The more your poem looks like the work of a child the better. Keep it flowing. Don't think — just write, following your gut reaction.

Glimmers of gold
In your dreams
When your recurring dream stops or changes to embrace a happier ending, you are making good progress.

Some symbols from your dream alchemy practice may appear in your dreams. For example, you may dream of standing in front of your old home performing your 'farewell' poem.

Your dreams may release grief or anger about your past that you have kept buried. This marks great progress. It is your dream's way of releasing you so that you are free to embrace the new beliefs you have chosen and to see them work for you.

Look out for dreams of calm seas, beautiful panoramic window views or stunning landscapes seen from the top of a mountain.

In your waking life
You feel older and wiser, more confident yet more energetic.

You notice huge positive changes within six months in at least one area of your life.

You spend more time thinking of today and tomorrow. Until now you hadn't realised how much time you had spent thinking about the past.

You experience life from many different perspectives and it surprises you how one-eyed many people can be.

24: Snakes

Snakes

(Also see 20: The awesome wild animal)

The dream

There is a snake, or several snakes. How are you going
to handle this situation?

*Shed your skin. It is time to break through the pain that
sealed your shield and became your prison.*

In your dream perhaps ...

- The snake is threatening to bite you, or does bite you.
- You are running away from a snake for fear of being bitten.
- The snake is staring you in the eyes.
- You see a snake slithering, half-hidden, towards you or away from you.
- You are struggling to overcome or kill a snake.
- You are phoning the emergency services or rushing to hospital after being bitten.
- The snake is shedding its skin.
- You have snakes around your feet or in your bed.
- You are handling a harmless snake.
- A dead or hibernating snake comes to life.

How do you feel in your dream?

Fearful. Shocked. Vulnerable. Paralysed. Hurt. In pain.
Overpowered. Powerful. Determined. Strong. Inadequate.
Awed. Transformed. Threatened. Enlightened. Anguished.
Deceived.

How does your dream end?

Positive changes are on the way if ...

- The snake bites you and you recover.
- You get through to emergency services or arrive at the hospital.

- A snake sheds its skin.
- You look the snake in the eye.
- You discover that the snake or snakes are harmless.
- You are somehow transformed through your encounter with a snake.
- You feel the pain of the bite.
- You express anguish, pain, grief or anger.

It's time for a new approach if ...

- You run away from the snake and it continues to chase you.
- You cannot get through to emergency services.
- You get the feeling that the dream snake is a 'snake in the grass' deceiver.

What your dream means

Your way forward may be blocked by ...

Past unhealed emotional pain that you are not facing. Old skins (old ways of being) needing to be shed. Energy blocks in your body.

Moving forward

Face your unhealed pain so that you can shed unnecessary protective skins and emerge bigger, stronger and more enlightened. Approach the pain as an initiation or spiritual awakening because that is exactly what this is.

◆

Freud saw the snake as a penis and he does have a point. There is a connection between the fertility associated with the penis and the fertility of a snake dream. No — your snake dream does not mean you are pregnant or about to become a father, but it does indicate great potency for change. The Western world's medical logo (the caduceus) features two snakes entwined on a staff. Intrigued? Here's the story.

In Ancient Greece, for close to a thousand years leading up to the birth of Christ, whenever you got sick you went to a healing temple. There you were met by your healer, taken through a cleansing and meditation ritual and sent off to sleep in a room full of snakes. These were harmless snakes. In the morning you told your dream to your healer and he or she interpreted the dream to deduce your cure. The reason for the snakes was that the God of Healing, in Ancient Greece, was Asclepius, and his symbol was the snake.

In the fourth century BCE, there was a student healer by the name of Hippocrates working in one of the temples. He noticed that some dreams predicted disease accurately. He called these dreams 'prodromic dreams'. (Your dreaming mind picks up on disease before it builds to a level where it begins to have noticeable physical effects.) Hippocrates is saluted by history as the Father of Medicine for his contributions. The Hippocratic Oath refers to the same Hippocrates; as for those snakes on the staff, they have their origins in the power of dream interpretation to heal.

Across so many cultures and times the snake has come up as a symbol of healing and change, as it does in dreams. Why should this be?

Snakes can bite and kill. They can slither up from a hidden position and suddenly deliver unexpected pain. In waking life and in dreams, the way to heal emotional hurt is to face the original pain and let it go. If you ignore or bury the hurt, it festers, leaving you with anger and an open wound. When life brings you to a point where an old issue slithers up on you and reminds you of the old pain, you have an opportunity to re-examine the past and heal the old hurts. But first there is the pain. And before that, often, the dream snake rearing its head at the first whiff of the return of the hurt.

Snakes are strongly linked with change and transformation in that they shed their old skin many times, emerging renewed, bigger and stronger than before, leaving their old cover behind. Snakes in your dreams, especially if they cover you like a skin, are part of your shedding, your emerging and breaking through from the old you to the new you.

Look at how snakes move! As land creatures with no legs they have a sliding, slithering, waving or whipping energy. Without legs they seem to move as if by magic. When you dream of animals you are generally dreaming of your instincts and energies, especially those you associate with each animal. (See common dream 20: The awesome wild animal.)

Your dream snakes may mirror the movement of your basic, particularly sexual, energies.

Yoga and other disciplines also focus on the seven body chakras. These are invisible to the physical eye but experienced as a sense of magnetic flow once you're tuned into feeling them. The chakras may appear in dreams, either as colours or as magnetic-flowing sensations. Each one symbolises a different form of energy, just as the nerves emanating from different vertebrae are connected to specific sensory and motor functions. For example, the throat chakra (blue) is about healing through communicating and is felt as a flowing, tingling sensation around the throat. There are specific yoga exercises that result in a tingling rush of energy travelling from the base of the spine to the top of the head that are about clearing chakras that otherwise tend to stagnate or block the flow.

Chakras are examples of real but invisible energy flows in the body that feel like the movement of a snake. You may dream of snakes when this energy is flowing in your body, or when you have an energy block that is about to be cleared if you handle your waking life correctly.

The yoga tradition pictures the potency of this chakra energy as a coiled snake asleep at the base of the spine. It is called the Kundalini. When something happens to bring you to a new level of awareness, the Kundalini is awakened and snakes its way up your spine to clear and awaken your chakras. In this way, your dream snake combines sexuality, potency for spiritual awakening and potential for personal transformation — if you allow it to do its work. Pain and hurt, grief, anger and shock (all the things that have been blocking your energy flow) may be released on the way, both in your dream and in your waking life.

And so you shed your skin and emerge from the emergency, pain gone, transformed and in touch with a new form of energy. Initiated, you could say.

In your life this could be about ...

- The pain you felt when you were sent to boarding school or a childhood friend died.

- The pain you felt when your partner cheated on you or rejected you.
- Your experience of any other deeply painful event.

Your unique dream contains personal clues only you may recognise

- If the snake's size seemed significant, its dimensions may give you a clue about when the pain and your protective skin layering first began. A five-metre snake may indicate 'five years old' or 'five years ago', perhaps.
- The colour of the snake may be a clue. First ask yourself what the colour means to you personally. Then consider the colours of the chakra energy centres to see if they resonate with something that's happening with you. These are:
  - red: the physical and material world
  - orange: harmony, balance, creativity
  - yellow: intellect and concept of self
  - green: unconditional love, personal growth
  - blue: healing, communication
  - indigo: insight, psychic self
  - violet: spiritual connection, unity with all things

  Black may symbolise what is unknown (unconscious) or a fear, while white may symbolise purity and all colours combined.

Why has this dream come up for you now?

Your answers to these questions will reveal the reason:

- What feelings and emotions did you experience in your dream?
- Which situation in your life now do these feelings remind you of?
- Has a physical disease or symptom just presented for you?
- Has a painful memory just reared its head or has someone just delivered a biting remark that upset you more than seemed reasonable?
- Has a situation just come into your life that seems full of promise but scares you because of your past experiences?

Your answer to the last question may reveal the reason your dream has come up for you now. Transformation is on your doorstep but to cross the threshold you need to face and heal unresolved emotional pain.

Dream alchemy practice
Starting the inner work
This is what to *do* if you hope to see dramatic transformations in your life.

A. Do this dream alchemy visualisation regularly:

Imagine going back into your dream and facing your snake. Walk up and look it straight in the eyes. Know that it brings you to face pain but does not bring you pain; instead it brings you love. Look deep into the snake's eyes until you see the pain you need to see. Feel it, know it and then let it fall away like a skin you are shedding. See the snake's skin shedding and feel a coat of armour sliding away from your body at the same time. See the snake's skin shed to reveal a mirror. Look into the mirror and see yourself shining with light energy. Step into the mirror and through to the other side, feeling the surge of energy you pick up as you emerge. Walk into your new world with confidence and look around to identify your first task.

B. For this dream alchemy practice collect small lengths of different coloured fabric — the more snake-like in pattern the better. These represent the skins that you are now shedding. Pick one piece of fabric for each pain you are growing through and discarding. Now paste your fabric skins onto a sheet of coloured card to frame and hang on the wall. The idea is to create artwork that looks like a museum piece — a sampler of real skins in an old-fashioned museum, a piece of ancient history. Under each fabric skin add an old-fashioned museum-style label bearing the name of the pain followed by the name of the spiritual lesson you have learned. For example, 'Rejected by Sam, Self-worth'. You may wish to add dates,

'Rejected by Sam 1998, Self-worth 2002'. Display your museum piece proudly until it's such old history that you can shed it too.

C. Here's an affirmation for you:

> I shed my snake skin and emerge, transformed and
> feeling ... (Insert the feeling you are welcoming
> into your life now that you are leaving your pain
> behind you.)

Glimmers of gold
In your dreams
When your recurring dream stops or changes to embrace a happier ending, you are making good progress.

Some symbols from your dream alchemy practice may appear in your dreams. For example, you may dream of collecting snake skins.

Your dreams may release a feeling of huge shock, the shock that you buried along with the original pain. Anger, grief, desolation, rejection and other strong emotions may follow. This is your dream's way of opening the door to a new level of spiritual awakening for you.

Look out for dreams of butterflies, feelings of emerging from sticky cobwebs and births. These are all symbols of personal transformation.

In your waking life
Life becomes easier. Some areas of your life are totally transformed.

You look back on your past through different eyes, seeing more struggling than you were aware of at the time but also seeing how simple the transformation was once you trusted the process and shed your skin.

You feel as if you have been initiated into a higher understanding and you may feel more equipped to use your natural talents in the world to benefit others in a similar way.

25: Cuts, wounds, blood, guts and vomit

Wounds, sickness

(Also see 22: Can't find a suitable toilet!; 39: Decapitated!; 41: Death and murder)

The dream

Blood, guts or vomit feature in your dream, or a body is cut or wounded.

To heal, flow.

In your dream perhaps ...

◆ Blood flows from a wound.
◆ Someone is vomiting.
◆ You have extreme diarrhoea.
◆ There are cuts and wounds to a body, whether or not blood flows.
◆ There is a headless body.

How do you feel in your dream?

Shocked. Nauseous. Peaceful. Distanced. Cool. Calm. Free. Expressive. Embarrassed. Released. A sense of grief or loss. Helpful. Helped. Repulsed. Restricted. Out of control. Focused. Unresolved.

How does your dream end?

Positive changes are on the way if ...

◆ Blood flows from a wound and you feel calm.
◆ There is vomit or diarrhoea — the more the better.
◆ You express hurt, grief, sadness or anger.
◆ A wounded or cut body functions perfectly well again.
◆ There is a death and you feel at peace with this.

It's time for a new approach if ...

◆ An untimely or early death occurs leaving you feeling that something was unresolved.

- ◆ A wounded person is unable to communicate with you, in words or through telepathy.
- ◆ You are unable to find a place to clean yourself up from your vomit or diarrhoea.

What your dream means
Your way forward may be blocked by ...
What you need to spill out, bring up or open up. Emotions and thoughts you have held inside for too long. Energies you have withheld that need expression. Emotional wounds that have not yet healed.

Moving forward
Let your pent-up feelings flow — understand them in order to let them go. Express them appropriately. Tend to your unhealed emotional wounds. Express yourself.

◆

What do cuts, open wounds, diarrhoea, vomit and visible blood and guts have in common? They're all about letting what's inside the body out. Or about not being able to keep what should be inside, in.

These are messy, embarrassing and sometimes chilling dreams that can leave you questioning your sanity, but fear not! These dreams *keep* you sane! They are about dealing with life's hurts and the emotional toxins that can build up as a result. They are about processing your feelings, opening up and expressing yourself. They are also about letting go so that you can move on.

You may question your sanity if you dream of slitting the throat of someone you love and watching the blood run out. But remember that the other people in your dreams are not themselves. They stand for your own beliefs, thoughts, feelings and memories. What you see in someone says far more about you than it says about them. The throat is the source of the voice, and to open (cut) the throat is perhaps to open the voice. Blood is the life force of the body, so to see blood flowing freely from the open throat may symbolise letting your vitality free up and flow out into the world by expressing yourself. The belief you are dreaming about (the person) is opening up and needing expression. If the person becomes drained of blood and dies, then you are draining the old belief of its life force and letting it die.

You may cut a stomach open to spill the guts. Dreams love playing puns and this one's a classic: 'spill your guts!' meaning 'open up, express yourself'. Think of your guts as being your gut feeling or gut instinct, your instant knowing as opposed to carefully thinking your way to a conclusion. Open up and let your gut instinct flow.

Then there's the other end of the guts: diarrhoea. As you go through life you digest your experiences, hopefully absorbing the good things and letting go of what you don't need. However, sometimes you hold onto the bad things, allowing them to weigh you down and poison your outlook. Diarrhoea dreams may help you to let go of toxic beliefs that are no good to you anymore. Let it flow, let it go.

Vomiting is the body's way of getting toxins out of the stomach before they can be digested. Dreams of vomiting are perhaps about dealing with things in life that you just can't stomach any longer.

Wounds in dreams may be the emotional wounds and hurts you have felt. Open up your wounds and look at them to let go of any toxic beliefs that have festered. Then you can heal and move on.

In your life this could be about ...
♦ The behaviour of someone close to you that you have been swallowing but just can't stomach anymore.
♦ Toxic thoughts you have been hanging onto about someone, and are now ready to let go.
♦ A gut instinct that you have been restraining — until now.
♦ A talent or gift you feel you have been holding back — until now.
♦ An addiction, attitude or pattern of relationship that is hurting you.
♦ A cutting or wounding remark someone made that has left you feeling upset.

Your unique dream contains personal clues only you may recognise

- People or places from your past may give you a clue about what you have been holding in and for how long.
- What you vomit up (a strange object) or what emerges from a cut (something unexpected) are clues to what needs to be got out.
- If you are cutting or hurting someone else in your dream, list three words to describe that person's approach to life. Now list the opposites to those three words. (For example, bitter, superficial, unkind and then forgiving, deep, kind.) The person you hurt in a dream represents a belief you have. Where, in your life, have these beliefs caused you hurt? (For example, beliefs about whether it is weak to show forgiveness or bad to reveal bitterness, or a belief that people do not want to know what makes you tick on a deep level or that more people will like you if you keep things light and superficial.)

Why has this dream come up for you now?

Your answers to these questions will reveal the reason:

- What feelings and emotions did you experience in your dream?
- Which situation in your life now do these feelings remind you of?
- Have you recently felt hurt and found yourself holding back your feelings yet again?
- Is there something you are 'dying' to do or say? If you did, what challenges do you feel you would face?

Your answer to the last question may reveal the reason your dream has come up for you now. It is time to express yourself clearly and appropriately but you are fearful about the changes this may bring.

Dream alchemy practice
Starting the inner work

This is what to *do* if you hope to see dramatic transformations in your life.

A. Write a conversation between yourself and the substance that escapes your body in your dream. Arrange the conversation like a script on your page. Start the conversation with you asking the substance how it feels to be released from your body. Let the dialogue flow from there.

B. Here's an affirmation for you.
I flow in harmony with the lifeblood of the universe.
I am in touch with my feelings and I know how to
express them in ways that heal me and bless others
with the opportunity to heal their lives too. All open
wounds are perfectly healed.

C. Write a quick poem. The title is 'Open'. Give yourself no longer than ten minutes to write a really simple poem. No rhyming or clever stuff is required. The more your poem looks like the work of a child the better. Keep it flowing — don't pause to think.

Glimmers of gold
In your dreams
When your recurring dream stops or changes to embrace a happier ending, you are making good progress.

Some symbols from your dream alchemy practice may appear in your dreams. For example, you may dream of being a healer of wounds.

As you do the alchemy, changes occur as a result of personal growth gained through working with this dream. Having further dreams of diarrhoea and so on is a sign of success as associated beliefs are purged.

Look out for dreams of swimming in clear water, gazing at crystal oceans or flying.

In your waking life
Things that had seemed stuck move along. Several areas of your life change dramatically for the better.

Bitterness and resentment leave your life. You know you once had these feelings, but now that they have gone you find it difficult to imagine how they felt or why you let things get to that stage.

You are less harsh on yourself and less judgemental of others.

You feel equal to others and fully entitled to express yourself and your talents.

You discover a depth to your talents you had not realised was there and you put these gifts to work for the greater good.

26: Wow! Extra rooms!

Rooms

(Also see 29: Renovations and house hunting)

The dream

You discover, to your complete surprise, that a house
has extra rooms you never knew existed!

Limitless horizons: infinite expansion.

In your dream perhaps ...

◆ The house is the one you live in now. The extra room or
rooms are accessed through a door or hallway that does
exist.

◆ The house is the one you live in now but it has an extra
door that leads to the extra room or rooms.

◆ The house in question is one you used to live in.

◆ The house is a dream house that reveals more and more
rooms as you explore it.

◆ Instead of a house, this is a school or building you once
knew.

◆ You have great ideas about how to use the extra rooms.

◆ The extra rooms are already furnished or their intended
use is obvious.

◆ The extra rooms seem to belong to the past, or to be
decorated in the style of a previous era.

◆ You are anxious that you may not be able to find these
rooms again once you leave them.

How do you feel in your dream?

Surprised. Amazed. Awed. Inspired. Excited. Expansive. Limitless. Rewarded. Abundant. Insightful. Privileged. Secretive.
Anxious. Unsafe. Tenuous. A sense of disbelief. Self-confident.
Fearful. Fragile. Small. Insecure. Secure. Threatened. Confronted. Unresolved. Uncomfortable.

How does your dream end?

Positive changes are on the way if ...

- You know exactly how to use these extra rooms.
- You feel inspired by the furnishings in the extra rooms.
- You communicate with people in the rooms.
- You feel positive about the existence of these extra rooms.
- You feel privileged that you have seen these rooms.

It's time for a new approach if ...

- You feel uncomfortable about the existence of these extra rooms.
- You fear entering these rooms.
- You lock up the rooms and decide to keep them secret.

What your dream means

Your way forward may be blocked by ...

The way you are limiting yourself by not exploring your greater potential. Living life according to your old expectations of yourself. Not allowing room for expansion.

Moving forward

Expand your mind and explore your potential. Know that there is more to you than you have realised until now. Develop your talents and draw on your extra resources.

◆

Wow! Extra rooms! Extra space! Something that has been there all this time and you didn't know about it! What a surprise! What potential!

And that's it. You thought you knew the size, shape and function of the various rooms in this dream house just as you thought you knew the size, shape and function of the various areas of your mind. Now your dream shows a different story. Your mind is bigger than you realised and there is both room and potential for you to extend yourself into those areas and use them.

Really, it's as simple as that, but this is such a common dream that it deserves a space and attention of its own, and so do you. So forget what you've learned about limits and stretch yourself. Why restrict yourself to living within your old expectations when you have so much talent to develop and use and so many extra resources to draw on?

In your life this could be about ...

◆ The course you have just completed, leaving you with free time to explore and develop new skills.

◆ Your children leaving home freeing up time and space for you to expand and develop the next phase of your life.

◆ That idea you have always put on hold because you didn't think you were talented enough to make it happen.

◆ That new idea that is beckoning you.

◆ A recent increase in finances that allows you to develop something new.

◆ The loss of a job or a relationship, which has thrown you back onto your own resources, enabling you to discover that they are greater than you had realised.

◆ A new friend who is challenging you to open your mind further.

Your unique dream contains personal clues only you may recognise

◆ What you find in the extra rooms is a clue to what you are about to discover in your waking life. A pen and desk might be a clue about writing; a peaceful lion might be a clue about a new form of inner strength.

◆ How you think about using the extra rooms in your dream is a clue to how you might apply your extra resources or hidden talents.

◆ If someone from your past is in the extra room, this is a clue about when you first glimpsed this potential, the approach you need to take, or something you need to heal before you can continue.

Why has this dream come up for you now?

Your answers to these questions will reveal the reason:

◆ What feelings and emotions did you experience in your dream?

◆ Which situation in your life now do these feelings remind you of?

♦ Have you recently found yourself with time on your hands or feeling stuck?

Your answer to the last question may reveal the reason your dream has come up for you now. Your dream is picking up on a prime opportunity for you to develop further.

Dream alchemy practice
Starting the inner work

This is what to *do* if you hope to see dramatic transformations in your life.

A. Take a good look around your home. Find a corner or window area that you can clear to create a new space. Be harsh! If you live in a big house, choose a room you can totally clear. Live with the space for a few days. Take time to sit in it, to meditate and to see what ideas come up for you. Then collect, make or buy the items or furnishings you need to decorate your space or room to symbolise your exploration into new territory. As you set up your room, dedicate it by saying, 'I dedicate this extra room in my life to explore and express my greater being.' Sit in this place at least once a day. Let the dream alchemy practice unfold its use.

B. Choose an animal that represents, for you, the kind of energy you would like to explore in your extra room. Find a picture of this animal and frame it. Place your animal energy portrait somewhere you will see it every day. Every time you look at the picture, summon up the energy of the animal. *Feel* the energy moving throughout your body, reaching beyond your old limits and touching the world around you.

C. Here's an affirmation for you.
> I feel confident as I move into my extra rooms. I know how to use them. Here I meet my greater, wiser self.

Glimmers of gold
In your dreams

When your recurring dream stops or changes to embrace a happier ending, you are making good progress.

Some symbols from your dream alchemy practice may appear in your dreams. For example, you may dream of being the animal you have framed as your animal portrait.

Your dreams may deliver some creative ideas to extend your own, including some great practical applications.

Look out for dreams of walls falling down, glass breaking (breaking through invisible barriers or mental limits) and open windows.

In your waking life
You experience a shift of focus away from things that were past their use-by date or that you had been hanging onto because of routine.

You take more risks. You feel 'now or never' carefree in at least one area of your life and you reap the rewards of this.

You become more confident. You feel your feet on the ground — your practical applications are sound.

You develop interests in a wider range of matters. Your instincts and intuition become stronger.

27: Was that a past life?

Past life

The dream

Everything about your dream — the clothes, the
setting — seems to point to a past era. If, added to
that, the 'you' in your dream is a different you or a
different sex, then you may be left wondering,
'Was that dream a past life?'

Your moment of choice is, and always has been, now.

In your dream perhaps ...

- The setting is historical but you are yourself, no matter how you are dressed.
- The setting is historical and you seem to be someone other than yourself.
- The other people in the dream are people you know from waking life, but in period costume.
- The other people in the dream are all unknown to you.
- You die and then see your dead body as you continue on your way.

How do you feel in your dream?

Embraced. Anchored. Steady. A sense of belonging. Traditional. Safe. Accepted. Reunited. Sad. A sense of loss. Joyful. Peaceful. Distanced. Separated. Alone. Defensive. Attacked. Insecure. Lost. Fearful. Betrayed. Restricted.

How does your dream end?

Positive changes are on the way if ...

- You embrace someone or are embraced and feel good about this.
- You gain an insight into life or into your dream character through experiencing this drama.
- The historical theme changes to the present day.

- Historical characters become people you know from your waking life.
- You secure some kind of victory in a positive way — win a battle, save a nation, discover a cure for a disease.
- You express anger or grief.
- Castle walls fall down and the dream ends positively.
- You feel at peace when you walk away from your dead body.

It's time for a new approach if ...

- A battle or war remains unresolved.
- You are weighed down by the period costume.
- You feel frustrated because the old methods of transport are slow.
- You feel frustrated because the old-fashioned tools of trade hamper your progress.
- You feel out of place and unrecognised.
- You see your dead body and you are distressed that nobody acknowledges that you are still alive.

What your dream means

Your way forward may be blocked by ...

A decision that a dream is a glimpse of a past life to avoid interpreting it. An issue that has been with you so long it feels like history. A problem or situation that is summed up by the era of your dream, for example persecution, battle or sexual repression.

Moving forward

Whether or not your historical dream is a past-life memory, interpret it as you would any other dream. Explore the relationship dynamics and your dream feelings to understand why this dream has come up for you now and how it can help you to create a positive change.

◆

While dreams are mostly symbolic, memories can and do surface in dreams. You may dream accurate details of your seventh birthday party, or the long-forgotten smell of your puppy, or the exact pattern on the wallpaper of your granny's house you last visited when you were five. How far back can your dreams recall? Three years old, one year old, birth, beyond that?

If you find yourself enmeshed in an historical dream drama, could you be accessing a past-life memory? If we do have past lives, then this is presumably possible. It is sometimes possible to dream telepathically in the present, to tune into what is happening to someone close to you and weave this experience into your dream. If all memory exists, floating indestructibly and accessible to the unconscious then perhaps it is possible to tune into the thoughts and memories of people long gone in the same way as it is to dream telepathically about people still living.

Given all this, if you felt your historical dream was a window into a past life, how could you be sure that the dream was about *your* past life and not someone else's?

Imagine yourself flying high, up and up. Now, look down at Earth. Watch it spinning; watch people evolving through thousands of years. Now look to the past-life dream you have had. Of all the past-life days you might have dreamed, why did you dream of that one, that day, that drama? Perhaps you feel the past life held something you needed to know. Isn't that what all dreams do? Dreams show you, through drama, where you are now, what's holding you back today and what you can do now to move forward.

You might dream of going back to the house you lived in when you were eight and of being angry when the vet came and took your beloved dog away. You might wake up and wonder why you travelled back in time, and then see the connection. Perhaps the vet in your dream represents your belief that what you love is always taken away from you. You might realise that you have been angry with your partner because you're frightened he too will take his love away. Knowing this you can free yourself of the fear of being abandoned because it has nothing to do with your partner and everything to do with your experience when you were eight.

If your dream took you back to explore a past-life experience, the purpose of the dream would be the same. It would show you an experience that is affecting your life now or a belief you have carried forward that needs to be released.

Dreams are symbolic and they weave in bits and pieces

from your past, often in the shape of people, to help you to see your beliefs and thoughts more clearly and to see how these are affecting your life. There is no way you can know whether a dream has any past-life element in it or whether it is simply symbolic. Whether your historical dream was a past-life dream or a symbolic dream, the only way you can make good, practical use of it is to interpret it.

What then is the significance of the historical setting and clothes? Your dream of the French Revolution might be exploring your beliefs about class, for example. Finding yourself mummifying an Egyptian princess might be related to something you have tried to preserve, or it might be exploring your feelings about motherhood. Wearing heavy Victorian clothes in your dream might be drawing your attention to old-fashioned Victorian beliefs that are weighing you down. Fighting a battle in the Middle Ages might be a great dramatic plot for a dream exploring your mid-life crisis or your conflicts about ageing.

And dying and walking away from your dead body? If you are living your life well and making progress physically, mentally, emotionally and spiritually, then you are dying many small deaths as you shed the skins of old beliefs along your path to wisdom.

In your life this could be about ...

* A person at work whose personality and treatment of you reminds you of an historical character.
* A sexual relationship that reminds you of a different era, for example, Victorian times and its repression.
* An indulgent affair that reminds you of an historical extravaganza.
* A pioneering idea you have that people cannot understand, which leaves you feeling like a misunderstood historical visionary.

Your unique dream contains personal clues only you may recognise

* What role are you playing in your dream? (You may be a different sex — treat this question the same way —

consider this as a role you are playing.) In which area of your life do you sometimes feel you are playing this role, or being treated in this way?

- Look at your dream clothes for clues about your life situation. A suit of armour might give you a clue about a relationship where you feel a need to protect yourself, or a heavy caveman bearskin might give you a clue about something heavy you are 'bearing'.

- Imagine bringing one of the dream characters into your waking life today. Where would he or she feel most comfortable or most uncomfortable and with whom? This gives you a clue about the situation in waking-life that this dream is addressing.

Why has this dream come up for you now?

Your answers to these questions will reveal the reason:

- What feelings and emotions did you experience in your dream?

- Which situation in your life now do these feelings remind you of?

Your answer to the last question may reveal the reason your dream has come up for you now. Your dream is using the historical theme to drive home the message with high drama.

Dream alchemy practice

Starting the inner work

This is what to *do* if you hope to see dramatic transformations in your life.

A. Do this dream alchemy visualisation regularly:

Imagine going back into your dream but instead of being the character you were then, be yourself now. See yourself dressed in today's clothes as a film director. See yourself wearing a headset and carrying the film script. Stop the dream action and gather all the characters to you — they are now actors and extras, as they have indeed been all along. (You are the director of your own dreams.) Tell them you have a new script. Now direct them to act the rest of the dream scene in accordance with your positive ending. Get one of the actors to be you (or the character you played in the original dream) and make sure 'you' turn out to be the hero. Make sure, as you describe the part to the actor, that you *feel* all the positive hero feelings the actor needs to project to make this a great movie.

B. Write a conversation between yourself and one of the historical characters from your dream. Arrange the conversation like a script on your page. Start the conversation with you asking the character what he or she likes about you. Let the dialogue flow from there.

C. Imagine you are living back in the era of your dream. You have been asked to prepare a time capsule for a future generation to discover now. You can simply write a message or you can collect a variety of objects, stories and messages. For this dream alchemy practice, either draw the time capsule with the objects visible and with the messages written around the page, or create the capsule in artwork of your choice.

Glimmers of gold
In your dreams
When your recurring dream stops or changes to embrace a happier ending, you are making good progress.

Some symbols from your dream alchemy practice may appear in your dreams. For example, you may dream of collecting pieces for your time capsule.

Your dreams may release intense emotions, such as grief, anger or betrayal, that you have repressed. This is the dream's way of clearing your way so you can move forward.

Look out for dreams of role reversals or scenes set in the future.

In your waking life
You feel released. The life situation this dream was addressing is solved and you find yourself in a stronger position. You see at least one part of your life-history differently.

28: Doing yesterday's work

Work

The dream

You dream of repeating the work you have already done during the previous day. It is usually repetitive work and, on top of that, you repeat it over and over in your dream. You wake up feeling tired.

In the groove or in a rut? Who tied your strings?

In your dream perhaps ...

- A single task you have already accomplished successfully is repeated over and over. For example, weeding, serving customers, writing an essay.
- A single task you have already accomplished successfully is repeated, but in the dream things go wrong. You do not have the successful outcome you had in waking life.
- A task you are in the middle of doing in waking life is continued in your dream. For example, you finished writing chapter one yesterday and dream you are writing chapter two. This may or may not go well.
- Your daily work is repetitive and you feel your dream is more about doing tomorrow's work than yesterday's.

How do you feel in your dream?

Frustrated. Busy. Over-loaded. Stressed. Pressured. Bored. Tired. Exhausted. Trapped. Restricted. Lacking confidence. Anxious. Under-performing. A sense of failure. Fearful. Trampled upon. Subservient. Used. Powerless. Unrecognised. Resourceful. Creative. Tested. Judged. Criticised.

How does your dream end?

Positive changes are on the way if ...

- You get a creative idea or breakthrough from the dream.
- You get recognition for your efforts.

- You communicate your true feelings to someone.
- You express anger or grief.
- A window, glass or other item is broken.
- You walk away from the work with a feeling of freedom.
- A job is completed and you feel rewarded.

It's time for a new approach if ...

- The task is never finished and you always wake up tired.
- There are things you want to say in the dream but don't.
- The difficulties and obstacles to getting the task done increase.
- You feel heavily judged or criticised.
- Other people don't have to work as hard as you.

What your dream means

Your way forward may be blocked by ...

Making your work unnecessarily difficult or time-consuming. Unresolved issues with people at work, with why you have chosen this particular work or with how you do this work. A need for more balance in your life.

Moving forward

Look at changing your working pattern and at putting more balance into your life. Consider implementing the creative ideas and work solutions that your dream delivers. Consider your emotional reasons for doing this work and let your dreams put these in perspective. Spend time solving work issues while you are awake so that you do not load this job onto your dreams.

◆

You know the feeling you get when you just can't remember something and then the moment you stop thinking about it you get it: 'Todd! That's it!' Or you wake up in the middle of the night, mid-dream, and shout, 'Todd! It was Todd!' to no applause.

Or have you ever spent all evening doing something like adding up your accounts and not being able to work out why you're twenty dollars out only to wake up in the morning knowing exactly where that twenty dollars went?

Your thinking, conscious mind is not always the best at

dredging up facts or solving puzzles. Your dreaming mind is brilliant at it. You can make this work for you by taking a problem that needs to be solved to your dreams. It's known as dream incubation. You repeat the problem over and over as you fall asleep, knowing that the first problem a dream will usually tackle is the unresolved one on your lips as you fall asleep.

What's this all got to do with dreaming about doing yesterday's work? Easy! When you've been repeating or working on something all day your mind is still busy as you fall asleep, so your dream treats the work as a dream incubation puzzle to solve. It will approach this task in several ways. If the work takes up too much of your time, your dream is likely to communicate a need for more balance in your life. One way it may do this is to look for a creative way of making the task easier for you, so that you can complete it in less time. So if you've been weeding the garden all day your dream might come up with all sorts of weird weeding inventions. Then it will remind you how boring weeding is; then it will show you that weeding is a never-ending job so you might as well change your attitude towards your garden.

Next it may niggle you about your beliefs about perfection, followed by a quick replay of your fear of success in the shape of a never-ending, obstacle-ridden, over-weedy playing-field of a garden. It might have a go at your belief in hard work with a dream about why you designed a garden that fulfils your need to endlessly weed.

If you are still doing yesterday's work in your dream it is because something about the work is unresolved or is an issue for you, and your dream is puzzle-solving its way towards a solution. You can accelerate this by choosing a particular work problem to put to your dream in the form of a Dream Incubation or you can defuse the whole exhausting dream thing by changing your working pattern to put more balance into your life.

In your life this could be about ...
- Beliefs carried from childhood about the importance of working hard.

- A repetitive job that is not challenging enough for you.
- A relationship difficulty that you are avoiding by taking on more work or by complicating your work so it lasts longer.
- A project, committee or charity you are working too many hours for out of a misplaced sense of duty. Are you seeking the approval your parents didn't give you or compensating for some guilt you feel, for example?
- Customers whose attitudes upset you and to whom you feel unable to respond.

Your unique dream contains personal clues only you may recognise

- In your dream, which aspects of your work are out of control or not working out? These give you a clue about emotional issues and beliefs that you need to address.
- Look at people you know in your dream and write down three words to describe their approach to life, then write down the three opposites to these. Some, if not all, of these words will give you a clue about what is driving you to work so hard.
- Look for bizarre, out-of-place symbols appearing in your dream that have nothing to do with yesterday's work. For example, if you keep stopping to pull down a window blind this may be the clue to something you don't want to see about your work relationships or motivations.

Why has this dream come up for you now?

Your answers to these questions will reveal the reason:

- What feelings and emotions did you experience in your dream?
- Which situation in your life now do these feelings remind you of (apart from yesterday's work)?
- Which situation in your life in the past do these feelings remind you of?
- If you were asked never to do this kind of work again, what challenges do you feel this would present you?

Your answer to the last question may reveal the reason your dream has come up for you now. It is time for you to face what you are avoiding through keeping your life busy.

Dream alchemy practice
Starting the inner work

This is what to *do* if you hope to see dramatic transformations in your life.

A. Buy a notebook and put it in your bathroom. Before going to bed each night spend an extra ten minutes in the bathroom. (The bathroom symbolises cleansing.) Use that ten minutes to write continuously in your notebook. Just follow your gut reactions, and write about the work or task you have been doing all day. Keep the writing flowing. This is not a grammar and spelling test. Nobody else will read it. It's a way of getting rid of all the self-talk left in your brain at the end of the day's work. When you have finished, tear out the page and put it in your wastepaper basket. Wash your hands, visualising the water flushing away all that you have just purged. Now enter your bedroom at peace and ready to sleep. (Keep your bedroom as a sacred space. Don't pollute it with work worries.) As you fall asleep, picture white light washing over you, and ask for your dreams to bring you what you need to know in new and exciting ways.

B. Write a list of people who influenced you when you were a child. Include your parents or guardians, your sisters or brothers, friends, teachers and so on. Leave three lines free between each name on the list. When your list is complete, go back and imagine asking each person in turn the following two questions: What are my best skills for doing this job? Why do you think I chose this job? Imagine their replies and write these down.

C. What is the first step you can take to make your work easier? For example, can you leave out a task, delegate it to someone else or do it in a different way? Have you got your first step? No? Think again. There's *always* a first step! Now do it.

Glimmers of gold
In your dreams
When your recurring dream stops or changes to embrace a happier ending, you are making good progress.

Some symbols from your dream alchemy practice may appear in your dreams. For example, you may dream of chatting to one of your old teachers.

Don't be surprised if your dreams release some anger or grief. Working to keep these emotions at bay is common. When you are ready to move on you may discover even more anger at yourself for working hard instead of dealing with this, or grief for time and other activities lost. Let your dreams release what has to be released.

Look out for dreams giving creative ideas for managing your work or life better.

In your waking life
You are less fastidious about the way you work and find easier ways to reach the same quality of output. You are more comfortable with delegating work and with communicating with people who work for you or with you.

The feeling is one of releasing your tight grip on your work or your drive to work in the way that you do.

You are comfortable with measuring your own success and lose interest in the judgement of others.

You find yourself laughing a lot more when you work — seeing the funny side of things and smiling more. You take yourself and your work less seriously and are surprised to see that this improves the quality of your work.

29: Renovations and house hunting

Renovating house

(Also see 26: Wow! Extra rooms!)

The dream

You are looking for a new house, moving in or renovating.

Change is life and life is change. Even mountains flow.

In your dream perhaps ...

- You are looking at houses, searching for a new home. There are plenty of choices.
- You are looking at houses, searching for a new home but nothing is suitable.
- You find yourself in a perfect new home.
- You find yourself in a new home but it is not quite right.
- You are packing to move into a new home.
- The house is your waking-life house, but you are renovating it.
- The house is a dream house you are renovating.

How do you feel in your dream?

A sense of anticipation. Excited. Expectant. Free. Abundant. Fortunate. Happy. Fulfilled. Unfulfilled. Disappointed. Sad. Restricted.

How does your dream end?

Positive changes are on the way if ...

- You find a home you are happy with.
- You find yourself in a new house with many rooms.
- There is light and space in the new house or renovated house.
- There is an amazing view through a window.
- The bathroom, toilet or laundry is successfully renovated.
- There is plenty of fresh green growth in the garden.
- The packing is easy.

It's time for a new approach if ...

- You are not satisfied with the choices available.
- The new house is small, cramped or dark.
- The bathroom, toilet or laundry needs renovation.
- The garden is untended or the plants are withered and unhealthy.
- The packing is difficult: there are too many things to pack.

What your dream means

Your way forward may be blocked by ...

Your image or the way you present yourself to the world not being in alignment with changes within you. A need for change, for moving on to a more suitable way of being in at least one area of your life. A need to heal something unresolved within you. A need to explore a new perspective.

Moving forward

The successful renovations and moves in your dreams reflect changes you have just made — unconscious shifts. The less successful renovations in your dreams or the 'stuck' moves or endless hunting for the right house reveal a need for you to free things up by giving yourself permission to change. It's okay to let go.

◆

Drive down any road and look at all the houses. From the outside they are on view for all to see, but how many do you get to see inside? Who lives in each house, and what can you tell about a person from how the outside of the house looks? What can you tell about a person from seeing inside their house? What private world exists behind the facade and what memories are collected in the furniture, the books and the photo albums? What clues might the style, colour and tidiness give about the personality and feelings of the person who lives here? Which rooms are kept in darkness, which in light? Which rooms are well worn and lived in most? Which rooms are neglected or kept shut?

Just as you might begin to piece together a picture of a person by exploring their house, so your dream house is a picture of you — your mind, your beliefs, your feelings, your approach to life, your memories, your personality, what you think about most and what you neglect. The outside of your dream house is perhaps the facade you show the world. The inside may represent your private self. The many rooms may be the many aspects of your self. Perhaps the kitchen shows your self-nurturing, the dark basement your unconscious, the different levels in your house the different levels of your being, the ceiling your upper limits, the windows your view of the world, the bedroom your sexuality or most private self and so on.

Whichever room is being renovated in your dream illustrates the area of your mind or self undergoing change. And when you're doing the big dream-house hunt you're at a stage in life where you're ready to move on within yourself, changing your attitudes, beliefs and ways of being. Your dream search for the perfect house is your search for a new, more appropriate expression of yourself. As with every journey, it's what you discover about yourself (what you like and don't like in the houses you see) on the way that is enlightening.

In your life this could be about ...

- A talent you are ready to develop and expand.
- Feeling restrained by your housemates, partner or family from expressing yourself fully.
- A lifestyle that is leaving you feeling tired or restricted and in need of a change of perspective.
- Too much focus on one area of your life and not enough on another.
- A recent relationship break-up leaving you ready for change.
- A change in your job or financial situation that gives you the opportunity to seek a completely different lifestyle.

Your unique dream contains personal clues only you may recognise

- Take note of the room you are renovating in your dream, as it is a clue to the area of your mind or life needing change. A dream about the bedroom might indicate that sexuality and intimacy or rest and relaxation are the areas requiring change. A dream about the entrance hall might be a clue about how you approach your inner life or how you receive others.

♦   If the room you are renovating belongs to someone you know, write down three words to describe that person's personality or approach to life. Then write down the three opposites to those words. Those six words will give you a clue about an issue you are grappling to change within yourself. You may also be looking to heal something unresolved between you and this person.

♦   The features you are seeking in a new house give you a clue about the type of change you are seeking in your waking life. Big windows suggest a new view of life, space suggests room to think or potential to explore, an older style house might suggest a wish to return to traditional values.

Why has this dream come up for you now?

Your answers to these questions will reveal the reason:

♦   What feelings and emotions did you experience in your dream?

♦   Which situation in your life now do these feelings remind you of?

♦   Have you been forced to face change through a loss recently?

♦   Have you recently felt restricted or entrenched in routine? If you could move forward in this situation, what would you fear most or feel threatened by?

Your answers to the last two questions may reveal the reason your dream has come up for you now. Change is on your agenda, but so are your fears of change.

Dream alchemy practice
Starting the inner work

This is what to *do* if you hope to see dramatic transformations in your life.

A.   For this dream alchemy practice either use the perfect house if you have found it in your dream, or create the perfect house in your mind, correcting everything you weren't happy about with the houses in your dreams. Now visualise your perfect house and put yourself in it. What feeling does this give you? If any negative or fearful feelings come up, write them down and then destroy the list. Do this as many times as it takes until you are left with only positive feelings.

B. Now you have the right dream alchemy practice formula to do your visualisation. Imagine yourself standing in your dream house. Summon up one by one the positive feelings from the list you made in the first dream alchemy practice. Breathe and *feel* how it is to be in this space. Do this visualisation frequently.

C. Make or buy one small item that symbolises something you would choose for your perfect dream house. This might be a framed picture, a book, a coffee cup, a plant or a vase. Put it in a prominent place and look at it or use it every day. As you do so, summon up the positive feelings from the first dream alchemy practice.

Glimmers of gold
In your dreams
When your recurring dream stops or changes to embrace a happier ending, you are making good progress.

Some symbols from your dream alchemy practice may appear in your dreams. For example, you may dream of buying something for your dream home.

Your dreams may release some of the negative feelings you burned in the first dream alchemy practice. They may bring up images and memories associated with these feelings. This is your dream's way of clearing the path for you to have the changes you seek without the negatives.

Look out for dreams of easy, fast and successful journeys and admiring beautiful ocean views.

In your waking life
You surprise yourself by changing your outward image in a dramatic way.

You feel changes within you and become aware of interacting with people in a slightly different way and are comfortable with this.

Some old plans and wishes start to happen and new opportunities present themselves. At the same time, some dearly held plans dissolve as you realise they are no longer relevant to you.

You may lose weight if you were overweight.

Relationships that seemed stuck either change for the better or end.

30: A visit from spirit?

Spirit

The dream

Someone who has died appears to you in a dream.

What haunts you ails you.

In your dream perhaps ...

- The person appears in your dream within days of their actual death and offers you information or an embrace.
- You dream a person has visited you, then later discover your dream coincided with the time of their death.
- A person appears in your dream months or years after their death and offers you information or an embrace.
- The person has a different personality to the one you knew.
- It is not until you wake up that you remember the person in your dream is now dead.
- The person is angry or critical with you.
- You are angry with the person or terrified about their appearance.

How do you feel in your dream?

Terrified. Awed. Fearful. Peaceful. Chosen. Lonely. Alone. Forgiven. Forgiving. Forsaken. Betrayed. Upset. Angry. Judged. Criticised. A sense of loss or grief. Enlightened. Anxious. Sad. Released. Relieved. Settled. Guilty. Blessed. A sense of completion.

How does your dream end?

Positive changes are on the way if ...

- You forgive or are forgiven.
- You have a sense of completion or peace.
- You express extreme anger towards the person.
- You express extreme grief.

- You kiss or embrace the person or are kissed or embraced by them.
- You tell the person a few home truths.

It's time for a new approach if ...

- You are terrified or fearful of the person because you know they have died.
- You feel unsettled or unresolved.
- You think the dream foretells your imminent death.
- You think the person holds sway over you even in death.

What your dream means

Your way forward may be blocked by ...

Still needing to complete your grieving over the death of a loved one. Issues that were unresolved with a loved one when they died that are affecting you now. Believing a person in your dream to be there in spirit when they are not. Believing that someone in spirit is watching or judging you instead of taking that responsibility on yourself. Believing your dream predicts your own death.

Moving forward

Be kind to yourself and allow time for your grieving to follow its natural course. Find ways to resolve what was unresolved, to make peace with your memory of the person who has died. Know that while it is possible for people in spirit to appear in your dreams, this is rare and tends to occur more at the time of death and shortly after than at any other time. Remind yourself that most of your dreams feature people, many well known to you — the only difference here is that this person has passed on. People in your dreams are symbols of your own beliefs!

◆

The burning question is: was your dream visitor playing a part in your dream just as all dream characters do, or was he or she really there, contacting you through your dream from the other side?

It's quite common but very precious to dream of someone at their moment of death, even though you might have been unaware that they were ill or that their passing was near. Often the time of death is made clear in the dream, or the dreamer wakes up and notices the time, later confirmed as the time of death. Details of the death or information unknown to the dreamer are often shown to be correct.

Whether the person was actually there in spirit or whether you, the dreamer, were tuning into their dying thoughts at the time is more difficult to know.

People can feel extremely upset and rejected if they have not dreamed of the passing of a loved one, especially if other members of the family have. This is most likely to be due to a level of dream sensitivity and recall — you might have had the experience but not the memory. Some people dream of deaths more than others.

Days, weeks, months and years after someone has died you may find yourself dreaming about them. The more time has passed, the less likely that the person is there in spirit, and the more likely that they are in your dream just as any other dream character is — because your memory of them and your feelings about them have something to teach you about yourself.

The first thing to deal with in these dreams is grief, and anger is an early stage of grief. It is normal to feel angry with a mate for dying and leaving you on your own — it's irrational, but normal. When you are awake you may feel terrible about being angry with someone you love who couldn't help dying, so you suppress the anger, pretending it's not there. Eventually it appears in your dreams, because anger needs venting. You may find yourself being intensely angry — even violent — with your loved one in a dream, and wake up feeling shocked at your dream behaviour. All of this can be a healthy and normal expression of anger as an early stage of grief.

Eventually your dreams will help you to heal any unresolved issues you had with your loved one when they died. There will be forgiving — of yourself and of the person — before you can move on. There will be a letting go. All of this is part of the natural process of grieving the loss of a loved one. Relish the beautiful experiences where you dream you are together, but also know that these are part of your healing as you continue on life's path.

After the dreams of grief and release there will be many dreams featuring your loved one. These are the dreams that help you to understand yourself, to help you to move forward in your life. As in any other dream, each person stands for a belief, thought, feeling or memory you hold about that person. They are there as dream pictures of your beliefs.

A mother who was very critical of you in life may appear in a dream still lashing out with heavy judgement. But she is not there in spirit. Though you might have worked at not letting her criticism affect you when she was alive, you would have taken it on at some level. Within yourself a critical voice lives on, fulfilling your childhood belief that your actions are not worthy. Your critical mother is an excellent dream picture to portray your very own self-judgemental beliefs.

A person who has died cannot hold sway over you. They may appear in your dreams to symbolise the afterlife — its mystery and your faith — as you explore your feelings about death and mortality.

When your dreams edge into spooky ghost stories, ask yourself what memories and feelings are haunting you, what ghostly remnants of your past are shifting in and out of your consciousness.

In your life this could be about ...

- Your need to grieve for the person who has died, even after many years.
- An issue that was unresolved when the person died, leaving you ill at ease.
- Your beliefs, doubts and questions about life after death.
- Your fears about your mortality.
- Something from the past (not directly related to the person in the dream) that has come up to 'haunt' you.
- Any situation or relationship in your life now where this person fits as a perfect symbol. For example, if you saw the person as dismissive then look at where you might be being dismissive or all-embracing (the opposite), or feeling dismissed in your life now.

Your unique dream contains personal clues only you may recognise

◆ If the spirit in your dream is more of a ghost than the spirit of someone you knew, then this is the time to confront 'ghosts from the past'. Look for numbers, people and objects in your dream that give clues to a year or event that seems to be echoing in your life now.

◆ What message does the dream spirit bring? Where in your waking life does this message seem to apply?

◆ What was left unsaid between you and this person? This is a clue to a similar situation in your life now.

Why has this dream come up for you now?

Your answers to these questions will reveal the reason:

◆ What feelings and emotions did you experience in your dream?

◆ Which situation in your life now do these feelings remind you of?

◆ If you can identify this situation, how would you like it to turn out? If this change did happen, what challenges do you feel it would bring up for you?

Your answer to the last question may reveal the reason your dream has come up for you now. You are ready for change but either have grieving to complete first or fear handling the challenges you believe will come up.

Dream alchemy practice
Starting the inner work

This is what to *do* if you hope to see dramatic transformations in your life.

A. *This dream alchemy practice is especially for those dreams you feel are about your unresolved issues with someone who has died.*

Think of a gift that symbolises what you would like to say to the person in your dream. This is to be a parting gift, something that heals what you feel has been left unhealed, or something that expresses your gratitude for having known this person, or something of yourself for the person to take forward on their journey. Spend up to three days — no longer — deciding on your gift. On the fourth day light a candle, close your eyes and see yourself giving the gift to the person. Allow some conversation and then make it clear to them that this gift is to help them on the next part of their journey. You will see them at the end, but you have different paths to walk between now and then.

B. *This dream alchemy practice is especially for those dreams where you feel the person who has died is in your dream as a symbol of your beliefs.*

You have ten minutes to write a poem, so no clever stuff! No rhyming is necessary, just gut-instinct writing, and if your poem ends up looking like it has been written by a six-year-old, that's just fine! The title of your poem includes the name of the person in your dream. The title is 'Knowing [insert the name of the person in your dream].'

C. *This dream alchemy practice is especially for those dreams where you feel you are still dealing with anger or grief over the death of someone precious to you.*

Buy a beautiful blank-paged book to write in. Title it 'A Hundred Days'. This dream alchemy takes one hundred days. The recommended time to spend each day is ten minutes, but you can make this shorter or longer depending on what feels right to you. Give the first page the title 'Day 1', then put the date. Now write or draw whatever you wish as long as it comes from your heart. When you have finished, write a single word at the bottom of the page — whatever feels right to you. Continue this until the hundred days are complete. On the next day, Day 101, plant a tree in your garden or in a public place near your home.

Glimmers of gold
In your dreams
When your recurring dream stops or changes to embrace a happier ending you are making good progress.

217

Some symbols from your dream alchemy practice may appear in your dreams. For example, you may dream of buying that gift or you may dream the perfect gift you need for your dream alchemy.

Your dreams may release a range of emotions, especially if you are still dealing with grief. This is your dream's way of providing a safety valve for the emotions you have repressed.

Look out for dreams of birth.

In your waking life
When dealing with grief:

Grief takes time, but your dream alchemy soothes and smoothes the way when you are at the beginning of the journey.

If your grief has been stuck or if there have been unresolved issues to heal, dream alchemy speeds your healing and releases you to continue on your journey.

You may also wish to seek professional grief counselling.

When dealing with the other kinds of dreams:

You are released to continue your journey. Your life is transformed.

31: I'm being chased or followed

Chased

The dream

Someone or something is on your tail and you know it.

Recognise the pattern of your echoing footsteps.

In your dream perhaps ...

- You are being chased so you are running away as fast as you can.
- You are being chased and you are trying to run but getting nowhere fast.
- You cannot see who or what is following you, but you sense them.
- The follower appears to be in shadow.
- You do not run from the follower but you try to outwit him or her, or hide.

How do you feel in your dream?

Shivery. Terrified. Fearful. Spooked. Hounded. Under surveillance. Uncomfortable. Trapped. Stuck. Doomed. Guilty. Covert. Vulnerable. Threatened. Caught out. Revealed. Invaded.

How does your dream end?

Positive changes are on the way if ...

- You recognise the chaser or follower.
- You confront or embrace the chaser or follower.
- The follower steps out of the shadow.
- The chaser or follower transforms into something positive.

It's time for a new approach if ...

- You escape or try to escape.
- You hide or try to hide.
- There is no end to the chasing or following.

◆ You are too scared to turn around and see what or who is behind you.

What your dream means
Your way forward may be blocked by ...
Something you have turned your back on because you do not want to face or confront it. Something you do not admire in yourself. Guilt about the past. Your negativity.

Moving forward
Face or confront the feeling, attitude, event or belief that is still haunting you. See it as part of your history or part of your true self. Own it, feel it, explore it and *then* the haunting will be gone.

◆

Q. *What sticks so close to you that no matter where you go or how fast you travel you can't shake it off?*

A. Your shadow.

This is true as long as there's a light and you're running towards it. What is following you in your dream is attached to you and you are attached to it. It is a fear, experience or belief that you have turned your back on because you don't want to confront it. You think it belongs to the past, but unless you have dealt with it the past catches up with you. And it does eventually 'catch' you.

What is following you may look dark (for example, a dark-haired person wearing dark clothes) or shadowy because you prefer not to shine a light on it, to have a good look at it, to face it.

The things about yourself that you do not admire are bundled together and referred to as your 'shadow' or your 'shadow side'. But what you don't admire will not go away! It persists until you face what it is and why you feel negative about it. Often the shadow wears a cloak of fear of the future or guilt from the past. It may appear ugly, murderous or devilish, but these are only measures of your severe distaste — pictures of how you judge what you do not admire in yourself.

Your dream follower may be more invisible than shadowy,

showing that no matter how hard you try to make a feeling, attitude or belief disappear it will still haunt you. In extreme cases this dream can spill into your waking life. You might feel you are being followed or have the sensation that another person is getting into bed with you or sleeping beside you. The only way to lose your follower is to take the feeling, attitude or belief back on board, own it as a part of who you are and then begin the work of exploring the feeling or changing your attitude.

Your shadow is much easier to pin down when you begin to see it. In dreams you might turn round and get a glimpse, or you might have a feeling that it is Marion from work or Carl the butcher who is on your tail. Then it's over to you to be the detective and work out what beliefs you have about Marion or Carl, or what feelings you have towards them. Name the beliefs or feelings and you will have named what you deny or fight in yourself.

In your life this could be about ...

- A sum of money you owe someone from long ago.
- A dream or wish that is chasing you instead of you chasing it.
- Regret over the way you handled a situation with a friend — and lost the friendship.
- Regret about not finishing a course of study.
- The anger you deny about the way your partner treats you.
- An addiction you can't beat.
- Your inability to leave or change the highly stressed job that comes home with you each night and 'haunts you'.
- An injury or death that you feel some responsibility for and cannot face.
- An affair you had.

Your unique dream contains personal clues only you may recognise

- Look at the clothes or shoes you're wearing for clues about when you first started running. For example, you might be wearing a top you had in 2008 or boots that date back to the '90s.

- Look for clues in the names of the streets or places in your dream. Being chased along a riverbank might give you a clue about a financial problem (bank) or being chased and ending up at a fairground might indicate an affair (*a fair*ground).
- If you always manage to hide somewhere, look at your hiding place for clues. For example, if you always hide in a bunker in your dream this might give you a clue to a debt you owed and 'did a bunk' on.

Why has this dream come up for you now?

Your answers to these questions will reveal the reason:

- What feelings and emotions did you experience in your dream?
- Which situation in your life now do these feelings remind you of?
- If you have identified the situation you have been turning your back on, imagine facing it now and then imagine the situation being resolved to your satisfaction. What challenges do you feel this new life would deliver for you?

Your answer to the last question may reveal the reason your dream has come up for you now. You know that you need to face up to something that is holding you back, but you fear the consequences.

Dream alchemy practice
Starting the inner work

This is what to *do* if you hope to see dramatic transformations in your life.

A. Write a conversation between yourself and the person who follows you in your dream. Arrange the conversation like a script on your page. Start the conversation with you asking the person how he or she feels about following you. Let the dialogue flow from there.

B. If you have identified a guilt from your past that you feel is following you, and if this is not something you feel you can put right with anyone at this stage, here's the dream alchemy practice to put things right within yourself and create magic in your life.

Write a letter to yourself at the age you were back then. On the first page, express your feelings of guilt along with whatever else comes up. On the second page, write about the positive things you've learned from the whole experience. On the third page, tell your younger self that we all do what we think is right at the time and, really, that is what matters. On the fourth page, tell your younger self you would forgive him or her if there were something to forgive, but since we all do what we think is right at the time, there is nothing to forgive. On the fifth page, express your thanks to your younger self for shaping your life through this event and state what it has taught you.

Read the whole letter aloud to yourself, then destroy page one. Read pages 2 to 5 aloud, then destroy page 2. Continue this, reading the remaining pages aloud until the whole letter has been destroyed. As you destroy the last page, say aloud, 'Fresh life is nourished by this act.'

C. On your bathroom mirror write, 'Look. There is no one following me. I see only myself.'

Glimmers of gold
In your dreams
When your recurring dream stops or changes to embrace a happier ending you are making good progress.

Some symbols from your dream alchemy practice may appear in your dreams. For example, you may dream of facing the person who was following you in your old dream.

Your dreams may release emotions such as guilt, fear, grief and anger along with images of the event you had been running from. This is the dream's way of clearing the past so that you can walk forward in peace.

In your waking life
You are able to look back and see your past without guilt or anxiety. You see your history in a different light. You

see a path of challenge that has taught you good spiritual lessons.

Your see that your path ahead is wider and easier than it appeared to be before. There are more options.

You are more in harmony with daily decisions, making good ones but also experiencing a grounded steadiness, an unhurried pace. You notice a lack of pressure and are surprised to see how quickly positive changes occur for you when the pressure's off.

You have something precious to offer others who are still experiencing the kind of situation that had been haunting you. You feel wise enough and confident enough to offer support.

32: The talking baby

Baby

(Also see 7: Losing or forgetting the baby or child)

The dream

A baby or small child speaks wisely, using adult vocabulary.

When the student is ready, let there be growth.

In your dream perhaps ...

- The baby looks like a baby but speaks with adult wisdom.
- The baby looks more like a miniature adult and speaks with adult wisdom.
- A young child speaks with an adult voice. You have a rough idea of the child's age.
- The baby or child seems to be a spiritual guru or master.

How do you feel in your dream?

Accepting. Awed. Inspired. Surprised. Sad. Chosen. Privileged. Enlightened. Weighed down. Burdened. Subservient. Serious. Playful.

How does your dream end?

Positive changes are on the way if ...

- You are inspired by the baby's wisdom to take positive action.
- The baby helps you to understand something or see it in a different light.
- The baby or child's body grows into adult form.
- You kiss or embrace the child.
- You express sadness for the child who is not experiencing childhood.
- You express sadness for the adult mind trapped in the body of a child.

It's time for a new approach if ...

- You feel subservient to the baby or child.
- You are carrying the baby or child and feel the burden of its weight.

What your dream means

Your way forward may be blocked by ...

Stunting a talent, idea or personal growth. Something from your babyhood that needs to be acknowledged or understood. Something your early childhood experience can teach you about today. Acting the baby or child. A message you need to get about something new in your life.

Moving forward

Let whatever needs to grow, grow. Look back to your babyhood experiences to see today in a clearer light. When you catch yourself acting the child remember that you are equal to all other people — express yourself as an equal. Look to your dream for clues about how to handle a new situation in your life.

◆

These dream babies may look and move like babies or toddlers but their vocabulary and wisdom extends way beyond that stage of life!

There are three main approaches to your dream images of babies or children, especially when you have a good feeling for the children's ages.

Firstly, if the child is two and a half, then she may represent your own long-lost feelings from when you were two and a half (but seen through your adult eyes and spoken with your adult wisdom and vocabulary). In this case, your talking baby is an experience of your own from long ago speaking to you in your dream when you need that particular wisdom.

Secondly, she may represent something that has been in your life for two and a half years (perhaps a job, project or relationship). Thirdly, she may be your dream's way of showing you that you are an adult pretending to be a child to keep someone happy. If your parents have had difficulty letting go of their parental authority, you may behave with them as if you are still their little girl. You might also see this feeling pictured in a dream as an adult with a baby's head, showing you, grown-up putting on the face of a child.

Babies with adult voices may also show you what you're stunting or not allowing to develop within yourself. A baby who sings exquisitely may be your dream's way of showing you that you have a singing talent you are not nurturing, for example.

If your dream baby is more of a miniature adult, ask yourself what you are stunting (the adult is not fully grown) or what you are forcing too hard (the child is deprived of play and made to be an adult before his or her time). Or ask yourself if you have lost the playful edge and become too serious.

If you are carrying the dream baby and she is heavy, then you may be carrying the burden of a childhood experience, feeling or belief in your life now. Your dream may help you to express and release sadness and grief over any of these issues.

In your life this could be about ...

♦ An idea that you have been developing but delaying putting into action or that has been delayed excessively. Deep down you want to hang on to the baby stage longer to stay in your comfort zone.

♦ A relationship, project, business, job, study course or other activity that has only been in your life for about the same time as the age of the baby in your dream.

♦ The way you cope with feeling intimidated by someone through acting like a baby or child.

Your unique dream contains personal clues only you may recognise

♦ What is your feeling about the age of the baby or child? What has been in your life this long? What was happening for you when you were this age?

♦ Are there any signs of intimidation in your dream? For example, people you know who intimidate you, a feeling you have in the dream, an emphasis on being surrounded by tall people or high furniture or buildings.

◆ Recall what the baby says to you then write down the opposite message. Where would either the original message or the opposite seem to apply in your life now?

Why has this dream come up for you now?

Your answers to these questions will reveal the reason:

◆ What feelings and emotions did you experience in your dream?
◆ Which situation in your life now do these feelings remind you of?
◆ If you can identify this situation, what would be the best outcome? Imagine yourself living the best outcome. What challenges do you feel would come up for you?

Your answer to the last question may reveal the reason your dream has come up for you now. You are ready for a change in this situation but you fear facing the challenges you believe the change may deliver.

Dream alchemy practice
Starting the inner work

This is what to *do* if you hope to see dramatic transformations in your life.

A. Write a conversation between yourself and the baby in your dream. Arrange the conversation like a script on your page. Start the conversation with you asking the baby why he or she wants to talk to you. Let the dialogue flow from there.

B. This dream alchemy practice takes three days. On Day 1 take a piece of paper and divide it into two columns. Give one column the title, 'The parent' and the other, 'The baby'. Spend a morning contemplating the life you lead today, looking for situations where you are the parent and situations where you are the baby. Record these in your columns. For example, you might have, under 'The parent', 'caring for elderly aunt, encouraging friend to apply for job, picking up partner's clothes from floor, beginning new business'. You might have under 'The child', 'playing with the dog, keeping mum happy, relating to intimidating boss, letting partner make decisions for me'.

On Day 2, take a red pen and have another look at your list. Look for parent and child situations where you would prefer to be an equal. Write in red pen across each one you would like to change, 'become equal'.

On Day 3, take a large piece of paper and draw a big circle for each of the situations where you would prefer to be an equal. Choose a name for each circle — for example, 'equal to Mum', or 'pick up your own clothes'. In each circle write the first step to becoming equal — for example, 'tell Mum about something in my life that may make her sad but for which I need her support', or 'stop picking up partner's clothes.'

Now create the opportunities to carry out all these steps. Do them and then keep doing them until you have developed new ways of operating or relating.

C. Buy a twenty-first birthday card. Imagine the baby from your dream now being a wise and beautiful 21-year-old. Write a message in the card expressing how wonderful it has been watching her grow from a baby. Tell her (imagine!) what you have learned from her over the years. Address the card to yourself and post it. When the post is delivered open it, read it and keep it as a bookmark.

Glimmers of gold
In your dreams
When your recurring dream stops or changes to embrace a happier ending you are making good progress.

Some symbols from your dream alchemy practice may appear in your dreams. For example, you may dream of receiving a card with a special message.

Your dreams may release emotions such as grief, fear and anger as the dream alchemy releases the beliefs that kept you in your old comfort zone. This is the dream's way of removing the restrictions that were slowing your growing and blossoming.

Look out for dreams of fast growth, stretching movements and new clothes or shoes.

In your waking life
You walk taller and are more confident. You speak out more clearly. Your voice may be slightly deeper, coming from your diaphragm rather than your throat.

At least one area of your life changes very quickly for the better.

People close to you may take a while to become comfortable with the new you. You understand that how they respond is their decision. They may become closer to you or they may disappear from your life.

New people come into your life — people who respect you and support your growth.

You feel wiser on many levels. Your life becomes more complete.

33: Trapped and under attack

Trapped, attacked

(Also see 12: Intruders!; 36: Paralysed — can't move, can't shout!)

The dream
Someone or something has you trapped or is attacking you.

Is that not your own hand pulling the pin?

In your dream perhaps ...
♦ You are in your home or a building, barricading yourself against surrounding attackers.
♦ You are trapped or attacked by a wild animal or insect.
♦ You are in a war or battle, defending yourself against attack.
♦ You are being verbally attacked or shouted down.
♦ You have been taken hostage.
♦ You are fighting back or defending yourself.
♦ You are hiding from an attacker.

How do you feel in your dream?
Fearful. Hurt. In pain. Paralysed. Invaded. Defensive. Insecure. Strong. Weak. Vulnerable. Victorious. Heroic. Martyred. Victimised. Powerless. Excited. Hyped up. Motivated. Stuck. Unprepared. Indignant. Proud. Angry. Just.

How does your dream end?
Positive changes are on the way if ...
♦ You confront your attackers and they retreat or disappear.
♦ You express anger or grief.
♦ You talk your attacker or the animal into releasing you.
♦ Walls, barriers and other defences are broken or dismantled and you feel okay.

It's time for a new approach if ...
♦ You build more and more barriers or lock yourself in further.

- The dream ends in a state of fear.
- You are in the grip of your attacker and still frightened.
- You are unable to free yourself from being a hostage.

What your dream means
(If you feel more invaded than attacked in your dream, read common dream 12: Intruders, instead.)

Your way forward may be blocked by ...
Fighting (attacking and defending) instead of negotiating a win–win situation. Trying to control a person or situation that feels threatening to you instead of finding a solution that frees you both. Being your own worst enemy. Sabotaging yourself: not completing the final step, doing things to ensure your own failure. Fear of an unknown future.

Moving forward
Negotiate instead of attacking or defending. See both sides. Know that if you are controlling a person or situation, you are restricting your own freedom. Face your fears about the future and transform them into love — love yourself enough to trust your future. Take one step at a time towards the future you want and keep walking.

◆

When you find yourself in a war zone or battle in your dream, you are most likely working out how to deal with a conflict in your life that has you trapped and cornered. The strange thing is that you probably don't feel trapped and cornered at all in your life. You probably feel fighting fit and on top of things, in control of yourself and your life very nicely. So what's happening here?

If you feel more invaded than attacked in your dream, and if you can relate to feeling trapped or cornered in waking life, see common dream 12: Intruders. If you feel more attacked than invaded, and more involved in fighting back or working out a plan of attack, read on, then read common dream 12: Intruders.

This dream is about feeling attacked and how you cope with this feeling in waking life. There are two main ways of coping. One is to fight back, to attack. One is to resist attack, to defend. When you attack you speak out, abuse or hurt another party. When you defend you stand up for yourself whether you are in the right or in the wrong. Neither of these ways leads to a win–win situation. You end up on an attack–defend merry-go-round that is far from merry and never peaceful.

Attacking and defending are both ways of trying to control the person or situation that you are feeling threatened by. It's an act of war and you are the controller. If you wanted peace, you'd negotiate for peace. You wouldn't be there with guns blazing in attack or eyes and ears shut defensively to the cause of your attacker.

Feeling trapped by someone or something usually starts in childhood and then a pattern of attack and defence begins. Whenever you feel trapped you fight, defend and control your way as you have always done. In the end you achieve a strained peace. Not real peace, not harmony and certainly not freedom because your tightly guarded life works only by restricting yourself and others. In the end you are as trapped as you were in the beginning. But you don't realise this!

Another way of looking at the attack–defence way of controlling your fear of being trapped is to see yourself as your own worst enemy. After all, you're not gaining freedom or peace from your attitude, so you're not winning the battle, are you? As in all dreams, the other people represent your own feelings and attitudes. Those attackers are *you*. The person or situation trapping you is *you*. You are sabotaging your freedom to move forward away from conflict towards peace.

Could you be a self-saboteur? This is someone who has endless plans but always destroys them at the last minute, always stops short of completing a final step. A self-saboteur changes his mind, spends all his money, fails to turn up for the final exam, doesn't dress up for the interview, runs out of petrol on the way to a meeting, forgets to set the alarm and leaves his wallet visible for someone to steal. A self-saboteur keeps himself under attack so that he remains trapped and avoids the fear of stepping into an unknown future. Could this be you?

In your life this could be about ...

- Not having the money you need for something because you spend all your money no matter how much you start with.
- The relationship you should leave but choose to stay in because it protects you from facing an unknown future.
- A project you leave until the last minute and then find you don't have the resources to complete.
- The cold feet you get at the last minute for a business idea or job interview so something 'happens' to cause your failure.
- Your fear of change — no matter how much you say you want it — that keeps you stuck where you are.
- Your wish to keep a relationship (with your partner, children or parent) exactly as it is because you fear the unknown future, so you try to restrict the other person's natural development or expression.

Your unique dream contains personal clues only you may recognise

- Your attackers' weapons may give you a clue about what is trapping you in your waking life. For example, if the weapons are firebombs your anger about a past situation (fire in dreams often symbolises anger) may be keeping you trapped in the situation you are now in. If the weapons are vats of acid perhaps your acidic words (or acidic thoughts in reaction to someone else's acidic words) are trapping you.
- What you are trapped in may give you a clue about your trapped situation. For example, if you are trapped in a giant bird's nest, perhaps your fear of leaving your comfortably 'feathered nest' (the money that provides your luxury) is trapping you in that very situation.
- Look for other things that are trapped in your dream. For example, a dog trapped on a short leash is a clue to an instinct or energy you are restricting by fighting a

situation or fighting your fear of the unknown. What personality do you feel this dream dog has? If it is a loving and loveable puppy, for example, you may be denying love and loving expression in your life.

Why has this dream come up for you now?

Your answers to these questions will reveal the reason:

◆ What feelings and emotions did you experience in your dream?

◆ Which situation in your life now do these feelings remind you of?

◆ What is your greatest wish? Has something happened to bring that wish a little closer, or to drive it further away? Has this wish just come true for someone you know?

◆ If this wish were to come true for you tomorrow, what else would change in your life?

Your answer to the last question may reveal the reason your dream has come up for you now. Your fear of the changes your desired future might bring are battling away in your dreams, revealing the stalemate you are in — and the way out.

Dream alchemy practice
Starting the inner work

This is what to *do* if you hope to see dramatic transformations in your life.

A. Write a conversation between yourself and the leader of the attackers in your dream. Arrange the conversation like a script on your page. Start the conversation with you asking the leader what he is fighting for. Let the dialogue flow from there.

B. Imagine yourself back in your dream, trapped and under attack. Now see your attackers coming very close, so close you can look them in the eye. As you look into their eyes, see them transformed from a look of attack to a look of love. As you focus on their now loving eyes, feel a white light suffusing your body, bringing with it a feeling of peace and a surge of vitality. Now see whatever

235

was trapping you dissolving away and yourself standing in the open air, stretching and yawning as if you have woken from a deep sleep. Now look around you and see that the attackers have dissolved too. In their place are many blossoming flowers. In the distance you see a soft, welcoming light. Focus on the feeling of freedom and safety as you walk towards your future, safe in the knowledge that only love awaits you there.

Practise this dream alchemy visualisation regularly, summoning up positive and loving feelings.

C. This dream alchemy practice takes twenty days. Take twenty pieces of paper and write a small task on each one. Make about a third of these easy — the kind of task you do most days anyway, like 'wash the dishes' or 'check the email'. Make another third the kind of tasks that are easy to do but that you don't do regularly, like 'clean the garbage bin' or 'sort out your wardrobe, item by item'. Make the last third tasks that you know you have been avoiding, like 'check the last three months' bank statements' or 'send my résumé to ...'

Now fold each piece of paper so you can't see what's written on it and put them all in a dish. Each morning take out a piece of paper. You must do the task — whatever it is, even if you think it doesn't need to be done — before the day ends. This dream alchemy practice works (to beat self-sabotage) *only* if you do all twenty tasks on twenty consecutive days in the order you take them out of the dish. Do it or stay trapped.

Glimmers of gold
In your dreams
When your recurring dream stops or changes to embrace a happier ending you are making good progress.

Some symbols from your dream alchemy practice may appear in your dreams. For example, you may dream of setting all the pieces of folded paper free from your dish.

Your dreams may release emotions such as bitterness,

grief, fear and anger as the dream alchemy releases the beliefs that kept you trapped and 'safe' from facing your future. This is the dream's way of knocking down prison walls to set you free.

Look out for dreams of being a winner, receiving rewards and achieving difficult tasks with great ease.

In your waking life
At first you need to sleep more. Before doing your dream alchemy your adrenaline levels kept your energy up. Now that you no longer need to fight, your adrenaline levels return to normal and you discover that the fight had been exhausting you deep inside. You sleep and dream.

Your vitality and energy not only return but reach a higher level. You are surprised at how easily you see solutions, make decisions and carry out tasks without needing a shot of adrenaline or a feeling of fight to make it happen.

Your goals may change but you do achieve them.

You are a better negotiator. People and situations that you feared before are suddenly no threat. You lose the need to control others or to know what they are doing and when. You are truly free.

You trust your future, you trust others and you trust yourself.

34: On the cliff edge – or falling

Falling

(Also see 7: Losing or forgetting the baby or child)

> ## The dream
>
> Whether you are standing on the cliff or hanging by
> your fingertips from the edge, you can see and feel the
> drop. Or you may be watching someone else on the
> cliff edge about to fall. You or someone else may also
> fall from a window, plane or other high place.

*The pain you feel in letting go is the same pain that
bound you in the first place. Release your pain to find
your wings.*

In your dream perhaps ...

♦ You are standing on the edge of a cliff and the view over
  the edge is stunningly beautiful.

♦ Your stomach lurches and you feel the fear of heights as
  you peep over the edge of the cliff.

♦ You see the cliff crumbling or dissolving into the sea
  below.

♦ You see sharks, whales or other underwater details from
  your cliff edge.

♦ You feel in danger of falling from the cliff.

♦ You are hanging on by your fingertips, or in a car see-
  sawing on the edge.

♦ You fall from the cliff, window, tree, plane or other high
  place.

♦ You feel safe but you can't find your way back down.

♦ You are watching someone else on the cliff, window
  ledge, tree or other high place, about to fall, and you feel
  powerless about the outcome.

How do you feel in your dream?

Awed. Insightful. Ecstatic. Successful. Fearful. Unsafe. Doomed.
Indecisive. Pressed. Hesitant. Forced. Out of control. Trapped.

Restricted. Safe. Puzzled. Lost. Insignificant. Powerful. Power-less. Released. Relieved. Unsatisfied. Shocked.

How does your dream end?
Positive changes are on the way if ...
♦ You see something positive from your cliff edge.
♦ You feel enlightened by what you see from the top.
♦ You save yourself from a fall from the edge and every-thing feels good.
♦ You let yourself fall and all works out well.
♦ As someone else falls, you express huge grief, anger or shock.

It's time for a new approach if ...
♦ You save yourself from falling but you feel unsatisfied or trapped.
♦ You remain fearful of what you see.
♦ You can't shake the 'on the edge' feeling.
♦ You wake yourself up as you fall, in a state of panic.

What your dream means
Your way forward may be blocked by ...
Holding on too tightly to a situation, belief or feeling. Stay-ing 'in control'. Fear of change or loss. Pride (comes before a fall). Depression (falling into a hole). Not acting on what you see clearly from a higher view.

Moving forward
Acknowledge your feelings — name them. Ease up on tight control. Let go. Release and reach higher. Allow yourself to discover your wings. Fall in love. When you see your life clearly from a higher viewpoint, act on what you see. Allow the natural process of change to take you to a better place.

♦

Was it a 'screaming falling from a window' kind of falling or a 'wow, I'm free floating' kind of falling? The thing is how did you *feel* about falling in your dream? Or how did you feel watching someone else falling? Dream falling is a lot about feeling, and also about being in and out of control.

You know that funny little falling feeling you sometimes get when you're falling asleep? Well, that's *not* what we're talking about here. In true dreams you fall with meaning and feeling.

Mostly you fall in dreams in terror, or find yourself watching, helplessly, as others fall. A child falls off a cliff or from a window, a plane falls from the sky or you find yourself falling to a certain death. Your heart lurches and falls into the pit of your stomach. There's nothing you can do except let go.

'If you fall and hit the bottom in your dream, you'll die in your sleep.' So goes the old tale. Well, if you *do* hit bottom in a falling dream and wake up you'll tell a different tale. Most dreamers, when they hit bottom, stand aside from their body and walk away. Life goes on.

If your dream falling gives you a feeling of terror, helplessness or deep loss, your dream is most likely releasing feelings you have kept under control — feelings of losing touch with a lover, losing your sense of belonging, losing face, losing control or feeling helpless in some area of your life. Life works better if you acknowledge your feelings, if you name them, if you ease up on the tight control. Control is fear, letting go is love. You can fall from fear or you can fall in love. Which do you choose?

To understand a dream 'fall', you need to think 'feeling'. How do you feel in the dream and what could this tell you about feelings you're not acknowledging?

Dreams are real drama queens. They love to play out puns and clichés too. An ecstatic kind of falling in a dream may be drawing your attention to falling in love. You may dream-fall into depression (you might dream of falling into a black hole) or fall from grace.

Remember to look at other people in your dream as symbols of your beliefs. Someone you know to be tight-fisted may be a dream illustration of your beliefs about the flow of money; or your beliefs about control; or your beliefs about giving, receiving, generosity or faith in change. People in your dreams usually represent extremes of your beliefs, whether you are of the same or opposite belief to the person in your dream. If you are shocked to see an ambitious person fall to their death in your dream, you are most likely letting go of your own passé beliefs about ambition. You will also be letting go of the original emotion or memory that set you on a path of ambition. Death of the old has to take place before the birth of the new.

When you find yourself on a cliff edge looking down at a spectacular view, your dream is giving you a bird's-eye view of your life and your situation. Cliff-edge dreams are often bathed in vivid colour and intensity as all is revealed in clarity, depth and meaning. Looking directly down you see the depth of your being, the many layers of life that have brought you to where you now stand. You can see things differently from afar: you can see patterns more clearly, you can see further down a path, and you can see below the surface of the water. From this vantage point your life map is clearer: you can see the old obstacles and see the way forward.

What's the bottom line in cliff edges and falling? You either hit the bottom — and the only way from the bottom is up! — or you see a new vision as you peer over the edge or find wings as you fall. In either case, the way forward out of a tight situation is to ease the control — to let go and allow the natural process of change to take you to a better place.

In your life this could be about ...

- Hanging on too tightly to the job you've had for ten years even though you can see that times have changed and the job will not be there for you much longer.
- Hanging on too tightly to a relationship that is not working, choosing to believe that all is well.
- Trying not to fall in love even though you are already.
- Holding on to childhood beliefs and expectations even though they are not getting you anywhere.
- Not wanting to let go of a business, house or position that gives you prestige even though it is hurting you financially.
- Trying to control your children's decisions in life even though you know they have other hopes and plans.
- Not letting yourself go enough to express your feelings or release your talent or creativity.

Your unique dream contains personal clues only you may recognise

♦ If the person who falls in your dream is not you, write down three words to describe their personality or approach to life. Then write down the opposite to these three words. These six words are clues to the beliefs you are losing touch with or that you need to let go.

♦ What you, or the person who falls, try to hold onto in the dream is a clue to what you are trying to hold onto in your waking life.

♦ What you are wearing in your dream gives you a clue to the attitude or belief that you have been holding too tightly or losing touch with.

Why has this dream come up for you now?

Your answers to these questions will reveal the reason:

♦ What feelings and emotions did you experience in your dream?

♦ Which situation in your life now do these feelings remind you of?

♦ Name five situations and five relationships that you fear losing. Have you felt unsure about any of these recently?

♦ If you were to lose any of these, what would you fear most as you look ahead?

Your answer to the last question may reveal the reason your dream has come up for you now. You realise you are holding on too tightly to something or someone and this brings up the fears you have for your future.

Dream alchemy practice
Starting the inner work

This is what to *do* if you hope to see dramatic transformations in your life.

A. Write a conversation between the person who fell (yourself or another) and the thing they had been hanging onto (for example, a window frame) in your dream. Arrange the conversation like a script on your page. Start the conversation with the person asking the structure (window frame or whatever) why it let him go. Let the dialogue flow from there.

B. Inhale, clench your fists tightly and hold your breath for just a moment. Then open your hands wide, stretch your fingers and breathe out. Take a deep fresh breath in. On the first day do this cycle of one breath only (no hyperventilating!) once every hour. Between these times, whenever you remember, relax your hands. Continue this dream alchemy practice every day until you realise what the situation is that you have been gripping too tight. On the next day, when you are stretching your fingers, imagine yourself releasing your hold on the situation so that the best solution will unfold. Continue your dream alchemy practice, including your visualisation, for as long as you need.

C. Make or buy a small indoor fountain — or a huge outdoor one if you prefer. Pause each day to watch and hear the water flowing. Watch the patterns of ripples and light changing. Close your eyes and let the sound wash over you. Let your mind drift and see where it takes you.

Glimmers of gold
In your dreams
When your recurring dream stops or changes to embrace a happier ending you are making good progress.

Some symbols from your dream alchemy practice may appear in your dreams. For example, you may dream of releasing something beautiful from your hands — butterflies, perhaps.

Your dreams may release emotions and images from the past connected with the situation you have been hanging onto. This is the dream's way of erasing the need to grip, freeing your hands so that you can embrace life more fully.

Look out for dreams of plants growing and blossoming, adventurous journeys and wise characters showing you the way forward.

In your waking life

You laugh more and feel more relaxed. You worry less about the future and worry less about what other people choose to do or not to do.

You are less concerned with what other people think of you and what you do.

New opportunities appear and the speed of this surprises you. You are more willing to risk and less concerned about outcomes.

You may discover a new talent or ability.

You have a new respect for the process of change and how quickly good things can occur when you release yourself to reach higher.

35: I've lost my handbag, wallet, jewellery or ...

Lost, handbag or wallet

(Also see 7: Losing or forgetting the baby or child; 21: I've lost my way; 39: Decapitated!)

> ### The dream
> You've lost or misplaced something personal and of great value.

Who are you?

In your dream perhaps ...
- You've lost your handbag, purse or wallet.
- You've lost an item of jewellery.
- You've lost an engagement or wedding ring.
- You've lost your watch.

How do you feel in your dream?
Sad. Devastated. Disorganised. Guilty. Irresponsible. Responsible. Punished. A sense of grief. Powerless. Lost. Naked. Vulnerable. Free. Relieved. Angry. Panicked. Hopeful. Accepting. Stuck. Foolish. A sense of failure. Distressed. Upset.

How does your dream end?
Positive changes are on the way if ...
- You find the lost item or it is given back to you.
- You find the lost item and it has grown in value since you lost it.
- You find the lost item but it has changed and you feel good about this.
- You find something better than the item you had lost.
- You accept the loss and let it go. You plan replacing what you've lost with something better.

- You feel more powerful, or better in some way, without the item.
- You express grief.

It's time for a new approach if ...

- The search for the lost item becomes increasingly complicated.
- You find the item but it is broken or damaged and you feel sad about this.
- You discover the thief but you can't get the item back.

What your dream means

Your way forward may be blocked by ...

Loss of self-esteem, identity, a lover, a job, health, wealth, faith, direction or purpose. Feeling under-valued. Loss of personal power. What you need to find. Not feeling or being whole.

Moving forward

You need to lose the old before you can find the new. Allow yourself to let go of old values that are past their use-by date so that you can develop new ones. Life is about change and moving on. You may find what you have lost or you may find something much better.

◆

'I once was lost, but now I'm found ...', so the hymn goes, acknowledging the amazing grace that steers you through dark, lost times towards discovering a sense of wholeness — a sense of who you are and a sense of purpose in the world. There are times in life when you need to find what you have lost — a sense of peace, self-respect, purpose or moti-vation, for example. There are times when you need to let go of what you have lost so that you can move on: a sense of failure at losing a job, anger at an ex-partner for leaving you, grief over a death or an old lifestyle.

There are times when there is a space to fill following a loss. You need a new habit to replace smoking; you need to fill the space left in your heart after losing a lover, or in your life when your children left home or you retired.

There are times when you need to lose old ways that

keep you stuck so that you can grow. Perhaps you leave a job to lose your old definition of self, or stop wearing your watch to lose the restriction of time. Perhaps you move to live near the sea to lose the boundaries of your city-self, or leave a relationship that is no longer nurturing you or your partner.

There are times when you need to lose something of great value to appreciate it. For example, you may lose your income to later appreciate the value of choosing how you spend your money, or you may lose your health to be re-minded later of the simple joys of wellness.

In the material world you carry your personal and pri-vate valuables and identities in your handbag or wallet, so these are good dream symbols of losing your sense of per-sonal identity or private self. Wedding and engagement rings symbolise your relationships or social identity, so these are good dream symbols of loss in these areas of your life. In dreams, jewellery often draws attention to a body part to emphasise a special value or talent. A necklace can symbol-ise communication, speaking or singing, for example. Rings may symbolise your talents in handling people, in creating or using your hands, while earrings may draw dream atten-tion to what you are, or are not, listening to or hearing.

Dreams of loss are about what you are losing touch with, what you need to let go of and what you need to find. They are about how to discover your greater self hiding under the cover of a job title, a smoking habit, long working hours, ad-diction to the television or Internet, or an overly full social life. They are about taking your head out of the sand so that you can see where you are and show your whole self to the world.

In your life this could be about ...
- A job loss, leaving you without your old public identity.
- A loss of face in public — something that has embar-rassed you.
- A relationship in which you are feeling under-valued.
- A loss of personal power or independence due to a finan-cial loss.

- Menopause or mid-life leaving you feeling a loss of youth and fertility.
- A health problem or loss of mobility.
- Loss of a lover.

Your unique dream contains personal clues only you may recognise

- Your personal memories connected with the item you lost in your dream may be a clue to what you feel you have lost in your waking life. For example, if you dreamed you lost a bracelet that was given to you years ago by a charity in recognition of your voluntary service, you may be feeling a loss of recognition or purpose.
- Look for dream puns. (See 'Confessions of the bizarre and cheeky', page 328.) If you're in a sticky dream situation and you've lost your small change, this may give you a clue about a small change you need to make to get you out of a problem in your waking life. Ask yourself if you have lost your flexibility and openness to change.
- What you were trying to do in your dream before the loss is a clue about what you feel is lost. For example, if you were trying to make a phone call from a public call box and you discovered you had lost your purse, then perhaps you are feeling a loss of power to communicate.

Why has this dream come up for you now?

Your answers to these questions will reveal the reason:

- What feelings and emotions did you experience in your dream?
- Which situation in your life now do these feelings remind you of?
- Have you recently felt at a loss about something, or felt as if something is missing from your life?
- If that something that is missing could be found, or if a better version could be found, what challenges do you feel this would bring up for you?

Your answer to the last question may reveal the reason your dream has come up for you now. You know that something is missing or lost within you but your fear of what it would take to find it is holding you back.

Dream alchemy practice
Starting the inner work
This is what to *do* if you hope to see dramatic transformations in your life.

A. Write a conversation between yourself and the thing you have lost in your dream. Arrange the conversation like a script on your page. Start the conversation with you asking the lost thing how it is feeling. Let the dialogue flow from there.

B. Do this dream alchemy visualisation regularly:

Imagine yourself back in your dream but change the ending so that you find what you have lost or something better. See yourself discovering the lost item and *feel* the joy of rediscovery and any other feeling that you want to restore in your life.

C. If possible, buy yourself a new handbag, purse or wallet — an upgrade from the one you lost in your dream. Buy something of greater value than the dream item as this dream alchemy practice is about increasing your value. If the dream item is rather expensive, a diamond ring for example, then buy yourself an accessory to go with it. This works by increasing the value of the original item — and, by virtue of dream alchemy practice, increasing your value as you wear the two things together.

Glimmers of gold
In your dreams
When your recurring dream stops or changes to embrace a happier ending you are making good progress.

Some symbols from your dream alchemy practice may appear in your dreams. For example, you may dream of the ideal accessory item.

Your dreams may release emotions such as grief and these may spill over into a few teary days. This is the dream's way of helping you to acknowledge your sadness over what has been lost within you so that you can let it go and be ready to fill the space with something precious.

Look out for dreams of feeling powerful and having your say, or of famous or revered people.

In your waking life
You see the past in a different light. You see your old identity as a stepping stone to where you are now rather than as something lost. You see lessons learned and skills gained.

You feel more energetic, more empowered and more whole. Health problems start to heal, or you start to see their lessons and are richer for the experience.

Your sense of purpose is restored, though your purpose now may be quite different from what it was previously.

You feel comfortable about who you are and about how you express yourself. You do not hold back to suit other's expectations of what your role is.

At least one area of your life changes quite dramatically for the better.

36: Paralysed – can't move, can't shout!

Paralysed

(Also see 12: Intruders; 16: Slo mo running or walking; 19: A scary presence in the room; 33: Trapped and under attack)

The dream

You are scared and feel paralysed. You can't move or shout out for help.

In the yawning stretch of 'freeze-frame' is reflected the beauty of each transient snowflake. Explore the infinite array of possibilities.

In your dream perhaps ...

♦ Someone is in the house or attacking you and you become frozen with fear.

♦ Someone or something is pushing down on your chest. You can't move.

♦ You can't breathe. You struggle and eventually wake up to take a breath.

♦ You feel terror and cannot move to help yourself.

♦ You are trying to wake up, believing someone is in the room, but you can't move, talk or scream.

♦ You are trying to shout for help, but only a tiny voice comes out. You may actually speak these words in your sleep.

How do you feel in your dream?

Terrified. Fearful. Paralysed. Frozen. Freezing. Weighed down. Powerless. Manipulated. Weak. Vulnerable. Overpowered. Heavy. Incapable. Exhausted. Forced. Threatened. Denied.

How does your dream end?

Positive changes are on the way if ...

♦ Someone helps you.

♦ The danger or threat disappears.

- You confront the danger.
- You take a deep breath.

It's time for a new approach if ...
- You wake up terrified.
- You are unable to overcome the dream paralysis.
- You are afraid to go back to sleep.

What your dream means

Note: This dream also has an alternative physiological cause — see the dream interpretation below.

Your way forward may be blocked by ...

Not communicating what needs to be said. Being emotionally suffocated: not having your own breathing space. Feeling under great pressure. Putting too many restrictions on yourself. Fear.

Moving forward

Face your fears. Acknowledge your feelings and talk about them. Discuss ways of finding space to be yourself without feeling suffocated by someone else or by a situation that is too restricting for you.

◆

You've heard the expression, 'scared stiff' and felt the goose-bump chill of fear. Here's a dream that lives out the stiff and frozen side of your fears; but first here's a little body chemistry.

When you fall asleep, the nerves and muscles that normally move your limbs take time off too. This is your body's protective survival mechanism: how dangerous would life be if your muscles responded to your dream actions and you got up and acted out your dreams! All that's left is a twitch here and there and a fair bit of facial expression giving a hint of your dream drama. Apart from the odd burst of talking in your sleep, major chatter is out of the question too.

When you wake up, your motor nerves and muscles do too. Well, that's the way it's supposed to work. If you find yourself half awake and half dreaming you may become aware of the dead weight of your limbs and even feel a sensation of a dead weight or force pushing your chest down. Talk about scary! Things go out of control when you find yourself still half dreaming that something or someone is pushing you down or paralysing you, and you just can't move or shout for help.

Many of these dreams occur because your mind starts to wake up before your body does, but you continue in the dream state and dream up demons to explain your paralysis.

Can't breathe? If your nose gets blocked, or your head gets buried in your pillow, you may dream of being suffocated or unable to breathe. This is very scary to dream, but you usually figure this one out when you wake up to discover the cause. But sometimes you wake from these dreams and all appears to be well, bodywise. No blocked nose, no deadweight muscles. So it's back to symbolism — almost.

Your hormones and other chemical messengers keep up the good body work as you sleep. When you meet fear in a dream your body duly responds by pumping up the adrenaline as if you were in an actual scary situation. Adrenaline, nature's powerful hormone, gives you the superpower of fight or flight, but when you can't decide whether it's stay or go you can end up frozen in fear. This is why you can wake up from a fear dream with your heart racing in a cold sweat, hyped up and either ready for action or frozen with panic.

These dreams are either about your mind and body being out of synch when you start waking up, or about fear. They may also be dream portraits of not being able to communicate (a great weight you need to get 'off your chest') or about being emotionally suffocated (no breathing space) or about feeling held back and restricted.

In your life this could be about ...
- Not having enough quiet time to yourself to think, process your feelings, absorb your experiences or plan ahead.
- A relationship that feels like a dead weight.
- A job that is weighing you down.
- Making life difficult for yourself by not talking about your feelings and worries.
- Any fear that you are not facing.

Your unique dream contains personal clues only you may recognise

◆ Most people have the basic dream then wake up in fear, leaving little room for dream detail and clues. If your dream is short, it is hard to identify the waking life situation it is reflecting. The best thing is to read the 'In your life this could be about ...' list again and ask yourself some serious questions. Remember, of course, that this dream does have an alternative physiological cause.

◆ If you can remember the dream leading up to the appearance of the scary presence, then find the nearest dream theme in this book and refer to the 'Your unique dream contains personal clues ...' list to discover the background to your fear.

Why has this dream come up for you now?
Your answers to these questions will reveal the reason:

◆ What feelings and emotions did you experience in your dream?

◆ Which situation in your life now do these feelings remind you of?

◆ If you can identify this situation, imagine a solution and the best possible outcome. What uneasy feelings does this bring up for you?

Your answer to the last question may reveal the reason your dream has come up for you now. You want things to improve in this area of your life, but you fear the other changes that may come with it.

Dream alchemy practice
Starting the inner work
This is what to *do* if you hope to see dramatic transformations in your life.

A. Whether you feel this dream is due to physiological causes or whether it is symbolic of a dead-weight situation in your life, this dream alchemy practice will help. You can do it as soon as you find yourself trapped in the dead-weight feeling and trying to wake up, or you can do it at any other time of day or night.

Start by feeling the weight on your chest and then imagining it gently lifting from your body, transforming itself from a heavy weight into a light rain cloud. Feel your chest rise and your lungs expand to take in a long, deep breath as the rain cloud lifts. Imagine the cloud gently floating out of your window and drifting until it is over a river. See the cloud gently dissolve away to nothing, the rain falling softly into the river and being carried away into the ocean.

B. For this dream alchemy practice take a large sheet of paper and write 'Under Pressure' in the centre. Now take fifteen minutes to quickly fill the paper with as many words, thoughts, feelings, drawings or images that spring to mind. Work as fast as you can. Write whatever comes up when you think 'Under Pressure'.

Three days later destroy the paper, saying goodbye to all the pressure you have felt in the past and welcome a new sense of peace.

C. Here's an affirmation for you:

I wake in peace each morning with a lightness in my heart and a breath of fresh air in my chest. There is time and space for me to breathe deep, full breaths. All is well in my world.

Glimmers of gold
In your dreams

When your recurring dream stops or changes to embrace a happier ending, you are making good progress.

Some symbols from your dream alchemy practice may appear in your dreams. For example, you may dream of a gentle shower of rain.

Your dreams may release emotions such as grief, anger and bitterness. This is your dream's way of unburdening you of the beliefs and fears you carry that weigh you down.

Look out for dreams of vomit, diarrhoea or spilling guts — yes, it sounds foul, but these are positive signs! (See common dream 25: Cuts, wounds, blood, guts and vomit.)

In your waking life
You feel lighter and less stressed. You see solutions to problems or situations that had seemed impossible before.

Other people seem more supportive and capable. You share more of your thoughts and feelings with them.

You have more space to breathe and you wonder why this seemed so difficult to arrange before.

You may change your priorities in life. Some things that seemed important lose their urgency.

37: I can't see clearly

Blind

The dream

You can't see clearly. Your view is clouded, blocked or you are blind.

Lift the veil.

In your dream perhaps ...

♦ You are driving but the windscreen is frosted or misted.
♦ You can only see through one eye, giving the impression that you can only see the right but not the left, or the left but not the right.
♦ Bright light is blinding your vision.
♦ It is too dark to see.
♦ You cannot see because of a wall or obstacle in front of you.
♦ You are blind, partially blind, or your vision is out of focus.
♦ Your vision seems normal, but you cannot read a book, a number or a sign.
♦ You cannot see something everyone else can see.

How do you feel in your dream?

Frustrated. Panicked. Incapacitated. Determined. A sense of danger. Distressed. A sense of denial. Denied. Accepting. Adaptable. Unsafe. Safe. Lost. Struggling. Fearful.

How does your dream end?
Positive changes are on the way if ...

♦ Your sight is restored.
♦ You see with the help of glasses or some other aid.
♦ You sense what you cannot see and function perfectly, not needing sight.
♦ You understand something differently.
♦ The frosted or misted glass breaks.

- You find a position from which you can see and this is enlightening to you.

It's time for a new approach if ...
- Your sight remains unclear or deteriorates.
- You become lost or powerless because of your failing eyesight.
- You can't find a way through fear.

What your dream means
Your way forward may be blocked by ...
What you do not understand. What you choose to turn a blind eye to — to deny. What is right in front of your eyes but you're just not understanding. Not being able to project ahead or not being tuned into your intuition. Not having the insight you need or not being your authentic self.

Moving forward
Be prepared to see or understand something you may not want to acknowledge. Once you understand your situation you have the choice and the power to do something about it. When you can't see ahead, look within: use your intuition, be guided by what is right for you.

◆

How often do you say 'I see' when you mean 'I understand' or 'I get it'? When you dream about what you can or can't see, you are often dreaming about what you can or can't understand or 'get'.

What you see or can't see in your dreams may be what you understand or can't understand about yourself and how the world works. You need to see ahead to know where you're going so you can plan for the short term and the long term. You need clear focus in your near and far vision. How far can you see in your dreams and in your waking life?

Your left eye may portray your understanding of your inner world. Are you blind to your inner vision, perhaps? Your right eye, being linked to your left brain, may tell you about your outer world. (See 'I'll see you in my dreams', pages 310–11.) Your right eye may also be about your 'right I' — your correct sense of self, your true or authentic self.

In dreams there should be no problem seeing in the dark. The dark is your unconscious or what you are 'in the dark' about. To see your way in the dark in a dream is to perhaps follow your intuition to gain insight and understanding.

Glasses or a window in your dream may help you adopt a different view, focus, frame or outlook. Breaking frosted glass may be about making a breakthrough.

Your sight may be selective in your dream. Take note about what you choose to see and what you choose not to see, and ask yourself why this may be.

In your life this could be about ...

♦ Someone deceiving you.

♦ A business idea you really want to believe in even though it is clear to everyone else that it is not going to work.

♦ An issue or problem that is taking up so much of your focus that it blocks out everything else.

♦ A financial situation that you cannot see your way past or through.

♦ A lack of faith in yourself — 'I just can't see it.'

Your unique dream contains personal clues only you may recognise

♦ Anything you bump into in your dream because you can't see clearly may give you a clue about what it is you are not seeing. A pile of rotting fruit, for example, might be a clue about something that is no longer reaping rewards — perhaps an investment gone wrong.

♦ Animals may pop up in your dream to hint at energies or instincts you are overlooking or that are diverting your attention. Perhaps that greedy pig is in your dream to draw your attention to someone's greed, or to show you that your own greed for money or love is blinding you to reality.

♦ Look for dream clichés for clues: can't see the forest for the trees, blinded by the light, turn a blind eye, can't see the big picture, can't see your way through, having the wool pulled over your eyes.

Why has this dream come up for you now?

Your answers to these questions will reveal the reason:

◆ What feelings and emotions did you experience in your dream?

◆ Which situation in your life now do these feelings remind you of?

◆ Which situation in your life now is the hardest to predict?

◆ Which situation in your life now makes you feel uneasy?

Your answer to the last question may reveal the reason your dream has come up for you now. You want things to turn out according to how you see them, but your dream shows a conflict between what you choose to see and what is actually happening.

Dream alchemy practice

Starting the inner work

This is what to *do* if you hope to see dramatic transformations in your life.

A. If you dream of not being able to see through a frosted window, here's an affirmation for you. (If your dream is different, use this affirmation as a model to create your own.)

> The window is now clear. I clearly see a view
> of light, colour and clarity. I feel uplifted and
> empowered by what I now understand. I am free
> to choose my next step.

B. Take a walk outside for at least ten minutes every day for a few weeks. Find somewhere to sit or stand and just look at everything. Zoom in on something small and pan back to something big. Take one photo a day to remind you of what you have seen. Or bring home something to remind you — a leaf, a stone or perhaps a poem. Then arrange your photos or memories in an artwork to give the 'big picture' of everything you have *clearly seen* in this dream alchemy practice.

C. Do this visualisation regularly:

Imagine you are sitting in a room with a book on your lap opposite a window with a view to a distant mountain. Look at everything in the room, and everything you can see outside. See the people standing on top of the distant mountain, the drops of glistening rain forming a rainbow, the worm in the beak of the bird flying high. This dream alchemy is about being able to see everything in perfect focus, no matter how near or how far. It's important to look at small things in great detail over a range of distances each time you do this visualisation. You can look at different things each time you do this. Summon up the feeling throughout your visualisation of the power of insight and sharp focus.

Glimmers of gold
In your dreams
When your recurring dream stops or changes to embrace a happier ending, you are making good progress.

Some symbols from your dream alchemy practice may appear in your dreams. For example, you may dream of taking photos or joining people on a mountaintop.

Your dreams may release strong emotions such as the shock or anger that sent you into denial, or the hurt that caused your confusion. This is your dream's way of opening your eyes so that you can use them to make positive choices.

Look out for dreams where *all* your senses are vividly awake, and for dreams of solving puzzles.

In your waking life
All your senses are heightened, not only your sight. You are aware of small details and large-scale patterns.

You are more insightful and your intuition is stronger. You have a better feeling for the 'big picture' in every situation.

You are less concerned about keeping things as they were and more interested in considering the range of possibilities at your fingertips. You are willing to introduce change into situations to make them viable. You are willing to let some things go, knowing that when one door closes another opens.

You are more empowered to make choices and more trusting of the future.

38: Stormy weather

The dream

Dark clouds or a storm gather on the horizon, or are advancing towards you.

Take the silver-lined path, gathering the pearls gifted by the darkest storms.

In your dream perhaps ...
- You feel threatened when you see dark clouds or a whirlwind or tornado on the horizon.
- You hear thunder, or sense an oppressive storm, but cannot see it.
- You are being chased by a tornado.
- You are caught in a storm.
- You see lightning in the distance.

How do you feel in your dream?
Threatened. Oppressed. Heavy. Depressed. Frustrated. Fearful. Unsafe. Puzzled. Haunted. Angry. Doomed. Amazed. Awed. Enlightened. Inspired. Freed. Refreshed.

How does your dream end?
Positive changes are on the way if ...
- The air clears.
- You express anger or grief.
- You confront someone and resolve a conflict.
- You learn something new, or see something in a different light.
- You feel inspired.
- It rains and the rain feels good.

It's time for a new approach if ...
- The clouds or storm remain and you still feel threatened.

♦ You run away from the tornado, or try to hide.
♦ You are incapacitated in some way by the storm.

What your dream means
Your way forward may be blocked by ...
Anger or grief you have denied or not expressed. Feeling threatened or overburdened. Tension or a building depression. Fear of change or resistance to change. Feeling out of control with changes in your life. A lack of inspiration or a need to be enlightened about something.

Moving forward
Acknowledge and express anger or grief in an appropriate way. Give yourself permission to be sad, to cry, to release the tension and clear the air. Remember that every dark cloud has a silver lining, gift-wrapped in one of life's lessons. Let your dream show you what lies behind your emotional storm and address those issues. Work with change instead of allowing it to blow you around without your input, or instead of fighting it. Stay alert for that inspirational silver lining.

♦

Think of the rumbling roll of distant thunder as your grumbling anger ready to bellow out what has been held back, brewing and gathering force until it must be released.

It is as far away, in your dream, as you have pushed or denied it in your waking life. What you push away or deny needs to be expressed in an appropriate way. Once the thunder is overhead in your dream, you are really letting your anger rip as you sleep. Expect to wake up feeling exhausted, sad and teary for a few days as the emotions and feelings your anger tried to hide are exposed and let go. Anger is a temporary cover, a lid for the emotions you find hard to face. However, it is not a socially acceptable emotion so your dream may help you to understand the source of your anger as well as help you to work out the best way of expressing it.

As you dream you tune into feelings and emotions that are not so easy to detect awake. These feelings and emotions will creep up on you and explode in a major way if you don't take the dream warning and defuse them ahead of time. That's 'defuse' (applying thought and action) not deny.

Think of dream dark clouds as anger, negative thoughts or depression in waiting. When clouds rain in your dreams, you are releasing the heaviness, letting the depression out, letting tears do their healing work, washing the air and your mind clear and clean. Attending to and dispersing whatever part of your waking life the cloud represents reveals the silver lining all the sooner. Beyond the dark there is a gift of light, the solution to the problem or issue.

In dreams, air often represents your mind — those invisible thoughts that you then turn into a physical form like a painting, a story, a building or a new business. Wild and windy air is perhaps your mind in transition, changing pressure and speed, and capable of reshaping everything.

Tornadoes and whirlwinds (both in and out of dreams) are strong, dangerous and frightening winds made visible. Think of them as the winds of change gone wild. Your fear of them lies in their unpredictability — which way will they turn and how fast? These dreams show the wild, unpredictable changes shaping your life and how you are, or are not, dealing with them. Are they really so unpredictable, or do your dreams give you clues? Let your dreams show you how to work with the winds of change to gain control of your direction.

If you hide from your dream clouds and gathering storms, the threat will remain until it bursts into your waking life leaving you unprepared to deal with the situation in a positive, empowered way. You will run from your dream tornado until you drop because you cannot run from change. It will catch up with you and mould you unless you turn around and work with it.

The zigzag flash of brilliant lightning makes all visible, defuses the positive–negative atmospheric charge, and brings cool air and cleansing rain. We all need lightning in our life to bring balance and clear the air from time to time! Lightning *en*lightens, brings consciousness, clarity, light and understanding. Yes, sometimes it kills too, but death in dreams is usually about the death of the old to make way for the birth of the new — and *that* is what enlightenment is all about. Look around the edges of the lightning in your dream for the flash of inspiration, the moment of an insight that brings you light, and cool, easy breathing.

In your life this could be about ...

* The argument that left you feeling angry and unresolved.
* Mounting tension resulting from holding back your feelings.
* Emotional issues from the past stirred up by a phone call or situation that brought back memories.
* Unfinished grief following a death or loss of a job.
* Changes at work with job losses threatened.
* Sudden change — even exciting change.

Your unique dream contains personal clues only you may recognise

* If you are talking with someone in the dream when you notice the gathering storm, this gives you a clue about the emotional issue. Write down three words to describe the person's personality or approach to life and then write down the opposites to these. For example, you might have 'inconsiderate, selfish, tactless, considerate, unselfish, tactful'. The six words you have written are your clue. In this example, your struggle with finding the right balance of consideration for yourself and others and how tactfully (or not) you get your message across may be causing you tension.
* Keep a diary of how often these stormy weather dreams come up. You may see a pattern between the dreams and your menstrual cycle, or your meetings with a person at work, or a recurring issue with a friend or relation. Stormy weather dreams are about what's brewing, so your dream may precede the waking-life event.
* The position of the storm is a clue. If it is behind you, it is likely to be an emotional issue connected with the past or one that sneaks up on you. If it is in front of you, it

is likely to be a fear of a future threat or an emotional issue you can predict because of a pattern in your life. If it is to your right, it may relate to something happening in your outer world as your right side links with your left brain. (See 'I'll see you in my dreams', page 310.) If it is to your left it may be about what is going on within you.

Why has this dream come up for you now?

Your answers to these questions will reveal the reason:

- What feelings and emotions did you experience in your dream?
- Which situation in your life now do these feelings remind you of?
- If you voiced in a considerate way the things that upset you or make you angry, and if you were heard, what new challenges do you feel this could bring up for you?

Your answer to the last question may reveal the reason your dream has come up for you now. You want the emotional issues resolved, but you fear moving out of your present comfort zone.

Dream alchemy practice

Starting the inner work

This is what to *do* if you hope to see dramatic transformations in your life.

A. Write a conversation on paper (arrange this dream dialogue like a script) between the storm cloud in your dream and the sun that lights up the silver lining of the cloud. Start with the sun asking the cloud, 'What's brewing?' See what develops.

B. Do this dream alchemy visualisation:

Imagine the storm cloud (adapt this visualisation to suit your stormy dream symbol) in front of you and see yourself looking at it. Now imagine reaching forward to give it a comforting hug, as if offering a shoulder to cry on. As you touch the cloud pour love and support out to it and, as you do this, see it turn to light, float up and become a glorious rainbow. Now see yourself reaching to the pot of gold you can see at the end of the rainbow. Dip your hands inside and feel the cool liquid gold within. Bring out as much gold as you want and make it into a piece of jewellery to wear. Put it on and *feel* a sense of reward, joy and peace.

C. Here's an affirmation for you:

> My skin shimmers with all the silver linings of all the
> storms that have come my way. Guided by the light
> of this wisdom I have the skills to disperse any storm
> even before it gathers.

Glimmers of gold
In your dreams
When your recurring dream stops or changes to embrace a happier ending, you are making good progress.

Some symbols from your dream alchemy practice may appear in your dreams. For example, you may dream of dipping your hands into the rainbow's golden pot.

Your dreams may release your old storms, bringing anger, grief and tears that run free for a few days. This is your dream's way of clearing the air to give you a fresh start.

Look out for dreams in peaceful, serene settings; calm waters; and gentle fountains.

In your waking life
You are more confident about expressing your feelings and find ways to do so without causing unnecessary hurt.

You are more aware of the emotional patterns in your life, within both your body rhythms and your relationship and work cycles. In understanding the patterns, you see at first how to anticipate them and later how to break them.

You are more open to change and to changing attitudes and approaches.

You accept that some people may disappear from your life, knowing that the emotional storms that bound you together have now dispersed. New people and new situations enter your life as surely as the sun rises to greet a new dawn.

39: Decapitated!

Decapitated

The dream
You see a headless body or a decapitated head.

Attend to balancing your alchemy scales. Mix equal parts of thinking and feeling to balance the equation.

In your dream perhaps ...
- The headless body is alive and functioning normally despite being headless.
- The headless body holds its decapitated head. The head has a life of its own.
- The headless body is dead, but the decapitated head is alive and functioning.
- You see no body, only a detached but living head, or heads.
- You see no body, only dead heads.

How do you feel in your dream?
Shocked. Unfeeling. Detached. Fearful. Remote. Horrified. Accepting. Undisturbed. Confused. Curious.

How does your dream end?
Positive changes are on the way if ...
- The head or body gives you a message or enlightens you.
- You express shock or another deep feeling.
- The head and body are restored — the person becomes whole and lives.
- Either the headless body or the head dies and you are okay with this.

It's time for a new approach if ...
- You remain detached or unfeeling.

What your dream means

Your way forward may be blocked by ...

Too much head (thinking) and not enough heart (feeling). Being detached from feeling to shut away past hurt. Too much heart (feeling) and not enough head (thinking). Basically not taking a balanced head–heart approach.

Moving forward

Acknowledge your feelings (reattach your heart) or get your brain working (reattach your head) to sense the world and communicate with it through a perfectly balanced thinking–feeling mix.

◆

Shocking though this dream is, it is simple to interpret and awesome in its power to enrich your waking life if you take heed of its message.

In dreams your head generally symbolises your thinking, your heart generally symbolises your feelings and your gut generally symbolises your gut instinct. Next time you're overwhelmed by strong feelings, perhaps grief, anger, rejection, despondency or fear, close your eyes and ask yourself where the feeling is located in your body. The physical sensation you feel in response will probably not be in your head. In dreams, emotions and feelings tend to be pictured as belonging to the body, not the head.

Your throat or neck — the point of decapitation — may be the location for many feelings. Think of your neck as being a bridge between your head and heart, the place where your thoughts and feelings mingle and blend to produce a balanced response. Shouldn't life be a balanced head–heart approach? It's not surprising, perhaps, that your voice box is in your neck — the best place to communicate your perfectly balanced thinking–feeling mix.

In yoga and in dreams, your neck is the location of the fifth chakra (energy point) and its function is communication and healing. With the right words you can heal yourself and others.

When feelings seem too difficult to deal with you repress them, shut off the source of the discomfort and move your

271

consciousness into your head. You leave the 'heart person' of your being buried and unexpressed. You become detached from your feelings, like a head detached from a body, as this dream depicts. Ask someone to listen to the way you talk. If your conversation is peppered with 'I think' and not 'I feel' then you may be in that head space.

How is it that you can end up retreating into head space, leaving your heart shut down? Hurt or rejection are usually at the basis of your withdrawal. Your shutdown is usually so complete that when your dreams draw your attention to what you have done the full force of your feelings comes as a shock. You may feel the shock in your dream, or you or someone else may show it with a classic wide-eyed, dropped-jaw expression.

Have you withdrawn into a thinking head space or have you withdrawn into a feeling heart space? There are times when you can't think through a situation because your emotions are too intense. You lose your cool; you lose your head!

Watch this dream to restore the balance between thinking and feeling.

In your life this could be about ...

- A crisis in your life that you have not yet cried about
- A difficulty you have in relating to someone you see as 'emotional'.
- A sense of being out of touch with other people or not being on the same planet as them.
- Your loss of passion and excitement.
- Your pride in being rational or scientific.
- A crisis that has left you with intense emotions that you cannot get past.
- Your fear of resolving a situation because it will take away the emotional drama that you thrive on.

Your unique dream contains personal clues only you may recognise

- Look for what else is missing in your dream as a clue to the situation in your life that is out of balance. Perhaps colour is missing in your dream, giving you a clue to a situation in your life that is bland.

♦ Look for location dream puns to pinpoint your waking-life situation. For example, if the dream is set in a desert, where are you isolated in waking life or where has there been a desertion? If the head is found in a well, where is health an issue for you (wellness), or what are you wishing for (wishing well) but not getting?

♦ Evidence of what you are out of touch with in waking life may be shown in your dream as something you can't reach or touch. A laughing child always one step beyond your reach may give you a clue about your detachment from play and fun in a situation that you are taking too seriously, for example.

Why has this dream come up for you now?

Your answers to these questions will reveal the reason:

♦ What feelings and emotions did you experience in your dream?

♦ Which situation in your life now do these feelings remind you of?

♦ Who or what puzzles you most in your life right now? Has this person or situation been particularly challenging or in the forefront of your mind recently?

♦ What would be your greatest fear if you woke up and found yourself in this situation or living as this person (from your answer to the question above)?

Your answer to the last question may reveal the reason your dream has come up for you now. The thing you fear is the reason you are escaping into your head or heart in a way that is out of balance. Dreams draw your attention to what is out of balance in your life and why.

Dream alchemy practice
Starting the inner work

This is what to *do* if you hope to see dramatic transformations in your life.

A. Here's an affirmation for you:

> My body is whole and complete, from the top of my
> head to the tips of my fingers and toes. I am thought
> and feeling. I am head and heart. I speak and move as
> one. I am perfect balance and harmony.

B. *This dream alchemy practice puts you back in touch with your heart:*

Find photos of yourself from as far back as you can. If you have no photos, dig out other memorabilia from your past. If you have nothing like this, find music, books or videos to take you back down memory lane. (Altogether, collect at least twenty items.) Also buy a good quality notebook or diary.

Each day pick one photo, piece of music or memento and let it take you back. Close your eyes and ask yourself one question only, 'Where do I *feel* this memory in my body?' Be patient with yourself as you may find this difficult when you have been out of touch with your heart. Just wait until you become aware of a part of your body and that is your answer. Make a record in your notebook. Simply write the date, a brief description of the item ('photo of me when I was seven at the beach with my father') and the place in your body where you feel the memory ('I feel this memory in my stomach'). If you are inspired, write more! Repeat this every day for a different item. As this dream alchemy practice involves at least twenty items, this will take you at least twenty days.

C. *This dream alchemy practice puts you back in touch with your head:*

Choose your weapon. Pick a game or puzzle that demands thought and reasoning (for example, chess, crossword puzzles), enrol for a course in logic or philosophy or teach yourself a practical logical skill.

Glimmers of gold
In your dreams
When your recurring dream stops or changes to embrace a happier ending, you are making good progress.

Some symbols from your dream alchemy practice may appear in your dreams. For example, you may dream of looking through old photo albums.

Your dreams may release a rush of emotions and feelings you've held back and some of these may spill over into your waking life. Let it happen. This is your dream's way of getting you fully functional again.

Look out for sensual dreams in vivid colour (if you're getting back in touch with your heart) and dreams of machines and puzzle solutions (if you're getting back in touch with your head).

In your waking life
You are more aware of everything going on around you. Your senses are heightened and you feel whole.

You understand and empathise with other people more easily and enjoy communicating more than you did before.

You feel that you belong rather than feeling you are out on a limb. You are more interested in sharing feelings as well as ideas.

You see solutions to problems more quickly. You have a better feel for the 'big picture'. Your lateral and creative thinking expands — you might have thought it was good before, but it is even sharper now!

40: Plane crash

Plane crash
(Also see 1: I'm flying; 33: Trapped and under attack; 34: On the cliff edge or falling)

The dream

A plane crashes, or people or things fall from a plane.

To manifest gold, work with air. Make the invisible visible, toss the rejects, perfect the formula and then pilot the dream.

In your dream perhaps ...

- You watch a plane climb too steeply, go into a spin and explode.
- You watch or hear a plane exploding in mid-air or being shot down.
- You watch or hear a plane fall from the sky.
- You watch a plane crash into something.
- You are the pilot of the crashing plane.
- You are in the plane when it starts to fall.
- People or things fall from a plane and may die.
- You see the site of a plane crash or help survivors.
- People fall from a plane and survive, unhurt.

How do you feel in your dream?

Terrified. Shocked. Out of control. Powerless. Unsafe. Sad. Amazed. Relieved. Heroic. A sense of inevitability. Doomed. A sense of grief. A sense of gratitude. Guilty. Responsible.

How does your dream end?

Positive changes are on the way if ...

- There are survivors.
- You are falling, in the plane, with a feeling of letting go and acceptance.
- The crash seems inevitable and you accept this.

- You express grief or gratitude.
- You feel relieved by the end of the dream.

It's time for a new approach if ...
- You are falling, in the plane, terrified.
- People are suffering.
- You realise that the plane was flying dangerously.

What your dream means
Your way forward may be blocked by ...
Ideas that are falling short of taking material form. Ways of thinking and fears that threaten a successful outcome. Losing impetus. Holes in your thinking or hesitation about taking the final steps to see an idea become a material reality. Bad planning. Fear of failure, fear of success. Self-sabotage. An idea that is outdated and needs to be dropped.

Moving forward
There are times to build ideas all the way to fruition and there are times to let them go. Life is full of change and there comes a time to let go of old ways of thinking. Question whether you are your own worst enemy, sabotaging your best ideas because of self-doubt or fear of success or failure. Plan well but also play your best ideas all the way through to fruition.

◆

The fear of flying is a big issue for many people. There is fear about having your feet off the ground, about crashing, about being at the mercy of the pilot or weather conditions, about being taken hostage and about being blown up. Particular plane crashes can play their way into your dreams, symbolising whatever fears were raised for you personally.

While planes may dream-crash their way through expressing your fears, consider them in dreams as planes of thought.

Let's go to the basics. Consider the ground as the physical and material world you make manifest. For instance, you have an idea that you may or may not take action on to bring to fruition. You conjure up something out of the 'thin air' and an idea becomes a thing. Look up from this book and look around you. Everything manmade that you can see started as an idea. Even the placement of some of the natural features you see started as ideas — the planting of a garden, the stream protected from pollution, the extra-green grass made possible by a watering system. You are reading words on a page in a book that are manifesting as typed letters on my computer screen at 3.59 p.m. on 16 December. For every thing there is a moment of transition from invisible thought to visible matter.

Many ideas fall short of becoming matter. You lose impetus or you see holes in your thinking and instead of safely landing these planes of thought, bringing your ideas to fruition, they implode. And so a dream plane crashes.

Your dream planes may show how you handle your ideas, your 'air'. You pilot the concept, but can you land the plane, or is this an idea destined to crash? Fly an idea too fast, too soon or run it too steeply overlooking the practicalities and you may go into a spin, overshoot the mark, burn out or explode. Fly it too slow and you may lose momentum and crash. Forget to plan for obstacles or ignore those huge barriers of your own fears and hesitations and you crash again.

Your crashing planes may be your crashing ideas. The circumstances of the crash expound the reason. Sometimes it is your own fears and expectations (of failure, perhaps) that sabotage the idea, and sometimes it is your own realisation that this idea is not really ready to land. Perhaps it no longer applies to where you are in your waking life.

You may hear a faraway plane crash in your dream and, strangely, feel okay about this. There are times to build ideas and times to let them go. See the people who die in these dream-plane crashes as standing for ideas and thinking patterns that have to go.

Bombs in your plane-crash dream should send you looking into the mirror to see if you are sabotaging yourself. Hostage situations should get you thinking about how or why you could be holding your ideas or yourself to ransom, placing restrictions on yourself or feeling restricted for some kind of cause.

Clear that airspace of fears, relax your mind, let go of

clutter, ride that plane of thought and, if it all seems to hang together well, pilot it to a successful landing.

In your life this could be about ...

- The project that almost succeeded but seems now to have run out of momentum.
- A long-term course of study that you are thinking of dropping.
- Your early excitement for a business venture, followed by your frustration that the whole thing takes time to come to fruition.
- An adventure you've been planning for so long that it's time to face the fact that your fear is stopping you from making your plans a reality.
- A change in your life that has a domino effect on older plans — they are no longer important.
- Your new way of seeing the world (a new spiritual or personal approach, or the result of doing dream alchemy) which puts a natural end to old ways of thinking.

Your unique dream contains personal clues only you may recognise

- How the plane crashes gives you a clue about why your idea is not shaping up. For example, fire may suggest recent anger, burning enthusiasm or burnout.
- Where the plane was headed is a clue. For example, New Zealand might be a clue for something you're newly passionate about (new zeal).
- Anyone on your dream plane from the past may give you a clue about the beginning of the plane of thought now crashing, according to your current frame of mind.

Why has this dream come up for you now?

Your answers to these questions will reveal the reason:

- What feelings and emotions did you experience in your dream?
- Which situation in your life now do these feelings remind you of?
- Has there been a change of priorities in your life recently?

◆ Has anyone recently challenged you about your plans or ideas in a way that has caused you to doubt?

◆ If your most cherished plan or idea were to come to successful fruition, what new challenges do you feel this would bring up for you?

Your answer to the last question may reveal the reason your dream has come up for you now. Your plans will succeed when you overcome your fear of what the success may bring.

Dream alchemy practice
Starting the inner work

This is what to *do* if you hope to see dramatic transformations in your life.

A. If you have decided your dream was not about a necessary letting go, and you really want your plan or idea to materialise, here's your dream alchemy practice. Do this visualisation regularly:

Imagine yourself back in your dream, only this time you are flying the plane and you can do it easily. Take the dream back to the point of take-off, before the trouble began. *Feel* a sense of calm confidence in yourself as a capable pilot and allow yourself also to feel the excitement of knowing that this plane is going to land successfully. Land your plane in a place of your choice — perhaps somewhere that symbolises what you want to achieve in waking life.

B. If someone from your past was in your dream plane, imagine they knew that the plane would crash and they had time to write you a letter. Write that letter yourself. Keep it for a day then read it again. Reply, this time as yourself writing a thank-you letter. If you have decided your dream was about a necessary letting go, write the letter to be read aloud at the memorial service. If you have decided your dream crash was a warning and you want to keep the plane in the air and successfully land it, write it as a 'Wasn't it amazing that the plane was saved after all? I want to take this opportunity to thank you ...' letter.

C. If you tend to sabotage your own plans, falling short of grounding your ideas into physical reality, here's your dream alchemy. Buy a sapling tree — perhaps a 'plane tree' or a type of tree that symbolises what you want to manifest — and plant it in your garden or get permission to plant it in a public space you regularly visit. Water it, look after it and watch it grow. Talk to it of your progress. Your healthy growing tree is your constant reminder that you *can* change the shape of the world around you through grounding your ideas and carrying them through to completion.

Glimmers of gold
In your dreams
When your recurring dream stops or changes to embrace a happier ending, you are making good progress.

Some symbols from your dream alchemy practice may appear in your dreams. For example, you may dream of piloting a plane to a successful landing.

Your dreams may release emotions and images from your past related to your fear of landing this particular dream plane, or many before it. This is your dream's way of pulling the pin on the self-sabotage! Next trip, it's all the way!

Look out for dreams of earthworks, landscaping and building as well as some practical pointers to how to successfully realise your idea or business.

In your waking life
You are more confident in a grounded, calm way rather than in a motivated, hyped-up way.

You see more reasons for doing than reasons for not doing. The positives far outweigh the negatives. You see solutions for the negatives.

You look forward instead of looking for escape routes or excuses.

Your planning skills are more sound and you know when to bring others 'on board' and how to involve them. You are focused on outcomes, but you are comfortable with the lead-up unfolding at a steady pace.

You get off the merry-go-round and arrive somewhere. You harvest the rewards of at least one of your ideas.

41: Death and murder

Death, murder

(Also see 2: Dead body discovered; 7: Losing or forgetting the baby or child; 25: Cuts, wounds, blood, guts and vomit; 30: A visit from spirit?; 34: On the cliff edge — or falling; 39: Decapitated!)

The dream

Someone dies a natural death, is killed in an accident or is murdered.

To transform the stone into gold undo it until it is no longer a stone.

In your dream perhaps ...
- You witness a murder.
- You kill someone.
- Someone dies of disease or old age.
- You're at a funeral service.
- You are killed.
- You feel yourself dying.
- You witness a death at the scene of an accident.

How do you feel in your dream?
Angry. A sense of grief or loss. Hopeless. Defeated. Exhausted. Horrified. Detached. Devastated. Guilty. Fearful. Desolate. Shocked. Released. Freed. A sense of duty. Forgiving. At ease. Enlightened. Loving. Inspired.

How does your dream end?
Positive changes are on the way if ...
- You express anger or grief in the dream.
- You express forgiveness.
- You see a loving spirit leave the dead body.
- There is a sense of relief and ease following the death.
- There is a sense of destiny in the outcome.
- You witness the burial with love and letting go.
- You move on to do something positive.

It's time for a new approach if ...

◆ You feel something was unfinished or unsaid between you and the person who died.

◆ You feel guilty at the end of the dream.

◆ You feel haunted in the dream.

What your dream means

Your way forward may be blocked by ...

A dead-end situation or old ways of thinking and being that need to be ended. Attitudes, appearances, beliefs, habits, jobs or relationships no longer working for you. Something you're killing off too early, such as a skill you still need, support and care for a child leaving home, an exercise regime or a valuable relationship.

Moving forward

Life is about growing and changing. Let your dreams show you when to let go and where you might be ending something too early.

◆

So you wake up in shock because you've just killed your housemate, witnessed a gruesome fatal road accident or attended your own funeral. The last thing on your mind is telling anyone about your dream — surely there's something massively wrong with such dark dreaming? Right? Wrong!

Many people stay stuck in old ruts, missing life's best adventures. They are dead bored and unhappy, feeling that something is missing but not quite knowing what. Life is about *change*. As you grow and change, physically, mentally, emotionally and spiritually, you experience little deaths and births. Death of the old you and of your old appearance, self-image, thoughts, attitudes, habits, ways of solving problems, mental barriers, ways of being, relationships, courses, jobs ... The only way to move forward and change is to let these old ways die. Then you birth new ways of being, new relationships, new paths, new attitudes.

Dreams of death help us to 'exchange' dead-end situations for more fulfilling ones. Your dreams often use death to show what is dying off within you so that you are free to move forward.

Sometimes your death dreams warn you that you are killing off things (relationships, ways of thinking) that you would be better to keep alive, even to put more energy into.

Is your dream about letting something die so that you can move forward, or is it warning you to keep something alive? As always, the details in your dream provide the extra information you need.

What does it mean if the people dying in your dreams are people you know? Take a deep breath and remind yourself that the people you dream about are *not* going to die; they are *not* themselves. They stand for your thoughts and feelings about who they are — not for who they actually are. They represent the beliefs you've learned from them or the attitudes you've developed in response to knowing them. If they're dying or you're killing them, then the dream is about the particular *belief* you are ending.

You've got to forgive dreams for their love of high drama in getting a message across because it certainly works as an attention-grabbing device.

In your life this could be about ...

- Your years as a child ending so that your years as an adult can begin.
- Your life as a single person ending so that you can begin a new life with your partner.
- The need to end your habit of eating junk food and start eating healthily.
- The need to put an end to the way you allow yourself to be used by someone.
- Your decision to cut off financial support for someone who is now independent.
- The natural end of a cycle — divorce, menopause or retirement, for example.
- The need to end an addiction — to drugs, cigarettes or overwork, perhaps.

Your unique dream contains personal clues only you may recognise

- A natural death gives you a clue about a natural ending

of something in your life — the end of a natural cycle or the completion of grieving, for example. Be aware, though, that you might be seeing something die an apparently natural death prematurely through lack of attention and nurturing — your sex life, for example.

- A murder or killing that you feel okay about in your dream gives you a clue about something you need to kill off within yourself. Who is being killed? Write down three words to describe their personality or approach to life. Where, in your life now, are any of these approaches working against you?

- Look for dream puns or clichés as clues. A dying nun may be a clue to ending a habit (the nun's clothing). A dead body with the nose cut off might be a clue to a situation in which you are 'cutting off your nose to spite your face' and need to put an end to this.

Why has this dream come up for you now?
Your answers to these questions will reveal the reason:

- What feelings and emotions did you experience in your dream?
- Which situation in your life now do these feelings remind you of?
- Is something coming to a natural end in your life now?
- Is something coming to a premature end in your life now?
- Where are you feeling most stuck in your life right now?
- Has someone or something challenged you about this situation recently?
- Imagine yourself moving on from this situation. What new challenges do you feel this would bring you?

Either something is coming to a natural end in your life now or you are ready to make a change but are held back by the fear of the challenges you think this may bring.

Dream alchemy practice
Starting the inner work
This is what to *do* if you hope to see dramatic transformations in your life.

A. Write a conversation between the person who died in your dream and the cause of death (the weapon, old age, for example). Arrange the conversation like a script on your page. Start the conversation with the person asking the weapon (or cause of death), 'Why you?' Let the dialogue flow from there.

B. *This dream alchemy practice is designed for when you have identified something in your life that is dying off because you have let it slip away (your art, or time to play and have fun, for example) but you want to keep it alive and put energy into it.*

Do this visualisation regularly:

Imagine yourself back in the dream and take yourself back to the point just before the death. Now change the ending. See yourself putting energy into the person, breathing life into them, spending time with them or whatever feels right to you. Visualise a glow of white light energy around the person and *feel* the vitality of this rebirth within your own body. *Feel* the feelings you want to experience by bringing this quality back into your life. Embrace the now vibrantly living person.

C. *This dream alchemy practice is for when you have identified something in your life that you are ready to let die.*

Take three days to collect things to build a small temporary shrine in gratitude and memory of what must now be put to rest. (Whatever you leave behind and no matter how keen you are to move on, there must be a thanksgiving for what you have learned and there must be a grieving process. Without thanks and without grief, you will find yourself looking back with guilt or with a feeling of something being unresolved.)

On the fourth day, build your shrine in a corner of your home or on a shelf or in your garden. On the fifth day, write a thank-you card or letter and place it on the shrine. On the sixth day, plant a seed or cutting in a small pot and place it on the shrine, or buy a bunch of flowers still in bud and place them in a vase of water on the shrine. Watch the growth of the seedling or the blossoming of the flowers over the next days, seeing and *feeling* new life springing from the old. When you are ready, move the seedling or flowers to a new place (or make pot-pourri or something new and creative from the petals) and take down (or dig in) the shrine.

Glimmers of gold
In your dreams
When your recurring dream stops or changes to embrace a happier ending, you are making good progress.

Some symbols from your dream alchemy practice may appear in your dreams. For example, you may dream of visiting a shrine.

Your dreams may release emotions such as grief and you may be teary for a few days while you say your goodbyes to the old way. This is your dream's way of helping you to close this door in peace so that the next door can open fully to reveal its treasures.

Look out for dreams of births.

In your waking life
You are more energetic and feel more alive. You may surprise yourself and others by a dramatic change in the way you look. You may get your hair styled or coloured differently or choose a new look in clothes, but you may also notice a change in weight (without dieting), body shape or facial expression.

Where something seemed to be missing before, life now feels rounded and more whole.

Your priorities change. You become more aware of changing seasons, in the weather, and in people, cultures, attitudes and the times.

You feel wiser.

Our uncommon dreams

For successful alchemy, precipitate the invisible and amalgamate the indivisible.

Once upon a dream time

Your quest is to precipitate the solution, to find the magical combination of elements that together create a solid vision which can be transformed in waking life ...

When you have a dream that is not described by any of the 41 common dreams, using the Storyline Method is your starting point. Always begin, as with any good story, at the beginning.

The Storyline Method

How would you feel if you went to the theatre and saw a play that did not have a satisfactory final scene? Imagine sitting in the audience taking in all the details, keeping track of the twists and turns of the plot only to be left hanging. What happened next? Did the butler do it? Will you ever know?

Some plays are like that. Some dreams are too. But what conventional plays and dreams have in common is a storyline. The stage curtain opens and there is the first scene, the opening situation. The drama moves on and, pretty soon, some tension is introduced in the form of a question or a problem to be resolved. Now you're sitting on the edge of your seat. What is the answer? How will they solve this? The play then moves to action. Various things are tried out, some moving the characters closer to a solution and some leading them up the garden path. Now, this is where you *don't* want the final curtain to come down! You eagerly await the resolution to the whole drama and here it comes, the final scene. How did it turn out? Which of all those actions and thoughts were the ones that led to the perfect solution? Or, if the resolution was not so desirable, where did it all start to go wrong? How could a better outcome have been achieved? What was the lesson to be learned or the moral of the story?

You leave the theatre contemplating the final scenes. What if they could have turned back the clock and done things differently? A tear surprises you, a choke in your throat. 'What's wrong?' asks your companion. 'Oh, it's just, well, that bit in the play where they … it just reminded me of when I …'

Talking of tears, let's call a quick scene change. There you are now sitting in the dark cinema. The movie is almost finished. How many soggy tissues are you squeezing in your hand? How often do you watch a movie that has nothing to do with you and your life and yet something in it resonates with something in you and calls forth a cascade of tears? (And do you feel better afterwards or not?)

Plays and movies carry you along in their drama until they trigger an element of recognition. You may consider it strange that something fictional and so removed from your everyday life could have such an effect, but it isn't really. This is the stuff dreams are made of. Your dreams are stories, every bit as dramatic and apparently removed from everyday life as the play or movie you last saw.

Your dreams speak in stories. Between the lines of your dream story, your waking life emerges. But first, you need to learn the art of looking between these lines.

How to use the Storyline Method

The Storyline Method of dream interpretation sometimes reveals everything you need to know, but sometimes it needs to be used along with the other methods described.

Now, if you are sitting comfortably we'll begin. Once upon a dream time …

Start by writing or telling your dream as a story.

Many good stories can be divided into four parts. These are:

The situation: the opening theme.

The question or problem: the first question or problem to come up.

The action: what happens next — there may be one action or there may be more than one.

The resolution: what happens at the end of the story or how it turns out.

(Some dream stories don't get to the end, so don't worry if yours doesn't! This is covered later in this chapter.)

Step one
Divide your dream into four parts

To help you divide your dream story into these four parts, consider Taya's dream.

The dream: Extra room

> I discover an expansive room hidden in my home. What I see there changes my attitude to my house. A cat helps guide me.

I'm living in this small apartment. I'm not ecstatic about it, but I feel comfortable and safe. Everything feels familiar, right down to a whole lot of old furniture and posters from my house-sharing student days. There's just me and this feeling of pride at what I've made of this tiny space because I've arranged the old furniture to fit so perfectly. Then I discover a door I've never seen before and I'm amazed. I open it and there's a sensational room. This enormous room has been hidden inside the small apartment all this time. It's all light and space and art. Not much furniture but totally 'right'. It's expansive and free, not calculated and careful like the rest of the place. Suddenly my old apartment rooms seem cramped. I'm worried that if I leave this room I won't be able to find the door again. I see a bright-eyed cat curled on a window-seat cushion. I pick her up and carry her into the apartment. Like a compass, she will lead me if I forget my way back. Back in the old rooms I decide to toss out some of the old stuff. I picture converting the whole place in the style of the extra room.

Now here is Taya's dream again, divided into the four parts:

The situation

I'm living in this small apartment. I'm not ecstatic about it, but I feel comfortable and safe. Everything feels familiar, right down to a whole lot of old furniture and posters from my house-sharing student days. There's just me and this feeling of pride at what I've made of this tiny space because I've arranged the old furniture to fit so perfectly.

The question or problem
Then I discover a door I've never seen before and I'm amazed. I open it and there's a sensational room. This enormous room has been hidden inside the small apartment all this time. It's all light and space and art. Not much furniture but totally 'right'. It's expansive and free, not calculated and careful like the rest of the place. Suddenly my old apartment rooms seem cramped. I'm worried that if I leave this room I won't be able to find the door again.

The action
I see a bright-eyed cat curled on a window-seat cushion. I pick her up and carry her into the apartment. Like a compass, she will lead me if I forget my way back.

The resolution
Back in the old rooms I decide to toss out some of the old stuff. I picture converting the whole place in the style of the extra room.

When you've done this for your dream, the next step is to reduce each part to a summary. Here's a sample from Taya's dream:

Step two
Reduce the parts of your dream to summaries
Situation summary
I am proud of the way I have made the most of a restricted space and I feel safe having old, familiar things around me.

Question summary
How could this extra room have been here all this time, why is it so different from the rest of the house, and how will I ever be able to find it again?

Action summary
Take the cat from the extra room into the old space because cats always know their way home.

Resolution summary
It's time to toss out some of the old, familiar stuff and bring in the free, expansive, arty feel of the extra room.

The next step is to relate your dream story to your waking life. This is how it's done.

Step three
In your life this could be about …
Take each summary and turn it into a question about your waking life. Then answer it. Follow Taya's example:

The situation
Q. *In which situation in my life do I feel proud about how I've managed some restriction to give me a safe feeling of familiarity?*
A. I feel restricted by my job but proud that I perform well. It sometimes reminds me of being at university, limited to studying the subject I chose at eighteen because my parents thought it would get me a well-paid job.

The question or problem
Q. *What is the extra space I have discovered? Why is it so different and how will I ever be able to find it again?*
A. I have been thinking of starting a new business — a very creative, art-based enterprise. Looking at this dream has brought back memories of my childhood when I was good at arty things, but I lost touch with these dreams when my parents warned me that art would not pay a regular wage. I did a 'sensible' degree at university. Can I really get back in touch with that feeling again: the feeling that I can make money from my interest in art?

The action
Q. *The effect of taking the cat from the extra room into the old space was to make me feel more confident that I could find my way back into the extra room again because cats always know their way home. What is it in my life that I can rely on to help me get back in touch with the feeling that I have*

extra room in my life for art, and that working with art may release me from the restrictions of my familiar, safe job?

A. Cats are independent creatures: cats wouldn't stop to listen to someone else's account of what's best for them. Cats just know what's good for them, just as they always know their way home. There is a part of me that is like a cat, intuitively knowing what's good for me. I can rely on my intuition to lead me to the best place.

The resolution

Q. *What old, familiar stuff can I toss out to bring in the feel of arty extra space?*

A. I can toss the old, familiar conditioning and expectations from my parents and university days that art and intuition do not pay the bills. This will open up my extra potential (extra room) to create my art business with more confidence.

Using the Storyline Method you can gain remarkable insight about your waking life and see new solutions to old problems. This is easier if your dream resolution is a positive one — a happy final scene to your night's drama. But if your dream resolution is not so great, or if it is entirely missing, you may need to use a variation of this method to arrive at your best waking-life solution.

If your dream resolution is not desirable ...

Let's go back to basics to remind us of how dream resolutions are made, or not made. Understand this and you have the key to turn problems in your waking life around.

Imagine your dream being coordinated and produced in a huge old-fashioned filing room. Filing cabinets line the room, some drawers are open and files going back a long way are scattered over the floor. Detectives, researchers and historians are hard at work. The movie director stands close by, ready to cast the next dream scene. The clock is ticking. They have till dawn to create your dream.

Why a filing room? Your dreams are the result of your mind sorting out everything that you experienced in the forty-eight hours before you fell asleep. As well as your conscious daytime experiences, there are your unconscious ones. So much happens in a day that you don't consciously note it, but your unconscious mind takes it all in. It hears the clock ticking, it notices the fly zooming past just out of your normal range of sight and it notices the menacing tone in someone's voice that you choose to ignore.

As you dream, your mind sorts through these conscious and unconscious experiences and compares them with all your past experiences, memories, thoughts, feelings and beliefs. Your dream brings up old memories and feelings that are similar to these recent ones, so you see glimpses of the past in your dream. It notices where you have changed your feelings about something or changed your attitude so it brings up the past and files it in different drawers to mark the changes. Your dream reflects the changes you have made, showing you relating differently to how you have related in the past.

Every day you experience new things and it is your dreaming mind's task to follow through on your experiences and update your world view. As you dream, your mind looks for the latest best-fitting picture of your world as you know it. It picks up on the questions and unresolved business of the last forty-eight hours and shows you new creative possibilities and how these could turn out for you in the resolution part of the dream. Sometimes the creative solution that the dream tries misfires, leading to an uncomfortable resolution, a different problem or no resolution at all.

Think of your dreams as projecting ahead so that you can choose the best solutions. Or think of your dreams as trying out different combinations of jigsaw puzzle pieces so that you can choose the best of all possible pictures.

The hardest task for your dreaming mind is to sort out the conflicts between your conscious beliefs and your unconscious beliefs. When these are opposite to each other, things do not generally work out well for you in your waking life. Remember that your unconscious mind is far stronger than your conscious mind, so your unconscious beliefs and conditioned ways of thinking will always override your conscious ones. Dreams that end in conflict, that end unsatisfactorily, or that have no ending are often due to irreconcilable differences between your conscious and unconscious mind. The secret is to interpret your dream so that you can see the opposing beliefs and trace their origins. Then you apply your dream alchemy to change the unconscious beliefs that need to be changed to help you move forward.

Before moving on to see how the Storyline Method can help you to create the right dream alchemy, let's look at how to use the method to understand what dreams that are unresolved or have undesirable resolutions mean.

How to use the Storyline Method for dreams with undesirable resolutions

We'll apply this method to Catie's dream.

The dream: Missing the plane

I'm travelling alone, heading for the airport. My journey becomes a farce and prevents me from catching the plane. I'm on my way to the airport and I'm travelling alone. This is excitement! I'm heading for some exotic, adventurous destination that's more about conquering mountain peaks than slamming tequilas. More about untrodden valleys than downtrodden tourist routes. I get to the airport and queue for a ticket but then I don't have the right cash, so off I go to look for a bank. I get the money I need and return to the ticket counter, but now I'm at the end of the line again. Don't tell me I'm going to miss the plane! Okay, so then I do get my ticket and I'm waiting to get my baggage checked in. I've got one eye on the time and one eye on this cute guy who's also travelling alone and then my cabin bag bursts. My underwear starts falling out just as the cute guy decides to cast his eye my way and right when my unwashed underwear starts trailing from my bag as I run to hide my blushes ... Well then the dream just goes crazy. The gate is in sight, the plane engines are starting up and I realise I've got two odd shoes on so I can't run and ... I always wake up before I get there with my heart pounding and adrenaline pumping.

Step one
Divide your dream into four parts

Start in the same way as for Taya's dream example.

The situation

I'm on my way to the airport and I'm travelling alone. This is excitement! I'm heading for some exotic, adventurous destination that's more about conquering mountain peaks than slamming tequilas. More about untrodden valleys than downtrodden tourist routes.

The question or problem

I get to the airport and queue for a ticket but then I don't have the right cash, so off I go to look for a bank. I get the money I need and return to the ticket counter, but now I'm at the end of the line again. Don't tell me I'm going to miss the plane! Okay, so then I do get my ticket and I'm waiting to get my baggage checked in. I've got one eye on the time and one eye on this cute guy who's also travelling alone and then my cabin bag bursts. My underwear starts falling out just as the cute guy decides to cast his eye my way and right when my unwashed underwear starts trailing from my bag as I run to hide my blushes ... Well then the dream just goes crazy. The gate is in sight, the plane engines are starting up and I realise I've got two odd shoes on so I can't run and ...

The action

(This part is missing.)

The resolution

I always wake up before I get there with my heart pounding and adrenaline pumping.

Step two
Reduce the parts of your dream to summaries

Continue with the same method even though some of the four parts are missing.

Situation summary

I'm excited about travelling alone to a foreign destination with a sense of accomplishment and unique purpose.

Problem summary

I am constantly delayed.

Action summary

I take no action other than to go with the flow — or go with the obstacles.

Resolution summary

There is no resolution. The problem remains unsolved.

See already that there *was* an action? It was a decision for 'no action' (whether it was a conscious or unconscious decision) that Catie made — a decision to be passive.

Also, there may be no dream resolution, but this in itself gives information: the problem remains unsolved. This reminds us that there *is* a solution, but so far it hasn't been found or applied.

Step three
In your life this could be about …

Turn the summaries into questions — then answer them. Continue as for Taya's dream example:

The situation

Q. *Where, in my life, am I excited about going alone to a new destination with a sense of accomplishment and unique purpose?*

A. My relationship! Or should I say, 'not my relationship'. There are things I want to discover and explore about life that I can't do with my current partner. Lately I've been thinking of ending my four-year relationship and the prospect excites me.

The question or problem

Q. *What constantly delays me from taking off on this solo journey?*

A. Not wanting to upset my partner and being afraid of being on my own in unfamiliar territory. Anxiety about flying too high and losing sight of the things I like about being in a relationship.

The action

Q. *Why don't I take action?*

A. I have fear and anxiety of letting go of the present and of hurting my partner.

The resolution

Q. *Why is my situation unresolved?*

A. I am putting obstacles in my way so I don't have to face the fear and anxiety. I am delaying my take-off.

The Storyline Method, when used on unresolved dreams or dreams with undesirable resolutions, still gives you insight into what is happening — and why — in your waking life. What it doesn't do so well is guide you towards actions or beliefs that will improve things for you. This is where you need to do the dream alchemy practices to change the unconscious beliefs that are blocking your way.

Remember that the Storyline Method is just one of the dream interpretation tools you need to get a handle on your uncommon dreams and your life.

I'll see you in my dreams

Seek the second element in the mirror of belief.

The people who appear in your dream are the keys to identifying the burning issues and beliefs your dream is exploring.

The Identity Method

Have you ever wondered how often you appear in other people's dreams and what roles you play in them? It could be quite a worrying thought, but you can be certain that you, or at least a dream character that looks and sounds like you, stars, co-stars and has cameo parts in many other dreamers' night movies.

If you think you're not important enough to be the stuff of other people's dreams, think again. How many people have you dreamed about who have been only fleetingly a part of your life? A student from your schooldays that you hardly knew at the time, the old lady you never spoke to who lived on the corner of your street, the homeless man who sleeps at the bus stop? Frequently the people you hardly notice with your eyes open make sure they're seen and heard in your dreams alongside those who annoy or inspire you and those you share your life with. Think again about your list of dream-film credits!

Just as you are not responsible for anything you say or do in other people's dreams, people featuring in your dreams are not responsible for their words or actions. They are there because your dreaming mind has put them there to help you to understand more about yourself.

When you were born you didn't know you were separate from the world and the people around you. Your senses were totally bombarded. In your early weeks and months you dreamed long hours looking for the picture to best fit this strange new world and your place in it.

Little by little you began to distinguish between you and

not-you, though this was never easy. It was the hardest task and still is. You learn where your body begins and ends but you are still unsure about the boundaries of your mind and your soul. Your head and heart entwine with the heads and hearts of others as you dance the complicated dynamics of relating to family, friends, colleagues and strangers. In order to 'get on' with others or in the world you agree, disagree, compromise, influence or are influenced; you express and repress your thoughts, feelings and beliefs.

You became a complex individual, shaped by your experiences of the people around you. Or should that be 'you shaped yourself through your experiences of the people around you'?

Are you shaped by others or do you shape yourself according to your experience of others? This question — and your answer — is crucial to understanding the meaning behind the cast of characters who appear in your dreams.

The people in your dreams are there to represent your beliefs about them, or the beliefs you have borrowed from them. Some beliefs may work well for you, but others result in long and painful journeys.

The key to personal transformation — to discovering how to turn base metal into gold — is to see, through your dreams, which beliefs need to be given back to their owners. Once you have identified the beliefs you are ready to release, you then choose better ones to replace them and get down to doing the dream alchemy practice that brings about the change.

How to use the Identity Method
People you know
Magic mirrors
Imagine a person named Mary. Sarah may see her as critical. Ben may see her as a rigid thinker. Mary herself may be neither critical nor rigid in her thinking, but people misunderstand others all the time.

Why does Sarah see Mary as critical? Perhaps because Sarah's sensitive to criticism. Why does Ben see Mary as a rigid thinker? Perhaps because she reminds him of another Mary he once knew who was a rigid thinker. The strangest truths can lie behind how you see other people, truths that say more about you, Sarah and Ben than they say about Mary.

When Sarah dreams of Mary, she is not dreaming about the real Mary. She is most likely dreaming about criticism and her beliefs around criticism — about how she handles criticism in her life and about how critical she is about her own life. Mary is a perfect symbol for criticism simply because that's how Sarah sees her.

When Ben dreams of Mary he is looking at his beliefs around rigid thinking, how he handles rigid thinking and how it affects his own life.

Both Sarah and Ben may dream of Mary but it is their own self they see in the mirror. The best starting point for the Identity Method is to look at the people in your dreams as mirrors reflecting back to you your own beliefs and how you handle them.

When you dream of someone — for example, Brian — start by writing down three words or phrases to describe his approach to life, or his personality. You might write 'easy-going, tranquil, can be inconsiderate'. It is most likely that you hold a conscious or unconscious belief about at least one of these aspects and that your dream is using Brian as a symbol of your belief.

Look at how you interact with Brian and feel about him in your dream, or look at what Brian gets up to in your dream. Then stop thinking 'Brian' and start thinking 'my belief about inconsiderate people' or 'how I deal with inconsiderate people', or 'what I do to make sure people don't see me as inconsiderate' or 'my inconsiderate approach'.

Brian, Mary or anyone else in your dreams symbolise something you are not comfortable with due to the beliefs you hold. Your dream urges you to examine your beliefs (some of them unconscious) to see which ones are beneficial and which ones you could replace. Use dream alchemy to speed this up.

The swinging pendulum
Make sure you read the previous section about magic mirrors before this section.

The swinging pendulum is the best Identity Method approach to use when there are at least two people you know in your dream, particularly when they are two people who don't know each other in waking life. In other words, these two people are unlikely to play in the same scene in your life.

Now list all the people who appear in your dream and then write down three words for each to describe their approach to life or their personality, exactly as explained in 'Magic mirrors' (on pages 303–4).

Look through your list for opposites. For example, you might have described one person as patient and another as impatient. Next look at your dream to see if these themes (for example, patience and impatience) show up in your dream drama. When your dream clearly brings up two opposites or extremes of an issue, it is pinpointing a belief that is out of balance within you. To explain how it works, consider the example of patience and impatience. These are two extremes of the same issue. It is easy to see where being impatient can mess things up for you, but there are times when extreme patience gets you nowhere. You may patiently await an answer from someone who has forgotten that you have asked them a question. You may be so patiently understanding with someone who is being abusive to you that your life suffers as a result. You may be so patient with the leaking roof that it collapses in the next rainstorm. The issue is one of judging the time or situation and knowing when to act or state your feelings.

Life generally works best when you know how and when to act or state your feelings. The concept of the Tao, the Middle Way, is the path between extremes. It is finding the middle point in an issue where neither extreme irritates or attracts you because you have found the point of balance — the issue is then a non-issue for you. There is no longer anything that requires you to be patient or impatient as you handle situations before they become an issue.

Many dreams help you to see where there are extremes in your life that need to be balanced. By showing you people who symbolise opposite beliefs (like patience and impatience) your dream is drawing you towards a point of balance. Your dream is showing you a swinging pendulum and indicating the still point — the middle of the extremes where you can leave the issue behind.

Why does the pendulum swing before you find the middle way? Think of it in the following way, still using the example of patience and impatience.

If you are very patient about something that is annoying, what happens? Eventually your temper explodes or you suffer a stress-related disease. If you are very impatient towards someone who is annoying you, that person will be so offended by your rudeness that they won't deliver. In the first case, after exploding you vow never to get to that stage again. In the second case, when you've lost your chance of getting what you want, you vow to be a little more patient next time. Either way, the closer you get to the *extremes* the closer you get to the *middle*. When you hit the end of the pendulum swing you return towards the middle and you will probably swing towards the other extreme first as you explore both approaches to find out what works best for you. Bit by bit the pendulum slows and the middle point is reached. This process is illustrated beautifully by the Yin Yang symbol.

Look to your past to work out where your extreme beliefs began. Here are two common scenarios still using the example of patience and impatience:

Scenario one: Someone is very patient. You love this person and admire their patience. You come to believe that it is good to be extremely patient. You become extremely patient.

Scenario two: Someone is very patient. You love this person dearly but you see how much their patience is taken for granted by others. You see how much they are hurt and miss out on good things. You come to believe (consciously or unconsciously) that patience hurts you, so your belief in impatience is planted.

The swinging pendulum variation of the Identity Method, combined with the Storyline Method, helps you to see what extreme beliefs you hold, how they began and why they are not working for you. You can then use dream alchemy to still that pendulum and move forward in your life.

Time travel

People in your dreams are sometimes there simply to provide you with a time clue. If you dream of Simon and you last saw Simon in 1982, then he may just symbolise '1982'. How neat is that for dream shorthand? Because so much of dreaming is about searching back to uncover the origin of a belief, year and date clues are extremely valuable.

Unfinished business

From time to time, your dreams will beg you to address unfinished business or to make peace within yourself about the past. For each person who appears in your dream, ask yourself whether you had unfinished business with them. If you did, then ponder the issues and use the Storyline Method to help you to find a resolution that heals the past and a dream alchemy practice to make it happen.

What's in a name?

Dreams love using word play to deliver a message. It's a bit like looking at a cartoon — it makes an impression through making you laugh. Your dreams will often use people for the punch of their names. For example, Frank might be about being frank, Sue might be about suing, Pat might be a dream pun on 'pat on the back', and Penny or Bill might refer to your finances. Sometimes you've just got to hand it to your dreaming mind for tongue-in-cheek accuracy.

Look for people in your dreams who have the same name as someone else in your life. When the dream concerns a sensitive issue sometimes it delivers the message softly. Tim B. might have really put your back up but your dream introduces Tim K. to make the dream easier to stomach. If the magic mirror, swinging pendulum or other variations of the Identity Method don't seem to be working, think of who else shares the same name as your dream character.

Changing faces, merging characters

When one person in your dream changes into someone else,

your dream may be showing you a changing belief, or the way one particular belief you hold always transforms into the other. To identify this, start by applying the magic mirrors approach to each person. For example, if Jim (busy) changes into Martin (bitter) then your dream may be showing you that when you are in busy mode you automatically become bitter. Then run your dream through the Storyline Method to get an accurate interpretation of what is happening for you here.

When two people share the one role or when you see Valerie in your dream but her personality reminds you more of Carolyn, your dream may be presenting you with an amalgamation of beliefs. Again, start by applying the magic mirrors approach and then merge your results. For example, when Valerie (cautious) merges with Carolyn (narrow-minded) your dream may be showing you a blending of caution and narrow-mindedness.

Alternatively, when two people share the one role, your dream may be reinforcing the message. For example, if you see Valerie as cautious and depressed and you see Carolyn as narrow-minded and depressed, then your dream may be saying, 'depressed — that's the one!'

Family members, partners and other role players

It's natural to wake up and feel upset with your partner for what they did or said to you in your dream, or to worry that because you dreamed your baby drowned you must be a bad parent. Take a *deep* breath and remember: your partner, child or any other person in your dream is *not* the real person!

Just as in any of the above examples, your partner, child, mother, teacher or priest may represent something about how you see them. They may be your magic mirror, your swinging pendulum, your dream pun, your year-marker and so on. Always apply the Identity Method first.

The same people can also play an important role in your dreams as archetypes. This is a big concept, but it boils down to the following.

You've probably heard the term 'inner child'. Your inner

child is a part of yourself that lives on, in your mind, as a nine-year-old or a four-year-old, or perhaps as a baby — or maybe all three. At nine years old you might have had your first experience of rejection, and the nine-year-old you lives on to reappear in your dreams still seeking recognition and love. As an adult, whenever you feel rejected, you may react more as the nine-year-old than as an adult. You may hear a childish voice, or use childish words as you react, or just feel small, vulnerable and helpless. In your dreams your own daughter or son may appear to represent your inner child. If your daughter drowns in your dream? Don't panic — this is not your daughter! This is you, emotionally 'drowning' at a younger age. This is your own inner child in trouble. (This dream is also about your feelings of losing touch with your Yin energy, your right brain. See the following and also common dream 7: Losing or forgetting the baby or child.)

In the same way you have all sorts of other 'inner' selves. In the previous example you can use dream alchemy practice to give the nine-year-old inner you the love she needs, heal the hurt and allow her to 'grow' to adulthood. There are plenty of other inner selves to nurture.

Everyone has an inner wise person — a wise woman or a wise man or both. She or he is the intuitively wise part of your mind that appears in dreams as a wise older person. She or he may also appear as your own grandmother, grandfather or elder in your community. This is where your grandmother in your dream is there as an archetype figure, *not* as a magic mirror or any of the other roles mentioned here.

Your partner is a special case. Your male partner in your dream usually represents your Yang energy, your left-brain functions or your outer world. Your female partner in your dream usually represents your Yin energy, your right-brain functions or your inner world. (For details see the next section, 'People you don't know'.)

Here's a sample checklist of possible archetype figures that may appear in your dreams:

Male partner Your Yang energy. Your left-brain functions, your outer world.

Female partner Your Yin energy. Your right-brain functions, your inner world.

Your child Your inner child.

Your son A new Yang energy, in contrast to the older, more familiar Yang energy represented by your male partner perhaps.

Your daughter A new Yin energy, in contrast to the older, more familiar Yin energy represented by your female partner perhaps.

Your grandparent Your inner wisdom.

Your mother Your inner mothering instincts or the mothering qualities you've learned from your own mother.

Your father Your inner fathering instincts or the fathering qualities you've learned from your own father.

Your priest, guru or spiritual advisor Your inner religious or spiritual authority.

People you don't know

You may believe you know someone very well in your dream, but when you wake up and can't relate the dream character to anyone you know in your waking life, consider the following.

A man or boy

The unknown man or boy in your dream probably represents your Yang energy (a type of 'male' energy that both women and men have). This energy is to do with rational thinking, intellect, assertiveness, doing rather than being, competition and looking at the world from a mechanical point of view (a view that everything is made up of parts). People usually apply these functions to handling the outer world, so the man or boy in your dream can sometimes be a symbol for your outer world.

Consider substituting your left-brain functions or Yang energy or the way you deal with the outer world for 'the man' when you interpret a dream featuring an unknown man.

Ideally you should approach your life with an equal balance of Yin and Yang energy.

A woman or girl

The unknown woman or girl in your dream probably represents your Yin energy (a type of 'female' energy that both women and men have). This energy is to do with intuition, creativity, emotions, being rather than doing, nurturing, spirituality and looking at the world from a holistic point of view. People usually apply these functions to handling the inner world, so the woman or girl in your dream can sometimes be a symbol for your inner world.

Consider substituting your right-brain functions or Yin energy or the way you deal with the inner world for 'the woman' when you are interpreting a dream featuring an unknown woman.

If all the people in your dream are the same sex, your Yin–Yang energy is probably way out of balance.

Kings, wise women, heroes, ugly sisters, hobbits, handsome princes and frogs

Frogs? Well, you get the message. We're talking about input from fairy tales, legends, myths, history, literature, films and television. You know their personalities and approaches to life from the characters they play, so go back to magic mirrors (people you know) and apply the same method.

And all the rest?

If your dream stranger is causing you interpretation headaches, go back to the magic mirror method. You met this character in your dream, so you have a good feel for his personality and approach to life. Failing hitting the jackpot with the magic mirror, check for clues, puns and word plays concerning his name, occupation, clothing or the even the way he walks. For example, he might be a joiner (what are you merging) or an accountant (what are you accounting for). He might be tiptoeing everywhere (what are you tiptoeing around).

The Identity Method Checklist

Here's your shortcut to the Identity Method. Answer the questions till something clicks:

1 What is the personality of this person (three words or phrases)?

2 How does this person approach life (three words or phrases)?

3 When was the last time you saw, heard of or interacted with this person?

4 What were the circumstances of answer 3?

5 How would you feel if you met this person today?

6 Who else does this person remind you of?

7 Is there a pun or different meaning in this person's name?

8 What role does this person play in the world?

9 What role does this person play in your life?

10 What three things do you admire about this person?

11 What three things do you dislike about this person (be honest with yourself!)?

12 Do you have any unresolved feelings or business with this person? If so, what?

13 What belief might you have borrowed from this person?

14 Do you need to make peace with this person?

15 If you were to meet this person today, what message would you like to deliver?

Remember, the Identity Method is just one of the dream interpretation tools you need.

Once more, with feeling!

Seek the third element in the tides of your heart.

This method of working with uncommon dreams goes straight to the heart of the matter. Use the Feelings Method for dreams with an emotional bite or when you're in a hurry and need a quick burst of insight.

The feelings method

'In my dream I was late. I came to a red traffic light and stopped. The light was red for ages! Then it turned green and I drove on my way.'

Let's run that one by once more, this time with feeling! 'In my dream I was late. I was feeling rushed. I came to a red traffic light and stopped. I felt frustrated and angry. The light was red for ages! I felt stupid for not leaving time. Then the light turned green and I drove on my way. I felt depressed, knowing I would be too late.'

That was Annie's dream. Now read Fin's:

'In my dream I was late. I was feeling rushed. I came to a red traffic light and stopped. The light was red for ages! I felt reflective. Then the light turned green and I felt refreshed. I drove on my way feeling confident and peaceful.'

As soon as you tell a dream once more, with feeling, everything changes. These are two different dreams with two different meanings.

As soon as you tell a dream once more, with feeling, you are so much closer to the heart of the matter.

How to use the feelings method

Firstly, revisit your dream and for each part add the feelings you had while you were in the dream. Next, write out your dream using only words that express the feelings. Make sure you list the feelings in the same order as they flow in your dream. Here are Annie's and Fin's results:

Annie's dream
Rushed. Frustrated. Angry. Stupid. Depressed.

Fin's dream
Rushed. Reflective. Refreshed. Confident. Peaceful.

A dream is like a play (see the Storyline Method), opening with the situation, posing the question or problem, working through one or more possible actions and finishing with the resolution. In your dream, the situation and question are about a situation you are in, and a question you are working out now, presented in dream code. The action part of your dream is the part where your unconscious mind is running through possible solutions. In your dreams your unconscious mind is in 'search' mode, seeking the best way forward for you. The happily-ever-after dream holds the key, in the actions, for you to follow. All you have to do is decode the dream actions so you know what to do to get alchemical gold.

On the way to finding that happily-ever-after resolution, your dreams may travel along some blind alleys. It all depends on the quality of the search engines your unconscious mind is using. If it keeps using the same old search engines, it will keep coming up with the same results, even though they're the dud results you've got many times before. This is the unsatisfactory recurring dream, the one that always takes the same route to an unfortunate ending or to a non-ending. When this happens to you, you know that your unconscious mind is stuck in a rut. You are stuck in a rut, applying the same old approach to a problem even though it's got you nowhere before.

If your unconscious mind uses a different approach it may come up with a novel action to run. Some of the actions may not work out too well and become dreams with unsatisfactory endings or non-endings, but at least your unconscious mind tried something new! But some of the actions may hit the jackpot. Decode the dream, follow the action and you're out of the rut and moving forward into a new groove. With this review in mind, you have all the information you need to take your next Feelings Method step.

Look at how a dream ends. If it has a fortunate or 'feel-good' ending then it is likely to offer you a new groove. If it's a recurring dream with an unsatisfactory ending or a non-ending, then it's likely to be reflecting your rut. If it's anywhere in-between, it's likely to be running through possibilities, moving out of the rut into adventurous ground, but not yet worthy of following until the happily-ever-after ending appears.

Annie's dream concerns the old rut. She's had this dream before and it always ends with her feeling stupid and depressed. Fin's dream moves into the new groove. His old recurring dream was similar to Annie's, but this new dream was his breakthrough.

Now forget their dream stories and look at the order of feelings in their old-rut and new-groove dreams.

Annie's old-rut pattern is: Rushed. Frustrated. Angry. Stupid. Depressed.

Whenever she feels rushed she gets frustrated and then angry. Once she acknowledges her anger, she sees the feeling underneath the anger — her feeling of stupidity linked with a lack of self-esteem. So she gets depressed. The story is probably more complex. She probably leaves things until the last minute because she lacks confidence and then rushes. The rushing makes the whole situation worse, but it also gives her an excuse for her poor performance, 'I was running late' instead of the truth, 'I wasn't feeling confident so I didn't prepare it properly.' And she always ends up feeling depressed.

An old-rut dream is incredibly valuable, especially when you use the Feelings Method. What you get is an accurate picture of a pattern of feelings — your unconscious conditioning is revealed. Your dream shows you which feeling or belief leads to the next, and so on for the whole chain of feelings all the way back to the same old-rut ending.

Next you have to break through the old pattern. Annie can start by acknowledging her pattern of leaving things until the last minute and make a change. She can plan ahead. When she feels frustration or anger welling up, she can say, 'This is my way of covering up for feeling stupid. I can cut the anger and tell myself I'm not stupid. I'm having a go at this whatever the outcome.'

Most importantly, she can create a dream alchemy practice to fast-track a breakthrough. She might choose to write an affirmation, for example:

> I am always well-prepared and ahead of time.
> Whether traffic lights are red or green, I enjoy the ride. I feel uplifted and confident as I arrive at my destination. I know my work is good.

Or she may choose to write a gut-reaction poem titled 'Red traffic light', knowing that it will reveal to her some of the reasons she had fallen into this destructive pattern.

When you have identified your old-rut feeling pattern, refer to the 'Dream alchemy practice guide' on pages 329–38 to create a dream alchemy practice to suit your needs.

Fin's new groove pattern is: Rushed. Reflective. Refreshed. Confident. Peaceful.

In Fin's old-rut dream he was in auto-pilot, moving from 'rushed' into 'frustrated', just like Annie. His new-groove dream replaces 'frustrated' with 'reflective' and from that point the whole dream is positive.

In Fin's dream the solution is to take time out (the red light opportunity in his dream) to reflect. This reflection refreshes him enough to feel confident and peaceful. Once he *feels* confident and peaceful, he *is* confident and peaceful. His old fear of being inadequate transforms into confidence and peacefulness through reflection. Without fear, the result is changed.

If Fin follows his dream, he is unlikely to leave things until the last minute, as he no longer needs to create a rush to excuse his fears. Instead he will use that time to reflect. His work will improve, in keeping with his confidence.

The formula for breaking through your old pattern is easy to pick in a new-groove dream when you use the Feelings

Method. Identify the point where the old chain changes and make the change yourself. (In Fin's dream, it changes between 'rushed' and 'reflective'.)

You can accelerate this change using dream alchemy practice, so check the 'Dream alchemy practice guide' to finetune your path to alchemical gold.

Fin might choose an affirmation for his dream alchemy practice, for example:

> I know when to take time out to reflect and I am
> guided by the time out the universe's red traffic lights
> present to me. As I reflect I feel refreshed, confident
> and peaceful. I drive peacefully through green lights.
> I feel uplifted as I arrive at my destination. I know my
> work is good.

Or he might choose to create a timetable as his dream alchemy, divided into red and green sections marking times for reflection and times for action as he plans a project or assignment.

Dreams with intense emotional outbursts

You can still apply the Feelings Method to dreams where you are wild with rage, anger, grief, shock or terror, but it's important to understand a little about these very frightening dream experiences.

Anger and rage

There are differing degrees of anger. And then there is rage. Many people who are quiet and considerate towards others in waking life dream of expressing such rage that it spills into violence. In dreams, you may find yourself feeling so angry that you shake someone violently, squash them or hurt them in ways that are not even physically possible in waking life. You may wake up with your heart pounding because of the adrenaline released by your real feeling of anger and rage in your dream.

Firstly, you need to know that these types of dream are normal. Why haven't you heard much about them? People are often frightened to tell others about such dreams.

Secondly, because the people in your dream represent

your beliefs, experiences, hurts and memories, when you are violently attacking Fernando in a dream it is not necessarily because you have repressed your anger towards Fernando himself. Pause and ask yourself what Fernando could represent to you. (Refer to the 'I'll see you in my dreams' section on pages 303–4.) You might decide that Fernando represents 'selfishness' or that he represents your belief that 'it is selfish to tell my friends about my feelings of depression and burden them with my negativity so I'll keep it quiet'. In your dream you see that you are extremely angry with yourself for feeling selfish because this feeling is stopping you from discussing your depression with your friends. In this example, your anger directs you to see the harm you are doing to *yourself* through believing that you are selfish. Your dream screams, 'Stop that belief!' It is a healthy dream with healthy advice.

The real question here is why are these emotions so explosive and frightening in a dream? Why is it that you can express feelings you didn't know you had at levels you didn't know you were capable of and that you would not allow yourself to do in waking life anyway?

It's all to do with holding back feelings, and that's why these types of dreams are more common for people who don't show their negative feelings much in waking life. If you hold back an emotion you've got to put it somewhere. It locks into your body as well as into your mind. Your repressed anger will lock into your jaw (grind those teeth), your hands (clench those fists) and your gall bladder (hard angry gallstones), among other places. Anger burns in your body in fever, rashes, irritation, heartburn and so on. Repressed anger festers in your mind, even though you try to push it into your unconscious! It's still in your mind because you haven't faced it or acknowledged it. The only way to let an emotion go is to face it, acknowledge it, see where it's coming from and feel it. Once you're enlightened and lightened, it's gone.

If you don't face your emotions they well up and eventually, no matter how hard you try to repress them, they explode into your dreams. (Also see common dream 4: Tidal waves and tsunamis.) This is a safe place for their expression. The drama of your dream also allows you to see where the anger is coming from and why you have held onto it.

Anger is a strong emotion but it is a surface emotion. Think of anger as being like the outer skin of an onion. Underneath anger there are many layers of emotions to peel away before you get to the core of the feelings you are trying to bury and hide from yourself and others. It's easy to use anger as a cover-up, to say, 'I'm angry because you hurt me.' It's not so easy to say, 'I feel angry because I felt alone and rejected when I was a baby and sometimes you say things that remind me of those feelings. I feel so hurt that I cannot bear to face it, so I'm angry with you because you are standing in front of me and I can blame you for my feelings. It's easier for me to do this than to look into my heart.'

Releasing anger in a dream is often a sign of a successful dream alchemy that is getting to the core of emotions and beliefs that need to be transformed. The explosive anger is the flying skin of the onion, discarded and no longer required because the real work is now underway on the deeper levels.

Grief, shock and terror

Grief, shock and terror are among the many emotions that are found hiding below anger. When someone close to you dies, hurts you or leaves you, the grief can feel too difficult to handle. It is common to swing between feeling the pain and feeling numb. It is common to feel angry with the person for dying (or leaving you) and to feel depressed when you look ahead at your life. After a while, hope creeps back in and you are on the way to recovery. Along the way, grief is felt or repressed depending on when you can or can't handle it. For many people, grief remains locked up inside for many years, along with unshed tears.

Grief is not only to do with dying. From babyhood there are many losses to grieve. As the eldest child you may grieve the loss of your parents' attention when your brothers and sisters were born. You may grieve the loss of your comfort blanket taken away from you when you were deemed too old to sleep with it. (Of course, you were grieving the security and comfort, not the blanket!) You may grieve a loss of love you felt when you were sent off to boarding school. The list goes on.

Whatever grief you cannot deal with may be covered with a top layer of anger, like that outer skin of an onion. When your dreams release the dry, brown top skin of the onion (your anger), the soft, white layers of grief underneath bring the unshed tears to your eyes. Grief is uncovered and free to flow. It gushes in torrents, it expresses itself overwhelmingly in your dreams and it even spills over into teary days in waking life. 'Why are you crying?' 'I don't know. I just feel sad.' Unexplained crying extending over a few days is often the result of grief being released in a dream, even if you didn't remember the dream.

Look at your dream for clues about your grief: what is the loss that you are grieving for, why have you tried to bury it and why has it come up for you now? Then face it, acknowledge it, cry about it (even if you do not fully understand your tears, and even though they may bring a thousand other memories and feelings) and then let it go.

Releasing grief in a dream is often a sign that a dream alchemy practice is successfully clearing your way forward of old obstacles.

Treat shock, terror and other strong emotions released in your dreams in the same way. Look for clues in your dreams about when you first felt the shock or terror, why you tried to bury it, how this denial has affected your life and why it has come up for release now. How can all this understanding unlock a better future for you? Thank your dreams for releasing your emotions safely and then move forward to the 'Dream alchemy practice guide' on page 329 to speed your healing.

Remember, the Feelings Method is just one of the dream interpretation tools you need in order to uncover the meaning of your uncommon dreams and to reveal the life-changing gifts they offer you.

Confessions of the bizarre and cheeky

Seek the fourth element in cryptic wit and rhyme-less reason.

Choose from the dialogue, poetry or cryptic crossword methods to discover the meaning of the weird and bizarre symbols in your dream. The bizarre symbols in your dreams are drawn from your life experiences. They talk to you in dream-speak, the language of your unconscious. But we have ways of making them talk, ways of making them speak their truth. These three methods give you what you need to extract the confessions of the bizarre and cheeky.

The Dialogue Method
This is one of the most enjoyable dream interpretation methods. It also doubles as a dream alchemy practice. You'll see why in the examples included and as you experience the magic when you use the method yourself.

How to use the Dialogue Method
Give yourself no longer than twenty minutes to do a dialogue. This is easier than it sounds because the next rule is that you must *not* think! This is a bit like writing a film script or play — but without the brain being involved. Take a piece of paper and a pen and start the dialogue by asking a question. You must keep your writing flowing, even though you think you're writing nonsense. If it ends up looking like the writing of a child, that's fine. No sophistication or literary content is required.

By not thinking, by keeping the words flowing, you are letting your right brain and your unconscious mind do most of the work. After all, it was your right brain and your unconscious that created the original dream, so they know what the symbol is all about. Dialogue is about playing and play gets you there!

There are two main kinds of Dialogue Method:

- *Dreamer–Symbol Chat:* Where you get to talk with one of your bizarre dream symbols (see Bryony's example).
- *Symbol–Symbol Chat:* Where you get two of your whacky dream symbols to talk to each other.

Dreamer–symbol chat

Bryony had a dream involving a silver hatpin. She used the Dreamer–Symbol Chat Dialogue Method to get the hatpin to reveal its meaning.

Bryony and the silver hatpin

The dialogue might start as follows, with Bryony interrogating the hatpin:

BRYONY   What were you doing in my dream?

HATPIN   I wasn't in your dream.

BRYONY   Yes you were. I saw you. I felt your sharp point when I put my hat on.

Banter between the two may continue for some time, but the meaning of the symbol is soon revealed:

HATPIN   I was in your dream to make a point. Did you get it?

BRYONY   It was a sharp and painful point. What is your point?

HATPIN   Let me ask you a question. Why did you feel the pain?

BRYONY   Because you're sharp.

HATPIN   Well, thank you. But no. Try again.

BRYONY   Because I put my hat on.

HATPIN   Yep. If you hadn't put the hat on, you wouldn't have felt the pain.

BRYONY   But I always wear that hat when I go out with my friends.

HATPIN	Why?
BRYONY	Because I look good in it.
HATPIN	Don't avoid the question.
BRYONY	Because it keeps the sun out of my eyes.
HATPIN	Don't avoid the question.
BRYONY	Because I can hide under the brim.
HATPIN	Hide what?
BRYONY	My shyness.
HATPIN	Thank you. Shyness is painful, isn't it?
BRYONY	Hmm. I wear the hat to hide my shyness so I don't feel the pain. But I do feel the pain.

The hatpin symbol goes on to offer a course of action:

BRYONY	So how do I get over my shyness?
HATPIN	Forget the hat. Brave it, girl. Show them who you are.
BRYONY	Don't know if I can.
HATPIN	You can. It's their problem how they respond to you.
BRYONY	What if I don't like how they respond to me?
HATPIN	Change your friends.

So Bryony's dream silver hatpin revealed its meaning and she was then able to understand her dream more clearly.

The magic with dialogue is that you can continue the conversation beyond identifying the meaning of the symbol and into solving an issue in life — in Bryony's case, her shyness. Her dream might have been pointing out the pain of hiding her shyness, but her dialogue took her well beyond seeing the pain and into finding a formula for healing it.

By keeping up the conversation with the hatpin, Bryony was practising dream alchemy: she was changing her unconscious beliefs by conversing in the language of her dreams. She was talking directly with her unconscious to make a change.

Symbol–symbol chat
In the symbol–symbol dialogue, two symbols that are prominent in the dream 'chat', revealing their meanings in a similar way to the dreamer–symbol dialogue.

The Poetry Method
Use the Poetry Method to identify a single bizarre symbol from your dream. This is an alternative to the Dialogue Method, but it takes less time to do. Use it to help you ring in the changes.

How to use the Poetry Method
Start with a blank piece of paper and a pen and set a timer for somewhere between five and ten minutes — no longer. As with the Dialogue Method, the Poetry Method works because you do not allow yourself to think. Keep that left brain out of action by keeping the words flowing. Keep on writing even if your poem seems childish or nonsensical. Your right brain and unconscious mind are happily and instinctively spilling out their dream symbolism. Let it flow and see what comes up.

Oh, and no rhyming or verses unless it comes out that way. The only definition of 'poetry' here is that you're not writing sentences and not using up all the space on your lines. Let your words find their shape on your page.

If you wish, write with your left hand (if you are right-handed, or vice versa if you are left-handed). When you write with your non-dominant hand you are more in touch with your unconscious mind.

Use a bizarre symbol from your dream as your title.

Peta's example
Peta's bizarre symbol in her dream was a blue salt twist. Remember when bags of potato chips were unsalted and came

with a little twist of paper containing salt inside the bag as an optional extra? Peta is English, so she'll call potato chips 'crisps'. Here's her result:

Blue salt twist

Packet of potato chips
nestling hidden
twist crisps
not chips
not fries
crisps
bland, tasteless, oily
until you find the old blue twist of salt
nestling hidden
special
transforming nothing into something special
if
you
can
find
one
in
your
packet
because
some packets didn't have blue twists of salt
and something special —
some promise of good things —
vanished into thin air
thin tasteless crisps
and I waited and I couldn't tell you
that the crisps you gave me
came
without
and I went
without
quietly
sad.

In this example, Peta sat back and looked at her poem and saw several linked themes. These were:

◆ something hidden
◆ something with potential to transform the bland into something special
◆ promise of good things sometimes not fulfilled
◆ feeling of abandonment (the packet without the promised twist)
◆ feeling of promise unfulfilled
◆ quiet sadness through not communicating regret.

Peta put all this together to see that the blue salt twist in her dream symbolised the promises her father had made but did not fulfil and the sadness, abandonment and isolation she had felt as a result in her childhood. As an adult she was, once again, on the receiving end of broken promises and her dream reminded her of her childhood hurt. Through her poem she could see that she had not talked about her regret and came to see that she had made things harder for herself by not communicating her feelings.

Did you notice the shape of Peta's poem? It looks a bit like a blue salt twist. The single words on separate lines create a feeling of isolation too.

Peta's poem is already working as a dream alchemy practice because, in writing the poem, she began to communicate her regret. Like the Dialogue Method, the Poetry Method often develops beyond an identification of the bizarre dream symbol and becomes a healing dream alchemy practice. This is because the poetry is written by your right brain and by your unconscious mind, the very same authors of your dreams, so you are communicating with your unconscious beliefs in dream language.

If Peta wished to extend her poetry dream alchemy practice she might write an affirmation, such as:

Every packet of crisps contains a blue salt twist.
Every promise made to me is met. The taste of
transformation and fulfilment is on my lips as
I communicate my true feelings.

As well as using a bizarre symbol from your dream as

your title for a poem when using the Poetry Method, you can introduce a deeper level of dream alchemy practice by introducing more complex titles. For example, Peta might like to write a second poem, now that she understands her dream better, this time titled, 'The taste of salt on my lips'.

The Cryptic Crossword Method

Tongue-in-cheek clichés, word plays and puns are at the top of the list for dreams communicating in right-brain short-hand. This is real detective stuff, so grab your magnifying glass and search your dream for 'cheeky' clues.

How to use the Cryptic Crossword Method

Search for word plays, puns and clichés. Here are some common examples to trigger your cryptic crossword mind.

Clichés

Clichés are done-to-death phrases that creep into our every-day conversation because they do a great job of delivering a shorthand message. Dreams shorten the message even more by delivering the clichés as visuals. The following dream scenes need no interpretation.

A horse refuses to drink water from a trough.
Cliché applying to your life:
You can lead a horse to water but you can't make it drink.

You have to walk across a floor of eggshells without breaking them.
Cliché applying to your life:
It's like walking on eggshells.

A man is trying to sell a dead horse.
Cliché applying to your life:
It's like flogging a dead horse.

The last example includes a play on words. 'Flogging' in the cliché means 'whipping'. But flogging can also mean selling. The man trying to sell the horse in the dream is a cryptic clue to 'flog'. These can be harder to identify in your dream but good fun when you catch them!

Puns and other word plays

Puns are either words that sound the same but have different meanings (like *weight* and *wait*) or words or phrases that carry double meanings in a cheeky way.

Consider the following dream examples.

A man is complaining to you. He is holding a glass of wine.
Pun applying to your life:
(Possibly) Who is whining?

A woman is doing a crossword puzzle.
Pun applying to your life:
(Possibly) What cross words are puzzling you?

Paired opposites

Search your dreams for word plays on pairs of opposites, as these most likely show you conflicts in your life.

For example, a dream may include 'weight', 'wait', 'a waiter', 'green traffic light' and 'go-go dancer'. The dream is about a conflict between waiting for something to happen and going ahead to make it happen.

Identify your conflict and you're more than halfway there!

Remember to combine elements from all the dream interpretation methods in the 'Our uncommon dreams' section to find the perfectly balanced meaning of your dream. Then move on to the dream alchemy practice guide to create the best formula for your dream alchemy practice.

The dream alchemy practice guide

The guide

For a description of alchemy, dream alchemy and dream alchemy practices, see 'Let the magic begin', pages 9–12.

There are over 120 individual dream alchemy practices for you to follow in this book. For your uncommon dreams you will need to design your own unique practices. Use this guide to help you do this.

The dream alchemy practices are presented here in nine categories:
- Visualisation
- Affirmation
- Dialogue
- Artwork
- Gut-reaction poetry
- Bodywork
- Giving back beliefs
- Story telling/writing
- Other adventures

Each category lists examples given in this book and describes how they work.

When you are ready to design your own dream alchemy practices for your uncommon dreams, this guide will help you to decide which category best suits your dream, and then guide you through creating your practice and using it.

Visualisation
Examples
Common Dreams:

4: Tidal waves and tsunamis — dream alchemy practice A, page 48

*16: Slo mo running or walking — dream alchemy
practice A, page 126*
24: Snakes — dream alchemy practice A, page 181
*35: I've lost my handbag, wallet, jewellery or … —
dream alchemy practice B, page 249*
38: Stormy weather — dream alchemy practice B, page 267

Best for …

Dreams with unresolved endings, or dreams that clearly
show (once you have interpreted them) that you are battling
with an unconscious obstacle, block or fear. Visualisations
can also be used to speed up positive outcomes using
dreams with effective resolutions.

Method

How to create it

Imagine a changed ending to your dream and include the
feelings you want to have when you achieve your result. To
speed up positive outcomes from dreams with good endings,
use the dream outcome as your visualisation and intensify
your positive feelings.

How to use it

To do the visualisation, close your eyes (or 'zone out') and
imagine the new scene you created in great sensual detail.
Make sure you *feel* this one! Experiencing the positive emotions is the most important part of the process. Your visualisation should take anywhere between ten and thirty seconds,
no longer. It is a short, sharp, sensual experience!

For best results, do the visualisation twenty times a day
for the first week, then ten times a day for the second week
and twice a day for the next month.

How it works

Your dream expressed your waking-life situation using dream
language — the language of your unconscious mind. By reliving the dream with changes (or reliving and intensifying
the dream in the case of a dream with a positive ending) you
are using vision and feeling to reprogram your unconscious
beliefs. The repetition reinforces the unconscious learning.

Affirmation
Examples
Common Dreams:

> *1: I'm flying — dream alchemy practice B, page 30*
> *8: Who's driving this car? — dream alchemy practice B, page 73*
> *14: Bags, baggage and cases — dream alchemy practice A, page 112*
> *21: I've lost my way — dream alchemy practice B, page 160*
> *38: Stormy weather — dream alchemy practice C, page 268*

Best for ...
The same conditions as for visualisation, but good for any dream where you have a firm understanding of the meaning of its symbols.

Method
How to create it

The best way to understand how to create an affirmation is to refer to the examples.

Make sure you understand your dream, then choose the main symbols that communicated the dream's message. Include at least one important symbol from your dream, the positive feelings you choose for yourself (how you want to feel when you achieve your result) and a description of your new relationship with the symbol (your new belief).

Write your affirmation (anything from one to six sentences) in the present tense with *no* negative words. Make sure you eliminate words like 'unafraid' or statements like 'not upset' — your unconscious picks these up as negatives and programs negativity.

How to use it

Say your affirmation *out loud* and *with feeling* thirty times a day for the first week. From the second week say your affirmation out loud and with feeling, once in the morning and once before you go to sleep for three more weeks. Saying the affirmation out loud is important for it to succeed.

How it works

The sound and shape of the spoken word when combined with great feeling (that is, feeling the emotion) make an impact on your unconscious mind. When you use an everyday kind of affirmation — nothing to do with dreams — such as 'I am now highly paid as a consultant', this will work for you *if*, and only if, your unconscious mind is in agreement.

Now, think about this! Why have you picked, 'I am now highly paid as a consultant' as your affirmation? Probably because you've wanted this to happen for some time and, since it hasn't, you've decided to do an affirmation. Could it be that your unconscious mind is not in agreement with the idea? By using this affirmation what you are really doing is challenging your unconscious mind with the very belief it is not happy with, so it works to reinforce the unconscious belief that, in this case perhaps, 'I don't know enough to be a consultant'. In this scenario your affirmation is driving you further away from achieving your goal.

Dream alchemy affirmations communicate with your unconscious using the same language — the language your dreams choose to express your situation.

Using the same example, imagine you had a dream about your goal to become a highly paid consultant, revealing your unconscious belief that you don't know enough to be a consultant. Imagine your dream showed your lack of confidence as a deflating yellow balloon, pricked by a pin. Wielding the pin was that old school teacher, Jack Mann, whose methods left you feeling very unsure of your abilities. Okay, so your dream used the language of a pin deflating a yellow ball to symbolise the start of your deflating confidence. Your unconscious mind has 'lack of confidence' stored away as 'pin deflating yellow balloon'. No matter how many times you say, 'I am now highly paid as a consultant', your unconscious mind is simply going to return 'pin deflating yellow balloon'. Here's a dream alchemy affirmation to suit working with this example:

'I give Jack Mann his pin back. I have a new yellow balloon. It is strong, knowledgeable and confident. I feel strong, knowledgeable and confident. I am highly paid as a consultant.'

The repetition reprograms and reinforces your new unconscious belief.

Dialogue
Examples
Common Dreams:

> *11: Back at school — dream alchemy practice A, page 92*
> *15: I had sex with …! — dream alchemy practice A, page 119*
> *23: Revisiting a past home — dream alchemy practice A, page 173*
> *35: I've lost my handbag, wallet, jewellery or … — dream alchemy practice A, page 249*
> *41: Death and murder — dream alchemy practice A, page 287*

Best for …
Dreams with one or two bizarre symbols that you are having difficulty interpreting or that you wish to open up and explore more deeply. It is great for time-efficiency as the dialogue takes no longer than twenty minutes and there are no repetitions to do.

Method and how it works
See the example on pages 321–4.

Artwork
Examples
Common Dreams:

> *1: I'm flying – dream alchemy practice A, page 30*
> *13: In a wheelchair — dream alchemy practice A, page 105*
> *14: Bags, baggage and cases — dream alchemy practice B, page 112*
> *15: I had sex with …! — dream alchemy practice B, page 120*
> *24: Snakes! — dream alchemy practice B, page 181*

Best for ...

Deep-seated issues you want to explore and heal over a longer period of time. It is a good alternative to writing and working with words. Artwork dream alchemy practice is also perfect for awakening and extending your creativity.

Method
How to create it

Artwork dream alchemy practice is unique to your dream. Be guided by the examples, noticing how elements of the dream are built into the dream alchemy practice. You may wish to start by using one of the examples as a blueprint, finding the one that most closely matches your dream and situation.

How to use it

Do your artwork dream alchemy practice alone. This is your contemplation time. Take as long as you want — but *do* start! Exploring your feelings as you do your artwork is an important part of this dream alchemy practice.

How it works

By working with dream elements and symbols in art form you are communicating with your unconscious mind in its own language to create change, to explore your feelings or to resolve past issues.

Gut-reaction poetry
Examples

Common Dreams:

Best for ...

Dreams including a bizarre symbol that you do not understand or want to explore more deeply. Perfect for time-efficiency as gut-reaction poetry takes no longer than ten minutes and there are no repetitions to do.

Method and how it works

See the example on pages 324–7.

Bodywork

Examples

Common Dreams:

> *13: In a wheelchair — dream alchemy practice C, page 105*
>
> *17: Aliens and UFOs — dream alchemy practice B, page 133*
>
> *33: Trapped and under attack — dream alchemy practice C, page 236*
>
> *34: On the cliff edge — or falling — dream alchemy practice B, page 243*
>
> *37: I can't see clearly — dream alchemy practice B, page 260*

Best for ...

Helping to ease physical disease and postural strains originating from the emotional issues and unconscious beliefs revealed by your dream. Bodywork dream alchemy practice is easy to do and a good alternative to writing and working with words.

Method

How to create it

Be guided by the examples. Include at least one symbol from your dream and build in the *feeling* that you want to have when you achieve your goal.

How to use it

Be guided by the examples. Repetition is good. Notice any feelings this bodywork brings up for you, name the feelings and then let them go. Focus on feeling the positive emotion you choose for yourself as you achieve your goal.

How it works

Your muscles hold emotions, memories and beliefs (think of hunched shoulders, a 'sick stomach' and frown-lines). In body-work dream alchemy practice you are releasing emotions, memories and beliefs from the parts of your body that are associated with your dream symbolism. By focusing on new, positive feelings you are reprogramming your unconscious mind by communicating with it through your physical body.

Giving back beliefs

Examples

Common Dreams:

7: Losing or forgetting the baby or child — dream alchemy practice C, page 66

8: Who's driving this car? — dream alchemy practice C, page 74

11: Back at school — dream alchemy practice B, page 92

14: Bags, baggage and cases — dream alchemy practices B and C, pages 112–13

23: Revisiting a past home — dream alchemy practice B, page 174

Best for ...

Dreams showing people from your past (or perhaps from now) as symbols of beliefs you have taken on board through knowing them — beliefs that are now blocking your progress. These may be conscious or unconscious beliefs. Also for dreams showing you beliefs you had when you were younger that are now blocking your progress.

Method

How to create it

Be guided by the examples. Find the example that is closest to your own dream and situation and then adapt it. Make sure that when you give back a belief you replace it with a better belief, otherwise it is likely to be filled by another unsuitable belief.

How to use it

Be guided by the examples.

How it works

The beliefs you carry are not set in concrete. You borrowed them from other people so you can give them back. Since dreams usually show the person you borrowed the belief from, that person is a perfect symbol to use to communicate with your unconscious mind. Like any symbol, the person lives on in your mind not as the actual person, but as part of your unconscious language. By communicating with the person–symbol through dream alchemy you give back your belief — you reprogram your unconscious mind.

Story telling/writing
Examples
Common Dreams:

> *3: Teeth falling out — dream alchemy practice B, page 42*
> *21: I've lost my way — dream alchemy practice A, page 160*
> *30: A visit from spirit? — dream alchemy practice C, page 217*
> *31: I'm being chased or followed — dream alchemy practice B, page 223*
> *40: Plane crash — dream alchemy practice B, page 280*

Best for ...

Dreams with unresolved endings or endings that are not satisfactory. Good for resolving unresolved issues you had with people in the past, or for finding peace within yourself about the past. Perfect for word-lovers and writers and for getting creativity flowing.

Method

How to create it

Be guided by the examples. Find the example that is closest to your own dream and situation and then adapt it.

How to use it

Be guided by the examples.

How it works

By working with dream elements and symbols in writing

form, you are communicating with your unconscious mind in its own language to create change, to explore your feelings and to resolve and heal past issues.

Other adventures
Examples
Common Dreams:

> *1: I'm flying — dream alchemy practice C, page 30*
> *20: The awesome wild animal — dream alchemy practice C, page 155*
> *27: Was that a past life? — dream alchemy practice C, page 199*
> *40: Plane crash — dream alchemy practice C, page 281*
> *41: Death and murder — dream alchemy practice C, page 287*

Best for ...
When you want to push your creativity, have fun, throw a party, create an event, make your mark, break a mould, do something completely different or celebrate a turning point with style. It's good for forcing a change in routine, taking yourself beyond your previous limits or exploring a different kind of creativity.

Method
How to create it
Be guided by the examples.

How to use it
Be guided by the examples.

How it works
The examples show different kinds of dream alchemy practices all working in slightly different ways. They all involve communicating with the unconscious using the language of the dream combined with feeling the positive feelings associated with success. The point of the communication is to change the unconscious belief system for the better.

Connections

Connect with Jane Teresa at JaneTeresa.com, where you can also listen to all episodes of The Dream Show, study dream interpretation, dream alchemy, and dream therapy courses online, and catch up with her blogs and media appearances.

Index

Acknowledgements

I am deeply thankful to every dreamer who has ever shared a dream with me. The insights you have given have helped to shape my understanding of dreams and how they relate to our waking lives.

I am grateful to those courageous souls who first tested the types of dream alchemy practice presented in this book back in the late 1990s. Personal challenges in my own life blessed me with the opportunity to experience powerful rewards through practising dream alchemy, and I am eternally thankful for these.

Thank you to everyone I have had the pleasure of meeting and working with through my work as a dream therapist. Witnessing your breakthroughs and achievements is always momentous for me.

Thank you to all the radio and television presenters and producers who have encouraged people across Australia to discuss their dreams with me publicly in the media. Your support and public endorsement of this work over so many years has been, and is, greatly appreciated.

Thank you also to the many thousands of people who have called in to radio stations over the years to discuss their personal dreams live to air. Your sharing helps more people than you would ever imagine. I know; I have heard from those whose lives have been changed as a result of listening.

Thank you to my agent, Margaret Kennedy, for discussing some of the early ideas for this book with me. Thank you also to the staff at Lothian Books for working with me to create the first edition of this book, *Dream Alchemy* (2003), and to the staff at Hachette for publishing subsequent editions, including this updated version, retitled *The Dream Handbook*.

Thank you to you, the reader, for buying *The Dream Handbook* and helping to spread dream light in the process.

Thank you to my greatest support team: my daughter, Rowan McKeown; my son, Euan Gray; and my husband, Michael Collins; as well as to many beautiful friends and communities across the world: you know who you are.

Notes

Notes

Notes